SHIPPING HOGSHEADS

THE MAKING OF
THE WEST INDIES

By F. R. Augier and S. C. Gordon

SOURCES OF WEST INDIAN
HISTORY

By S. C. Gordon

A CENTURY OF WEST INDIAN
EDUCATION

THE MAKING OF
The West Indies

F. R. AUGIER   S. C. GORDON

D. G. HALL   M. RECKORD

LONGMAN CARIBBEAN

LONGMAN CARIBBEAN LIMITED
Trinidad and Jamaica
LONGMAN GROUP UK LIMITED
Longman House, Burnt Mill, Harlow,
Essex CM20 2JE, England
and Associated Companies throughout the world.

First published 1960
Sixty-seventh impression 1993

ISBN 0 582 76304 5

Printed in Hong Kong
SWT/67

CONTENTS

ORDER OF PRESENTATION

Some topics in this book are more difficult than others for school children to appreciate. This is particularly true of sections dealing with the relationship of colonists with their mother country, prices and markets and government and constitutions.

We therefore suggest that the more descriptive chapters and sections be taken through first. The pupils will then build up a picture of the different peoples in the Caribbean at different times, and the changes in the societies as different groups arrived with their various motives, loyalties, standards, and beliefs.

The first year's work might consist of the following series of studies:

> The Spanish settlement and empire.
> Other European colonisation and settlement.
> The slave society.
> The estate society.
> The critics—missionaries and abolitionists.
> Post emancipation society.
> Immigrant and emigrant workers.

These studies could be supported by the following chapters and sections, with the relevant extracts from *Sources of West Indian History* and the additional reading recommended—

> CHAPTERS 1 and 2 (omitting the section *Government and Church*)
> CHAPTERS 3 and 4 (omitting the section *European Interest*)
> CHAPTER 5 *Sugar Revolution* and *Servants and Slaves* only.
> CHAPTER 6 *War by Buccaneer* only
> CHAPTER 7 and Chapter 8
> CHAPTER 9 *Garrisons and Militia* and *The Navies* only
> CHAPTER 11 *An Estate's Accounts* only
> CHAPTER 12 and Chapter 13
> CHAPTER 14 and Chapter 15
> CHAPTER 16 and Chapter 17
> CHAPTER 20 *Facing the Facts* and *Enterprise and Adversity* only.

By returning to sections and chapters omitted and then using the last chapters of the book the pupils would spend what is for the majority their last year studying history on government and relationships with European governments, the mercantile system, trade rivalries and war, the rise and fall of the sugar industry, the search for economic alternatives and the political, economic and social changes of the last century in the Caribbean area. These topics would then be a study of public activities and attitudes in different historical societies which the pupils have already studied descriptively. It should offer many opportunities for discussion and special studies on the modern history of the pupils' own territory.

Such a second year course would be supported by the following sections and chapters, with the relevant extracts from *Sources of West Indian History* and other reading recommended:

ILLUSTRATIONS

FOREWORD

THIS book has four authors. The reason for this will probably be the best way of illustrating the difficulties of writing West Indian history at this time. Two of the authors went to school in the West Indies and two in England, yet we all did the same course of history. That is, we are all more familiar with the chain of events that make up the political history of England than with what will come to be West Indian history. Since our school-days we have made special studies of small parts of West Indian history, and we have now pooled our knowledge to make a continuous story.

Sometimes, because what we are writing about is not readily available elsewhere, we have written fairly fully, as in, for example, the descriptions of estate life, planters' difficulties and the different phases in the relationships between the European countries and their West Indian colonies. Where the material has been discussed simply elsewhere we have tended to economise on our own writing and to give references for the pupils to pursue. This is why the book is balanced in a different way from other histories of the West Indies. Until the subject has grown a great deal more, it will be difficult for us to say finally whether we have weighted the most important parts or not. We do not claim that we have said the last word on the subject either for ourselves or for anyone else.

Our book is rather full because we intend to meet the requirements of three G.C.E. 'O' level syllabuses in West Indian history. The syllabus for the Oxford and Cambridge Examination Board was compiled mainly by the teachers of history in Barbados, after consultation with their colleagues in Guyana; it prescribes that the students shall do only two periods of West Indian history. This means that they will not require the whole book for preparation for the examination. They will, however, have to seek elsewhere some of the detailed material of European history required by their syllabus. The Cambridge Syndicate, on the other hand, prescribes no periods formally, and probably candidates will not require as much detail as we include.

It has been impossible to give a balanced account of the history of the whole Caribbean area. We have not told how the Latin American countries won their independence from Spain nor how the French islands developed after the eighteenth century, nor much of the part played in the area by the United States of America in the last century. We have only made reference to these important events. From the time when the British West Indies were finally determined, we have discussed them almost exclusively. It would have needed a much bigger book to do justice to the history of the whole area in the last century and a half, and we think this one is quite large enough.

We have made no attempt to write the full history of any one island, although it should be possible to work out a fairly consecutive story by looking up any particular territory in the index and reading the references. We have been concerned rather to show the background of life and events which have affected the whole area. Our readers should go to the printed laws of their territory, old newspapers, or to any available public documents for precise information on what happened there. One question has been suggested at the end of most chapters to encourage pupils to do this.

A joint endeavour such as this book needs many friends and advisers. We have never been without, and we wish to thank them all for their invaluable help.

We name only two. Prof. Elsa Goveia, of the Department of History, University of the West Indies, and Mr. John Hammond, headmaster of Harrison College, Barbados, both of whom gave invaluable advice in the preparation of the book. We are deeply indebted to them.

We would also like to thank warmly the history teachers and the pupils of the secondary schools who used early drafts of our chapters.

Fig. 4 is based on J. D. Fage: *An Introduction to the History of West Africa*, by permission of the Cambridge University Press.

Finally, we are extremely grateful to Commodity Services Co. (Jamaica) Ltd. for their generous and timely provision of secretarial services in producing the book.

This book has many imperfections. We wish we could have delayed publication until we felt more sure of our ground, but this would have kept some pupils waiting for the history of their own country; we preferred to invite them to join us in the beginning of the search for it. Our successors as West Indian historians will come from their ranks and we should like them to work in the setting of a general knowledge which we ourselves did not have.

F. R. A. S. C. G.

D. G. H. M. R.

1967

PART I
IMPORTING THE SOCIETY

PART 1

IMPORTING THE SOCIETY

CHAPTER ONE

Discovery and Settlement

THE AMERICAS

The native people of the West Indies and North and South America were Indians. For hundreds of years the Indian peoples, undisturbed by outsiders, developed ways of life which by the end of the fifteenth century varied considerably through the whole continent. For instance, the Algonkins living in the north-east of North America were hunters and fishermen who grew maize in gardens attached to their huts. On the plain of Mexico, on the other hand, the Aztec Indians had a more elaborate way of life. Great stone temples dominated towns connected by roads and causeways across the Lake of Mexico. In South America the Incas dominated an empire comparable in size and efficiency to the ancient Roman Empire in Europe. It stretched from Ecuador to Chile.

In the large islands of the Caribbean and in the Bahamas lived the Arawaks. They were skilled seamen using canoes manned by seventy or a hundred men to span the Caribbean from the Bahamas to Yucatan. The islands were not rich in animal life and the Arawaks depended chiefly on fishing; they made nets, pots, lines and spears tipped with fishbone. They lived in thatched villages, grew cassava and fattened a breed of barkless dog. Cotton fibre was used to make clothing and sleeping hammocks. Each village had a chief or *cacique* who acknowledged the authority of a greater *cacique* living in Cuba. Gold was found on some of the islands, where it was worked into ceremonial masks for chiefs and priests, decorated belts and nose ornaments. But it was not used as money, and trade was conducted by barter.

In 1492 Europeans first discovered the larger islands and from there the American continent. Adventurers quickly followed to make their fortune in what they called the New World. The violent process of colonisation had begun. The Europeans had the advantage of steel swords and gunpowder. Mexico City was captured. The Inca Empire was destroyed. Everywhere the interlopers met with resistance and in

3

North America the struggle for the old way of life and hunting grounds continued for centuries until the railway spanned the continent.

The Arawaks took the first impact of European colonisation. They are usually described as 'peace-loving' and do not seem to have spent their energies in perfecting weapons of war; but they were not meek or helpless. Their conquerors faced long years of resistance which only ended with the extermination of the Arawaks. The small islands to the south were inhabited by Caribs. They were cannibals and lived by attacking their neighbours. They were also skilled seamen and took great pride in physical endurance. As the European colonists penetrated into those islands, Carib resistance was fierce, aggressive and continued for a much longer time than that of the Arawaks who were invaded first.

THE AGE OF DISCOVERY

The West Indies were discovered by an expedition searching for the mainland of Asia. During the fifteenth century Europeans became interested in finding a sea route to increase their trade with India and China. Europe already had important eastern trade connections. One of these routes ran via the Red Sea, another followed the Euphrates valley and another went from the Black Sea through Bokhara and Samarkand. The routes were worked by merchants with caravans of pack animals, each caravan carrying the goods one stage on the journey. Many of the merchants were Arabs who sold to European dealers when the goods reached the Mediterranean.

These land connections were no longer adequate. The caravans made a long, dangerous journey through regions infested with brigands. The pack animals could only carry goods in comparatively small quantities. So the trade was confined to goods small in bulk and high in value. Spices like pepper were imported for flavouring meat, special dye-stuffs for the cloth-makers, medicinal plants, raw silk, perfume and precious stones. There was an increasing market in Europe for Eastern products; but during the fifteenth century two developments limited the trade. A group of merchants from Venice in Italy established a monopoly of the overland route; all the traders sold to Venetian merchants, who therefore profited most from the spice trade. Secondly, a powerful Turkish Empire was established stretching across the trade routes in the Middle East. The Turks imposed and collected heavy duties and export taxes which drained the merchants' profits and made the trade precarious.

The only way to by-pass the Turks, break the Venetian monopoly and satisfy the market for Eastern goods was to find a new trade route. A sea route had great advantages. The overland route brought only 420,000 lb. of pepper into Europe each year; one ship alone could carry half that amount in its hold. Asia, too, was rich in gold according to the Venetian, Marco Polo, the only European who had visited India and China and left a record of his journey. 'They have gold in the greatest abundance, its sources being inexhaustible,' he reported, 'the sovereign's palace has the entire roof covered with a plating of gold.' Gold was wanted for currency and sufficient quantities could only reach Europe by ship.

The pioneer country in the search for a sea route was Portugal. Prince Henry the Navigator, who lived from 1394 to 1460, was convinced that there must be a sea route round the south of Africa to India. Special èxpeditions were sent along the coast south of Cape Nun, each captain trying to push farther than his predecessors and bring back charts and information. The Portuguese found they could trade along the coast exchanging horses and Venetian beads for gold and ivory. As exploration progressed, trading centres were set up with the main one at Arguin. Prince Henry's work was continued by John II, King of Portugal from 1481, who built a new large trading centre, Sao Jorge da Mina (Elmina) on the Bight of Benin.

The early explorers faced many navigational problems. Prince Henry and John II employed mathematicians and astronomers to seek a solution to these difficulties and to use the findings of the captains in their study of geography. One of the chief problems of navigation was to establish the latitude of a ship. Charting an unknown coast could only be done if the ship's captain could calculate the latitude of landmarks like rivers and headlands; moreover, a journey between two distant points was certain only if the ship's position could be checked. In the northern hemisphere latitude was calculated by checking the altitude of the North, or Pole, Star, but in the southern hemisphere the North Star was not visible. In 1484 astronomers suggested that the height of the sun at midday might be a better universal guide. From this calculation they worked out tables of the sun's position north or south of the equator at noon on any given date. This they knew from Arab studies of the heavens. These tables were a revolutionary advance for navigation, and a Portuguese experimental expedition was sent to Guinea, in West Africa, to test the new method of observing latitude.

But even at the end of the fifteenth century many important geographical problems were still unsolved. Geographers agreed that the world was round and could be divided into 360 degrees; but how long was a degree of latitude? The works of the second century Greek geographer Ptolemy, who thought a degree was 50 nautical miles long, were still discussed as well as the views of Alfragen, a Moslem geographer, who said it was 45 nautical miles. It is in fact 60 nautical miles; so this meant that no one knew how big the earth was. At the same time no one knew how many miles lay between the easternmost point of Asia and the westernmost point of Europe. So apart from the careful exploration of the African coast being carried out by Portuguese sailors there was a profound ignorance of what lay beyond Africa or beyond the Atlantic. But the promise of the riches of Asia enticed Europeans to finance the voyages that would remodel their map of the world.

THE VOYAGES OF COLUMBUS

These were the circumstances that gave Christopher Columbus, an unknown Genoese sea captain, a chance to explain his particular theories about the distance between Europe and Asia, first to the King of Portugal and then to the rulers of Spain, in the hope of finding a patron to finance an expedition. Columbus based many of his ideas on the *Book of Ser Marco Polo*, where an island called Cipangu was reported 1,500 nautical miles east of China; this would be Japan. From Marco Polo's account Columbus calculated that this island was 283 degrees to the east, which meant it could be reached by sailing 77 degrees westward across the Atlantic. He also adopted Alfragen's theory that a degree of latitude was 45 nautical miles long. This meant that he thought that Asia lay only 2,400 miles west of the Canaries. When Columbus arrived at the Portuguese court John II allowed him to argue with his mathematicians, who were convinced that no less than 10,000 nautical miles separated Eastern Asia and Western Europe.

In any case the Portuguese were already committed to finding a route round Africa and John II turned down Columbus's plan while waiting for news of his latest expedition. As it happened Columbus was still in Lisbon when Bartholomew Diaz returned in December 1488 with the news that he had been driven by storms round the southernmost tip of the African continent. Diaz had therefore opened the route to India which Vasco da Gama completed ten years later.

6

With this discovery in his grasp there was no hope of interesting John II in speculation, and Columbus had to seek another patron.

The Spanish sovereigns, Ferdinand and Isabella, were anxious to compete with Portugal for trade and conquests. Bartholomew Diaz's successes meant that the African route was lost to Spain, so they were interested in Columbus's plan; it offered them a chance to reach Asia first. The Spanish court was not equipped with a body of professional geographers such as Columbus had to deal with in Portugal, and his ideas were not so closely investigated. Ferdinand and Isabella agreed to supply him with ships in his transatlantic search for Cipangu and the mainland of China. They expected to tap all the treasures of the East and at the same time to teach Christianity to the people of the newly found lands. This meant a great change in fortune for Columbus. He was no longer regarded as an untitled seaman with ideas, but embarked with the commission of Spain: 'It is our will and pleasure that you, the said Christobal Colon, after you have discovered and acquired the said islands and mainland . . . shall be our Admiral and Viceroy and Governor therein and shall be empowered henceforward to call and entitle yourself Don Christobal Colon.'

Columbus sailed for the Canaries on 3 August 1492, with his three ships, *Nina*, *Pinta* and *Santa Maria*. The *Santa Maria* was the largest of the three, probably about one hundred tons, and was made flagship. With a favourable wind the fleet could cover two hundred miles a day. They left the Canaries on 8 September. Columbus believed Cipangu was in the same latitude and so held a course due west. By good chance he had stumbled on part of the Atlantic wind system and was sailing with the easterlies. The ships made good time in perfect weather; 'like April in Andalusia', Columbus described it. But there was always the lurking dread of the time when the seamen would be afraid to go farther in an uncharted ocean. By the first week in October the ships had sailed beyond the point where Columbus expected to see land. By 10 October, the ships were running into freshening westerly winds. The men were alarmed, fearing they might never get back to Spain, and on the *Santa Maria* Columbus had to control a mutiny. The very next day they began to find signs of land, branches floating in the sea and bits of carved wood. A gale sprang up and Columbus, anxious to sight land despite the danger of running on to shoals or reefs off an unknown coast, let the ships run before it. At 2 a.m. on 12 October, the look-out on *Pinta* saw white sand cliffs in the moonlight. Sails were furled and the ships lay adrift

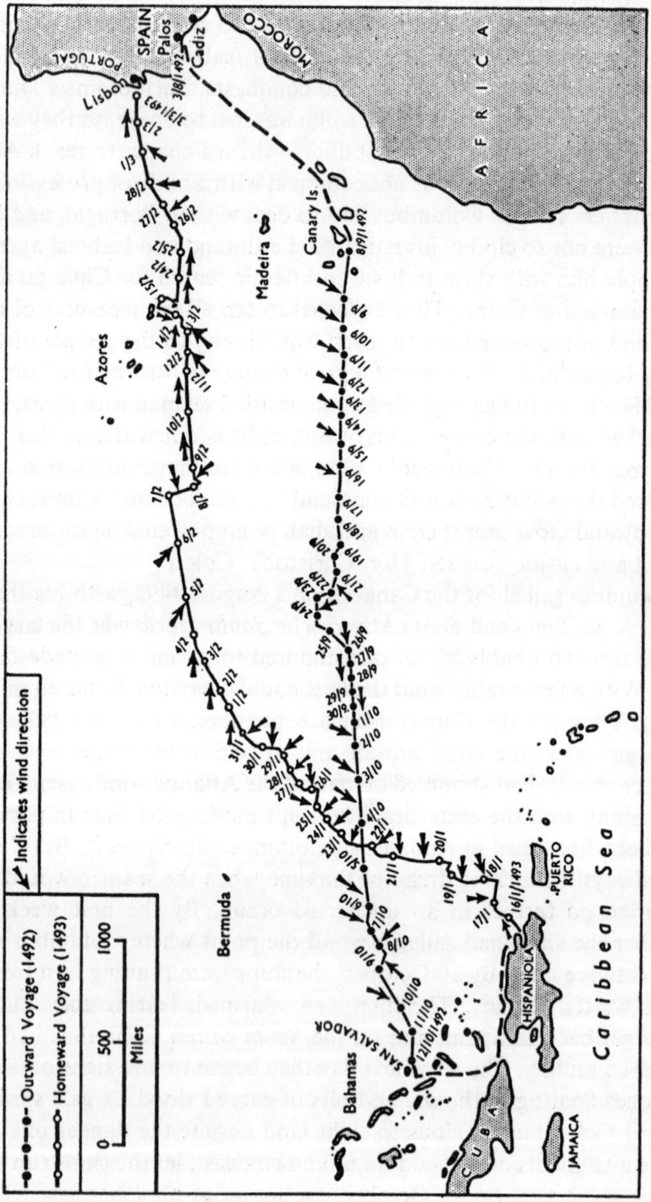

Fig. 1. The First Voyage of Columbus

until daylight revealed a safe harbour. Next day a service was held to thank God for their safe deliverance on the island Columbus named San Salvador, now called Watling Island.

At San Salvador Columbus first met the Arawaks. He took a few aboard to act as guides and interpreters and they led him without difficulty along their three-hundred-mile canoe route to Cuba. Columbus had accomplished the first object of his mission in reaching what he thought to be the eastern bounds of Asia; he was now anxious to discover the abundant gold, 'its sources being inexhaustible', that Marco Polo had reported to be in Japan. In Cuba the Indians described a great inland city, but Columbus found only a village of fifty huts. So he sailed to modern Haiti, which he called Hispaniola. Here a girl wearing a gold nose plug was captured, first evidence of the presence of gold; the local Indian *cacique* assured Columbus that much gold was to be found on the island.

The *Santa Maria* ran aground in Hispaniola and Columbus decided to leave the crew in a fort named La Navidad, with instructions to locate the gold mines reported there. Only his conviction that he had found Japan could justify his letter to the Spanish rulers announcing 'the great victory with which Our Lord has crowned my voyage'. He reported the capture of 'very many islands filled with people innumerable', from which he promised 'as much gold as their highnesses may need, spice and cotton, and mastic and aloes-wood and a thousand other things of value'.

Columbus's news promised Spain the opportunity to settle an extensive empire. From this time settlement and discovery went forward together. Seventeen ships with six months' supplies and carrying between twelve thousand and fifteen thousand colonists with seeds, farming implements, food and wine, left Spain for Hispaniola on 25 September 1493. It was the largest colonising expedition that had ever left Europe; many more people volunteered to go than the fleet could accommodate. They included officials, priests, soldiers and peasants, as well as two hundred gentlemen volunteers.

The official aims of this expedition, enumerated by Ferdinand and Isabella, were the conversion of the natives, the establishment of a trading colony and the exploration of Cuba to discover if it was an island or the mainland, since 'the Sovereign sagely suspected, and the Admiral declared, that a mainland should contain greater good things, riches and more secrets than any one of the islands'. The sovereign and the colonists alike were anxious for gold.

They were to be disappointed. The garrison at La Navidad, far from greeting Columbus on his return with news of gold, had been wiped out by a local chief who had grown tired of their endless demands for food and gold. This was the first of many clashes between the colonists and the Arawaks. Columbus had to start again on a new site, which he named Isabella, and send a fresh expedition inland in search of the gold mines. On return they reported a beautiful, fertile country and hospitable Indians who had nuggets and gold dust to trade, but no news of real riches to plunder or of great gold workings.

The colonists at Isabella were suffering in the meantime from bad health produced by changes in climate, diet and occupation, and within a month, twelve of the seventeen vessels had to be sent back to Spain for fresh supplies without any gold to pay for them. Eighteen months later supplies were still being imported because 'although the soil is very black and good they have not found the way nor the time to sow: the reason is that no one wants to live in these countries'. The colonists had come to make a quick fortune and return home; the favourite oath in Isabella was 'as God may take me back to Castille'. Many of them returned to Spain with their dreams of easy wealth shattered and spread discouraging stories about conditions in the Indies.

Things went from bad to worse. Columbus had left Hispaniola to explore the coast of Cuba at the end of April. When he returned in September, he found the settlers demoralised, roving the country in armed bands and provoking resistance from the Indians. He had to organise a campaign against the Indians, and sent five hundred of them back to Spain as slaves, in the hope that they would sell at a profit. He then tried to exact tribute from the Indian population in a desperate effort to make the colony pay; they were to give either a hawk's bell full of gold dust or 25 lb. of spun or woven cotton every three months.

This was the state of affairs when Columbus returned to Spain in June 1496. His exploration of the coast of Cuba had led some experienced seamen to believe Cuba was an island, not the mainland Columbus had promised his patrons. But Columbus could not afford to spread that news, and he made his subordinates swear they believed Cuba to be part of the mainland. Even so, the Spanish sovereigns were not impressed with the results of the first four years of West Indian settlement. The cargo of Indians proved unwelcome and

Discoveries of Columbus on his First and Second Voyages

- ← - 1st. Voyage (1492-93)
- ←·- 2nd. Voyage (1493-94)

FLORIDA

San Salvador

12/10/1492

A t l a n t i c
O c e a n

C u b a

13/6/1494

5/3/1494

Hispaniola

Puerto Rico

Virgin Is.

Montserrat

Guadeloupe
4/11/1493

16/1/1493

22/11/1493   11/11/1493

Jamaica

Dominica
3/11/1493

Martinique 3/11/1493

C a r i b b e a n
S e a

SOUTH AMERICA

Trinidad

0   300
Miles

HISPANIOLA

La Navidad   Isabella

S. Domingo

Discoveries of Columbus on his Third and Fourth Voyages

FLORIDA

A t l a n t i c
O c e a n

C u b a

Jamaica

Hispaniola

Puerto
Rico

Santa Cruz

Guadeloupe

Dominica

Martinique

30/7/1502

HONDURAS

C a r i b b e a n
S e a

Trinidad

Margarita
Islands

15/8/1498

31/7/1498

SOUTH AMERICA

0   300
Miles

- ← - 3rd. Voyage (1498)
- ←·- 4th. Voyage (1502)

Fig. 2. Discoveries of Columbus in the Caribbean

11

the Queen ordered the survivors to be freed. Expenses were mounting, and the Indies were acquiring a bad reputation.

In Hispaniola discontented Spanish colonists were forming factions. On Columbus's return on the third voyage, he found rebellion in progress against his brother Diego, whom he had left in charge, and even he was unable to impose order at once. Continued reports of disturbances and discontent persuaded the Spanish rulers to send out Francisco de Bobadilla with powers of Chief Justice and with a special commission to adjust grievances. On arrival Bobadilla was horrified to find that Columbus had hanged seven rebel Spanish colonists in an attempt to gain authority. He decided to send both the Columbus brothers back to Spain in chains.

Although Ferdinand and Isabella ordered his release, Columbus could make no headway in reclaiming his past position and honours, though he did make one more voyage of discovery in which he beat along the coast of Central America from Cape Honduras to Mosquito Point. By the time he returned, Don Nicolás de Ovando had taken over his post as the Spanish Governor and Supreme Justice of the islands and mainland of the Indies. A new type of settlement had been established in Hispaniola.

SETTLEMENT AND CONQUEST

Ovando arrived in Hispaniola in 1502 with 2,500 colonists, including seventy-three families. Of these, one thousand died so quickly that the clergy did not have time to bury them. It was not a very hopeful beginning, but under Ovando's government it was soon found that many crops brought from Spain flourished in the new climate and that livestock, pigs, goats, cattle and horses, multiplied rapidly. Wheat and barley were not very successful, but rice, date palms, oranges, olives and sugar-cane were found to grow well. Cattle ranches yielded hides and tallow to send to Spain and dried meat to supply the ships.

Ovando's business was to make the Indies profitable. This could only be done with a considerable number of workers. A settlement of Spaniards working for themselves at Santo Domingo, the newest town in Hispaniola, would have been hard put to it just to maintain themselves. Only if they had many people working for them could they have a surplus of goods to send to Spain. The Indians, as the conquered people, were expected to supply the labour force. A royal order sent to Ovando in 1503 explained the new policy: 'Because of the excessive liberty the Indians have been permitted,' it ran, 'they flee from Christians and do not work. Therefore they are to be compelled to work, so that the Kingdom and the Spaniard may be enriched and the Indians Christianised.' The order went on to authorise the *encomienda* system, which guaranteed the exploitation of the Indians without making effective provision for their conversion.

By the *encomienda* system, a Spanish colonist could be awarded a number of Indians to work for him. In return, the colonist was responsible for teaching them Christian principles, paying them wages and looking after them generally. In effect the Indian population of the islands was enslaved and, within half a century, practically exterminated. They were unaccustomed to long hours of forced labour and were driven beyond endurance by their taskmasters. They fell easy victims to European diseases such as smallpox; and their cassava was frequently destroyed by the wandering livestock brought in by the Spanish. As a labour force they were first supplemented by captives from the Bahamas, and then replaced by African slaves. But it was with the help of Indian labour in the early years that Hispaniola became the base from which the other islands of the Caribbean were settled.

Cuba, Jamaica and Puerto Rico were taken by well-armed expeditions under capable adventurer leaders still hoping to find gold in the islands. In Puerto Rico resistance by small groups of cannibal Caribs who had penetrated from the smaller islands made early capture more difficult; but elsewhere the Indians could not defend themselves. Jamaica was easily occupied in 1509 and was used for cattle-rearing by a small population of Spaniards. Cuba was conquered in a series of cruel attacks between 1511 and 1514; as the island was gradually taken over, a settlement under Velasquez developed on a similar pattern to the one in Hispaniola. Trinidad, discovered by Columbus on his third voyage, never had more than small groups of Spanish settlers.

Many of the colonists had no interest in agriculture and plantations; they still hoped to find gold. These were the men who set out to explore and conquer Central and South America. They were called *conquistadores*, and the most famous were Hernan Cortez and Pizarro. Cortez left Cuba in 1519 with six hundred men to try his luck in Mexico. There he found the cities and the gold Columbus had hoped for in Hispaniola. The rich empire of the Aztecs with its great temples and busy markets dazzled the Spaniards and prompted their greed. It took two years to secure Mexico for Spain; the ruler, Montezuma, defended his wealth with a cunning and persistence matched only by Cortez. Peru was conquered in 1530 and there

13

Pizarro found another empire rich in gold and silver. By the middle of the sixteenth century Spain had founded the first colonial empire in the Americas.

The conquest of the Main inevitably attracted many of the colonists from the islands. They had sought gold in the first place, and developing the soil of the islands seemed to them a poor alternative. Also, such problems as the risk of hurricanes and plagues of ants were discouraging. The islands became less important, and those not on the regular sea routes to the Main, such as Jamaica and Trinidad, were neglected in consequence. New immigrants were found for Hispaniola, Cuba and Puerto Rico from the overcrowded Portuguese islands of Madeira and the Azores on the other side of the Atlantic; the promise of new land attracted them.

At the same time the Portuguese were exploiting the great trading opportunities offered by the African route to India. Both Spain and Portugal were anxious to have an international agreement to settle the boundaries of their respective empires. So the world was divided between them. The Treaty of Tordesillas in 1494 fixed the western limit of Portuguese power 370 leagues west of the Azores. This in fact gave Portugal the right to colonise Brazil after its discovery by Cabral in 1500. Apart from this the Spanish American Empire held no European rival.

FURTHER READING

Sources of West Indian History, People of the Caribbean, pp. 1–4, Economic Life, pp. 31–2.

Parry and Sherlock, *A Short History of the West Indies*, Chapter 1, Discovery.

Ottley, *Spanish Trinidad*, Chapters I–VIII.

Williams, *History of the People of Trinidad and Tobago*, Chapters I and II.

QUESTIONS TO CONSIDER

1. Would you consider Columbus more important as a discoverer or as a colonist?
2. What do you consider was the most profitable use made of their West Indian islands by the Spanish colonists?
3. What conflicts were bound to occur between the Indians and the colonists in all the Spanish conquests?
4. How do you think that the Spanish rulers would organise their American Empire to make the most of it for themselves?

CHAPTER TWO

The Spanish Empire

THE PEOPLE

When the *conquistadores'* work was completed, Spain's West Indian islands formed a small part of an empire that stretched from Texas in North America to Patagonia in South America, and included the islands of Puerto Rico, Hispaniola, Cuba, Jamaica and Trinidad. With the exception of Jamaica and the western part of Hispaniola, this area belonged to the Spanish Crown for more than three hundred years. In the nineteenth century the Southern and Central American states fought for their independence; Texas became part of the United States, and Trinidad became part of the British West Indies.

The first Spanish colonists represented a cross-section of Spanish society. There were peasants who could not hope for prosperity in their own villages, soldiers who had fought and plundered for a living in Europe and now hoped to find an easier way of life in the New World, and there were the gentlemen volunteers. These were the sons of the lesser nobility who could not depend on inheriting enough wealth to support them and had to look out for themselves. The Empire offered them a chance to make their fortunes.

These colonists founded the 'creole' land-owning class. The creoles were Spanish by descent, but were born and lived in the Empire. This group organised the development of the colonies. The Indians of the mainland supplied their labour force. The *encomienda* system, first introduced in Hispaniola, was quickly brought into operation. Generations of Indians served generations of Spanish creole masters in the mines and on the plantations, bringing tremendous profit to Spain. From the Spanish and the Indians sprang the *mestizos*, half Spanish, half Indian. They formed a class of skilled workmen, overseers and domestic servants. The Indians did not provide the labour force throughout the Empire. African slaves, first used in the islands, were introduced for sugar planting and for mining in Venezuela and New Granada (modern Colombia); the knowledge of mining opera-

15

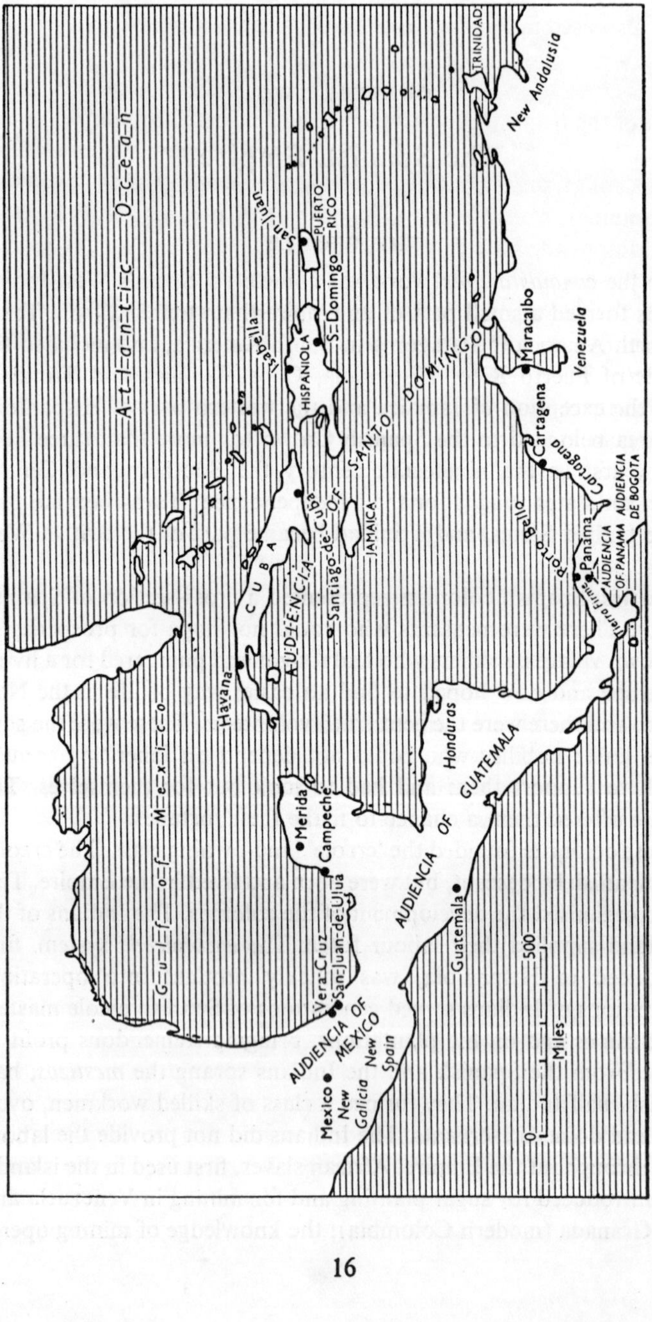

Fig. 3. The Spanish Empire

tions they brought from Africa was often vital to the Spanish. They were also used in Panama and the Gulf coast of Mexico.

PRODUCE AND TRADE

Most of the tropical products Spain had expected to find in the East were in fact supplied by the American Empire. From Venezuela came indigo, coffee, sugar and tobacco; from Peru, cacao and cinchona bark (for quinine); from Mexico, cochineal, vanilla, sugar and dye-woods. In addition, the vast cattle ranches of New Spain (part of modern Mexico) supplied oxhides, greatly in demand for boots, saddles and the leather jerkins that could turn a sword's point. These products sold in Europe at enormous profit; occasionally even at ten times their cost price.

Then there were the precious metals. Columbus had promised 'as much gold as their highnesses may wish'. The promise was fulfilled by the conquests of Cortez and Pizarro. In New Granada, Mexico and Peru, gold was found as well as emeralds, diamonds and other precious and semi-precious stones. But more important were the silver mines of Mexico, Bolivia and Peru. Silver production increased throughout the colonial period, yielding an increasing income to the Crown of Spain. It was Spain's possession of this vast mineral wealth that roused the fear and envy of her European neighbours.

The riches of the American continent made the Spaniards neglect their West Indian islands. Jamaica became the home of a few cattle ranchers whose production was infinitesimal compared with New Spain. The governors of Trinidad used the island as a base from which to seek gold on the mainland coast. Not until 1783 did the Spanish Government begin to encourage colonists to use the rich soil for sugar and cacao-planting. Hispaniola remained important as the administrative centre of the whole Spanish Caribbean, but from the beginning of the seventeenth century settlement was confined to the south, round the city of Santo Domingo.

Of the islands, Cuba became most important to Spain because of its position on the regular sea routes to the Main. Commanding the Florida passage, Havana, the chief port, was important for defence. It became the Spanish shipbuilding centre for the Caribbean and the rendezvous for the yearly convoys plying between Spain and the ports of the Empire. At first Cuban colonists also supplied indigo and tobacco; in the late seventeenth century they turned to sugar production. With great numbers of Negro slaves Cuba in time became the sugar centre of the New World.

Spain aimed to keep the wealth of her American Empire for herself. A special government department, the House of Trade, was set up in Seville to superintend all commerce between Spain and her colonies. Any trader wishing to do business in the Empire had to have a licence from the House of Trade. The cargoes he sent out were inspected to make sure the duties were properly paid; imported cargoes were inspected in the same way. All imports were checked at Seville before being distributed through Europe. The House of Trade also fixed duties and taxes to be paid on goods before they were sent to Spain from the colonies. This money was collected by revenue officials on the spot and remitted to Spain. The slave trade was another source of income. A special licence, the *asiento*, legalised the sale of a limited number of slaves to the Empire. As the demand for slaves increased, the *asiento* became a coveted privilege which sold for a good price.

This taxation system could only be successful if the products of the Empire reached market safely in Spain. As we shall see, the long Atlantic sea route gave Spain's enemies many opportunities for piracy. No trader wanted the expense of licences and taxation unless he could be reasonably certain of a cargo to sell. In the early years of the sixteenth century pirates became such a menace that Spain had to find some means of defending her trade. The solution was the convoy system.

Admiral Pedro Menéndez de Avilés established the convoy system in about 1560 and it lasted for a hundred and fifty years. Two fleets left Spain every year. One loaded at San Juan de Ulua, the port for Vera Cruz in Mexico. The other went first to Cartagena for the products of Venezuela and New Granada, and then to Nombre de Dios, or later Porto Bello, to load the products of Peru, brought by mule train across the isthmus of Panama. The two fleets met at Havana for revictualling and repairs before sailing in one convoy across the Atlantic. The whole fleet was captured only three times, though one or two ships were lost every year. So the plan was largely successful.

Unfortunately, these arrangements did not take into account the needs of the colonists. There was a constant demand in the colonies for manufactured goods such as hardware, tools, weapons, books and paper. The licensed traders travelling with the annual convoy could not satisfy these demands. The slave trade was also limited; the *asiento* allowed only a certain number of Negroes to be supplied for fear of slave rebellion. As a result the colonists were willing to buy goods and slaves from unlicensed traders. Many of these were French, English and Dutch merchants who seized this opportunity to take a share of the wealth of the Spanish Empire. So the legal traders who paid their lawful duties, the *asiento* and the convoy system did not secure all the profits of empire for the Spanish.

GOVERNMENT AND CHURCH

The government of the Spanish Empire was also rigidly organised. All colonial affairs, except the economic regulations in the hands of the House of Trade, were looked after by the Council for the Indies. The Council was appointed by the King who could attend its meetings and had to approve all its decisions. The Council framed regulations for the colonies and appointed all top-ranking officials.

The Empire was divided into four viceroyalties. New Spain and Peru were organised in the seventeenth century and, as the Empire developed, the viceroyalties of New Granada and La Plata (modern Argentina) were added in the eighteenth century. The viceroys held office for three years; they were responsible for the defence of the colonies, for putting into effect imperial legislation and making such appointments as were not made from Spain.

The viceroyalties were divided into *audiencias*, each administered by a council of lawyers appointed from Spain whose business was to report on their district to the viceroy, advise him and carry out his instructions. The *audiencias* also acted as the supreme courts of the colonies and were empowered to bring the viceroys themselves to trial if need be. The *audiencia* of Santo Domingo was permanently established in 1524 and its jurisdiction at first covered not only the Caribbean, but also the coast of Venezuela, Southern Mexico and Florida. With the growth of the mainland colonies, Florida alone remained with the Spanish islands under Santo Domingo. The *audiencia* was subdivided into provinces ruled by governors appointed in Spain. They held office for five years and one of their main duties was to make sure that taxes were collected.

In order to keep a check on these important officials the King had the right to order an investigation of an official's term of office by a *visita*—a special mission by an emissary with powers to take over the viceroyalty while he did his inspection. This imperial system was intended to keep the colonies loyal to Spain and so the Crown always preferred to appoint officials born in Spain. Thus, the most important

19

class in the Empire, the creoles, were treated as second-class citizens. Of seven hundred and seventy-two top appointments made in the history of the Empire only eighteen went to creoles. They were left to conduct local government and were only active in the *cabildos*, the town councils. The *cabildos* included only the wealthiest members of the community, but they represented the creole interest which eventually asserted itself in the wars of independence in the nineteenth century.

The Empire could not exist for ever as a mere adjunct of Spain. The products that swelled Spain's revenue also made the colonies and the colonists rich. As early as 1574 there were two hundred towns in the Empire. Traditional Indian crafts in textiles, woodcarving and the goldsmith's art were brought into service with the Spanish skills of the wheelwright and harness-maker to supply the rich with the carriages, house furnishings and other comforts their dignity demanded. The great fairs that marked the routes of the caravans from Mexico City, Lima, Quito and Santiago to Cartagena, Porto Bello and Vera Cruz to serve the yearly convoys also served the colonists. Intercolonial trade was extensive. Universities were founded at centres such as Lima, Bogota and Mexico City.

The Church in sixteenth-century Spain occupied a privileged position. It owned enough land to make its prelates the social equal of any titled lay lord. The rulers of Spain took the advice of churchmen and used their services in every sort of business; the Archdeacon of Seville, for instance, was put in charge of providing men, money and supplies for Columbus's second voyage. The Church became as important in the developing Empire as it was in Spain. The first colonists, accustomed to the Church in Spain, expected the priests to play a part in the colony. No frontier community was happy without a priest to minister absolution to the dying, and no town was complete without a church. The Crown supplied grants of land for the Church, free passages for priests, free wine and oil for the monasteries.

For the most part ordinary schools were attached to monasteries. Local colleges were usually run by priests, in particular the Jesuits who had twenty-three colleges in Mexico alone. In the Universities of Mexico and Santo Domingo, Lima and Bogota, clerics again predominated. In this way the Church was a powerful instrument for influencing the way people thought. The Crown added to the powers of the Church in this respect by giving it powers of censorship over all books entering the Empire. This was intended at first to keep out heretical Protestant works, but it could also be used against political books.

To make these powers more effective, a branch of the Inquisition, a special church court, was established from Spain. Its official powers were to prosecute those who broke the laws against blasphemy, bigamy, heresy and witchcraft; its punishments included penance, prison sentences, property confiscation and burning at the stake. Informers could remain anonymous and the crimes of 'heresy' and 'witchcraft' could have many interpretations. This tribunal was operating in Lima and Mexico by 1570. Protestant smugglers and raiders of all nationalities captured by the Spanish were brought before the Inquisition and charged as heretics. But more important for the government of the Empire, the Inquisition could be used against influential people who showed too great a tendency to criticise. In this way the Church played a part in keeping the colonies tied to Spain.

THE CHURCH AND THE INDIANS

In addition to its accustomed part in Spanish society, the Church in the Empire had a new role to play. It was responsible for the conversion and protection of the Indians. From the first, Ferdinand and Isabella were concerned that the people of the newly-won territories should be taught Christianity. The terms of the *encomienda* demanded that the masters should see that their labourers were converted to Christianity. But the colonists' attitude was summarised by Pizarro, the conqueror of Peru. When he was reminded of his duty to convert the Indians he said, 'I have not come for any such reason. I have come to take away from them their gold.'

A small group of churchmen in the sixteenth century decided that the Crown must offer greater protection to the Indians. The story of their efforts shows the way in which the Spanish Crown, the colonists and the Church faced a basic colonial problem, namely, how to treat the people of a captured territory.

The first protest against Indian exploitation was made by a Dominican friar called Montesinos. On the Sunday before Christmas 1511, he stood in the pulpit of the church in Santo Domingo before the wealthiest and most influential colonists in the island, and pronounced a dramatic indictment: 'In order to make your sins against the Indians known to you I have come up on this pulpit, I who am a voice of Christ crying in the wilderness of this island, and therefore

21

it behoves you to listen, not with careless attention, but with all your heart and senses . . . this voice says that you are in mortal sin, that you live and die in it for the cruelty and tyranny you use in dealing with these innocent people. Tell me, by what right and justice do you keep these Indians in such cruel and humble servitude? Why do you keep them so oppressed and weary, not giving them enough to eat nor taking care of them in their illness? For with the excessive work you demand of them they fall ill and die, or rather you kill them with your desire to extract and acquire gold every day. Are these not men? Are you not bound to love them as you love yourselves? Be certain that in such a state as this you can no more be saved than the Moors or Turks.'

His audience was shocked and indignant and protested to the Governor. But Montesinos went to Spain to present the case to the King. As a result Ferdinand set up a committee of churchmen to reconsider the question of Spain's right to exploit Indian labour. In 1512 they produced the Laws of Burgos whereby Spaniards were confirmed in their right to coerce the Indian, but their obligations to convert them and treat them humanely were set out in great detail, even to what food, clothes and beds they were to be supplied with; two inspectors were to be appointed in each town to see that the rules were kept.

This provided, even if the Laws were observed, only for Indians already under Spanish rule. But the Empire was growing daily; how was Spain to deal with the Indians in future and protect them from violent attacks as colonisation spread? This problem was considered urgent enough for an expedition of two thousand men, in which the King had invested money, to be held up until the churchmen decided what could be done. In the end a remarkable document was drawn up, designed to be read to Indians by a notary before Spaniards attacked them. This 'Requirement' demanded that the Indians must either acknowledge the rulers of Spain as their lords and superiors and accept Christian teaching, or the Spaniards would subdue the people, 'and we protest the deaths and losses which shall accrue from this are your fault and not that of their Highnesses'. This was clearly a device by which the Spaniards were absolved from the inevitable consequences of subjugating other peoples; it was little more than a sop to uneasy consciences. No one could seriously have thought that threatened Indians would stand by while a document, legally phrased in another language, was read to them.

PROTECTION OF THE INDIANS

Montesinos's protest and the discussions that followed convinced some priests, and from this time there were always spokesmen for Indian rights among the clergy at the Spanish court. It was to this group that Las Casas later gave his dynamic leadership. He had gone to Hispaniola, probably with Ovando's expedition, as a young man fresh from the university. He did very well for himself, was ordained a priest, took part in the conquest of Cuba and was there awarded lands and Indians. News of Montesinos's protest left him unmoved. He did not then share the Dominican idea that enslavement of the Indians was evil, even though by his own account, given in his *History of the Indies*, he was present when some of the worst outrages were committed against the Cuban Indians. Las Casas had no change of heart until, when working on his Whitsuntide sermon in 1514, he was struck by his text, 'He that sacrificeth of a thing wrongfully gotten, his offering is ridiculous and the gifts of unjust men are not accepted'. Within a few days his mind was changed. He freed his Indians and returned to Spain to join the Dominicans and to argue against Indian slavery.

Tireless lobbying by Las Casas of the Church hierarchy and the Crown itself persuaded the authorities to appoint him Protector of the Indians; he was sent back to Hispaniola to supervise a commission of friars investigating the fitness of the Indians for freedom. The friars took evidence from the colonists and eventually freed only one Indian. Las Casas protested against this decision and was threatened with arrest, so he returned to put the matter to the new ruler of Spain, the Emperor Charles V. His skill in negotiation won Charles's agreement to a number of social experiments designed to show that Indians could work as free men and live like Christians. The first attempt was carried out in Hispaniola. A group of Indians were supplied with food and left to work the gold mines voluntarily. But the Indians had no reason to show how hard they could work, and the result was that the amount of gold they produced did not even pay for the food they ate.

Las Casas's own attempts to prove that Spanish farmers and Indians could work together in a community on the coast of Tierra Firme (modern Panama) also failed. The Spanish colonists, determined to break up the attempt, sent slave traders to raid the coast and undermine any confidence Las Casas had managed to inspire in the Indians. They attacked their Spanish neighbours and, when Las Casas left for Hispaniola to protest against this interference, they turned on the priests as well. After this fiasco Las Casas spent ten years in a monastery in Hispaniola, where he began his great *History of the Indies*. He did not give up hope; his last and most successful experiment was based on his treatise, *The Only Method of Attracting People to the True Faith*, in which he suggested that peaceful means alone could convert the Indians to Christianity. This idea was put to the test between 1537 and 1550 in what is now Guatemala.

Near Vera Paz there was a tribe of Indians living in mountainous tropical jungle who were so fierce that the Spanish settlers had been unable to subdue them and had nicknamed the province Tierra de Guerra, Land of War. Las Casas and the friars accompanying him set about composing ballads in the Indian language which told the story of Christianity. They persuaded Indian merchants to entertain their customers with these; the merchants returned describing how they had repeated their performance eight nights running to their delighted fellow Indians, who were only too anxious for the friars to come and instruct them further. For a few years the success of the experiment seemed established, and the absence of Spanish colonists allowed the priests undisturbed progress with the Indians. The province was re-christened Vera Paz, Land of True Peace, and the Spanish Government sent out a succession of orders to encourage the peaceful conversion of all the Indians there. Las Casas was made Bishop of Chiapas in 1544 with the Land of True Peace as part of his province. But it all ended in bloodshed shortly after he retired from the bishopric in 1550 at the age of seventy-six. The pagan Indian priests had resentfully watched their power destroyed and their status dwindle; they now intrigued with neighbouring Indian tribes and provoked a rebellion. Two friars were murdered in church and another was sacrificed before an idol. In the end the King ordered reprisals and the experiment in peaceful conversion was at an end.

Protecting the Indians was an impossible task. It involved asking the settlers to abandon the profits of exploitation for the virtues of teaching Christianity, and asking the Indians to abandon their way of life and turn to the God of the Spaniards. While the Vera Paz experiment was in progress, the Spanish Government made a last great effort to abolish the basis of Indian exploitation by putting an end to the *encomienda* system. Charles V once again turned to Las Casas for advice in drafting a new system. The New Laws of 1542

24

made it illegal to enslave any more Indians and, when the present slave-owners died, their Indians were to become Crown slaves. But a law to end the *encomienda* system could not have been more than a magnificent gesture unless Spain had been willing to abandon her empire altogether. The Church in the New World joined with the settlers in vigorously opposing the Laws and they never came into effect.

The Church missions played an important part on the frontiers of the Empire and in the less developed islands such as Jamaica and Trinidad. The Indians were entirely in their charge and the missions represented the farthest outpost of Spanish rule. Some missions exploited the Indians; a group of fathers in Venezuela, for instance, indulged in the slave trade. In others, the Indians worked on the mission land, attended school to learn Spanish and new crafts, while the most intelligent were taught reading and writing in preparation for entry into the Church. All the missions sent back to Spain invaluable maps and information about these regions. They undoubtedly played a large part in extending the influence of the Spanish Empire.

FURTHER READING

Sources of West Indian History, Religion and Education, pp. 141–2.

Parry and Sherlock, *A Short History of the West Indies*, Chapter II, The Spanish Indies.

Williams, *Documents of West Indian History*, Chapter II, The Economic Organisation of the Spanish Caribbean, Chapter VI, The Spanish Colonial System.

Ottley, *Spanish Trinidad*, Chapters X, XIV–XVI.

Williams, *History of the People of Trinidad and Tobago*, Chapter III.

Evan Jones, *Protector of the Indians*.

QUESTIONS TO CONSIDER

1. How did the Imperial Government keep control of the Spanish Empire?

2. 'They undoubtedly played a large part in extending the influence of the Spanish Empire.' Do you agree with this statement about the Church in the Empire?

3. How would a churchman have argued both for and against the *encomienda* system?

4. How do you expect that other European powers reacted to the growth of this empire and what action do you anticipate that they took?

CHAPTER THREE

Pirates, Traders, Pioneers

RAIDS ON THE EMPIRE

Spanish wealth aroused much jealousy amongst other European nations, anxious themselves to expand and become rich. Furthermore, Spain used her wealth from America to finance long wars in Europe to extend her power there. Her rivals, the French, the Dutch and the English realised that, since Spanish colonists were in possession of the continent of South and Central America, they could never control Spain in Europe alone. To be successful they had to attack at sea and on this side of the Atlantic, at the source of Spanish wealth. They began with illicit trading and pirate attacks on Spanish ships in the Caribbean area. Later they settled in the small islands that Spain had neglected. By raids and infiltration, French, Dutch and English pioneers gradually established themselves on the Guiana coast and in the islands, deliberately disregarding Spanish claims to a monopoly as the firstcomer.

France was the first country to resent Spain's increasing power on both sides of the Atlantic. In a series of wars in the sixteenth century, the French tried to get some of the wealth of the Indies for themselves, both to weaken Spain and to help pay for the wars. This meant using sea power; but no government at this time had a big enough revenue to support a navy. So the French Government issued letters of *marque* which gave the owners of privateers a legal right to capture Spanish ships and hold towns to ransom. The privateers were fitted out by business men who expected to make a profit by trading the captured cargoes. In this way it was hoped that attacks on the Spanish Empire would more than pay for themselves.

At first the privateers were lucky to pick up a few cargoes of oxhides and gold dust, but in 1523 a French privateer lurking near the Azores took two galleons, part of a fleet sent by Cortez from Mexico with the treasures of Montezuma's palace aboard. News of the captured gold masks, jewelled head-dresses and feathered cloaks spread through the ports of Europe, exciting appetites for a further share of

26

Spanish treasure. Pirates crossed the Atlantic and centred their operations on the Bahamas where the privateers could lie in wait for the Spanish ships as they came through the Florida Channel. Spanish settlements were attacked from one end of the Caribbean to the other. In 1553, François le Clerc, one of the most successful French pirates, with ten ships pillaged almost every island settlement, including Santiago de Cuba where he took 80,000 pesos, worth £120,000, and the key town of Havana, which he utterly devastated.

Privateering was so thoroughly established that when the French and Spanish rulers signed the Treaty of Cateau-Cambresis to end the war in 1559, both acknowledged that there was no way of stopping it. As a recognition of this the convention of 'no peace beyond the line' was established; that is, European peace treaties would not operate west of the Azores. The privateers would be treated as pirates if captured by the Spanish at any time, but the French Government were not to be responsible for their attacks on Spanish property in America in time of peace. The convention of 'no peace beyond the line' lasted until the end of the seventeenth century, and the distinction between piracy and privateering was decided by whether there was war between the countries or not. The practice continued regardless.

In addition to fighting France, Spain became involved in a war with the Netherlands, then part of Spain's European possessions. The Dutch were so embittered by Spanish domination that they finally rebelled. As part of their resistance, the rebels followed the example of the French and sent out privateers to the Caribbean. Dutch wealth already depended on trading activity, so they had plenty of merchant ships ready to use in the challenge to Spain. Dutch privateers first made their appearance in 1569 and, from then until the truce of 1609, they were a permanent menace to Spanish settlements.

Spain's third rival was England, which, between 1559 and 1563, was established as a Protestant country. England was not at first powerful enough to declare open war, but private ventures against Spain were encouraged by the English Government. The Spanish Empire offered good prospects not only for piracy, but also for trade both in manufactured goods and slaves. For the first half of the sixteenth century this illicit trade was dominated by the Portuguese, owners of the West African slave forts. The most famous English trader to take a share of Spanish colonial trade was John Hawkins. At first he tried to get legal trading rights from the Spanish Government by offering his services against the French privateers. This offer was ignored, but Hawkins made his first voyage in 1562 regardless; he traded three cargoes of slaves at small settlements on the north coast of Hispaniola, taking hides and sugar as his return cargo. He was careful to apply for licences to trade from local officials, although they were not authorised to give them, and to pay all Spanish customs fees and duties.

Hawkins's second trip, two years later, took him to the coast of Tierra Firme and the Isthmus where he hoped to add gold and pearls to the return cargo. Investors in this second voyage made a profit of 60 per cent. On his last voyage in 1567, Hawkins kept up the show of being a legal trader, although the Spanish authorities had never accepted him and war between England and Spain was obviously coming soon. He could afford to take no risks but, when his ships were damaged by storm, he put in for repairs at San Juan de Ulua. Here he had the misfortune to meet with the Viceroy of New Spain, newly arrived from Spain with the annual convoy. The Spaniards attacked and sank four of Hawkins's six ships, leaving him aboard the *Minion* with two hundred survivors from his original complement of three hundred. Only fifteen arrived back in Plymouth.

Trading with the Spanish had proved profitable, however, and from this time forward English traders were to be found in the Caribbean. When the first English privateering voyages were made, England was on the verge of war with Spain. Francis Drake, one of the survivors of Hawkins's last venture, returned to the area in three successive years on trading expeditions. The third, in 1572, turned into a spectacular pirate raid when Drake made a land attack on the mule trains loaded with Peruvian silver before they reached Nombre de Dios. Three mule trains yielded enough booty to make every sailor rich for life; fifteen tons of silver had to be left behind when the crew made for the ships.

The Spanish settlers lived in fear of privateering raids and sent constant petitions to the government in Madrid. Eventually, as we have seen, Pedro Menéndez de Avíles was sent out. He realised that a regular police patrol of swift ships was needed, and by 1582 there were two squadrons on duty, one at Cartagena and one at Santo Domingo. Two squadrons could not defend all the Caribbean, however, and in any case they were never properly maintained. Most Spanish colonial towns had to rely on their own efforts, aided by such Spanish garrisons as could be spared from European duty.

As the colonies developed, the towns became bigger, more prosperous and better able to defend themselves, so that by the end of the century it was becoming more difficult for small bands of privateers to be successful. Drake's 'Indies' voyage of 1585 to 1586 resulted in booty worth more than £300,000, but his last voyage, from 1595 to 1596, with twenty-seven ships, was a disaster. The Spaniards defeated his attack on San Juan, Puerto Rico, blocked an attempt to cross the Isthmus of Panama, and finally, after Drake's death from dysentery, intercepted the fifteen remaining ships in the Florida Channel. The battle was indecisive, but there were no profits to take back to England.

The pirate raids could lead to spectacular successes or miserable failures, costly in life to the adventurers and in fortune to those who had financed them. Piracy went on for generations in the Caribbean; but in the seventeenth century European merchants and capitalists found more profitable and less uncertain ways of establishing themselves in the area.

DUTCH ENTERPRISE

It was the Dutch merchants who, by the beginning of the seventeenth century, were offering the most effective challenge to Spain's West Indian monopoly. While war against Spain was going on in Europe, merchants in the Netherlands were sending twenty ships a year to buy hides in Hispaniola alone, and ten ships a month collected salt at Araya under the nose of the Spanish Governor of Venezuela. All these ships arrived with trade goods which they sold at lower prices than their rivals, chiefly the Portuguese and English.

In many ways the Dutch were the most implacable enemy of Spain. By the time a twelve-year truce was agreed upon in 1609, they had laid the foundations of a great colonial empire in the East where a succession of Dutch traders had slowly edged a way through the Portuguese monopoly and founded trading stations in India. The Dutch East India Company, formed in 1602, was really an amalgamation of all the individual Dutch concerns which had gained a foothold for trade in India. A large fleet had been developed to support these activities.

It was therefore a powerful subject nation that came to terms with Spain in 1609. Not only did they gain a twelve-year independence from Spanish rule, but they refused to recognise Spain's monopoly rights in the West Indies. The Dutch would only recognise Spain's monopoly in areas 'effectively occupied', that is, in Hispaniola, Cuba, Jamaica and Puerto Rico, which the Spanish had actually settled. All other areas, the Leeward and Windward Islands, part of the South American coast and North America were to be left open. This challenge was made at a time when England, France and Holland were in a position to follow up their raids and illicit trading by planting colonies for themselves. The limits to the Spanish Empire were in fact now set, and new countries were ready to take part in oversea expansion.

The earliest attempts at settlement were made, not in the islands, but on the Guiana coast of South America. Between the Orinoco and the Portuguese colony of Brazil was the Wild Coast, reputedly rich in gold, which attracted Dutch, English and French adventurers, often in mixed groups. These settlements were unsuccessful. Supplies were difficult to maintain and the Carib Indians were hostile; attempt after attempt was made, only to fail eventually. It was not until 1616 that a lasting colony was founded on the banks of the Essequibo with a mixed group of English and Dutchmen, under Dutch leadership; this was the beginning of the history of Guiana.

The Dutch, however, were closely controlled by their government in Holland who were concerned above all with trade and wealth, but only with settlement if it was clearly to create more profitable trade. The Dutch West India Company was founded in 1621 at the instigation of William Usselinx, who had persuaded the government that the great commercial success of the East India Company could be repeated in the West Indies. Usselinx felt that wealth would follow from establishing colonies rather than from trade, but his rulers were more attracted by the idea of securing monopoly of the slave trade with the Spanish Empire. The Dutch company was therefore primarily concerned to secure trade in the developing Caribbean area and only secondarily to plant colonies there. As the most efficient European traders in the world, the Dutch became the 'foster-fathers' of the early West Indian colonies. Without them English and French settlers in the islands would have found it even harder to establish themselves than they did.

ISLAND COLONISTS

From the ranks of the French and English mainland adventurers who failed to found lasting colonies on the Wild Coast came some of the earliest settlers in the smaller islands. The leaders of the various mainland expeditions left the Caribbean; but their unknown followers were still anxious to find land and peace to grow tobacco, which was in ever-increasing demand in Europe and which the Dutch captains were very ready to trade.

Thomas Warner was an unsuccessful colonist who had been a member of the most promising English enterprise in Guiana, North's Amazon Company. Captain Roger North's expedition in 1620 had established themselves and planted tobacco despite the usual setbacks of disease, hardship and hostility from the Indians. Its failure came from another source. The settlement was very unpopular with the Spanish who wanted no rivals on the Main. In 1620 the Spanish ambassador in London managed to persuade the English King to withdraw his promised royal patent from the company.

Warner and some companions left the mainland two years later in search of a new area where they could plant again, 'free from the disorder that did grow in the Amazons for want of government amongst their countrymen and to be quiet amongst themselves'. He had heard of St. Christopher as a small fertile island where he would be free from interference and where his followers would have little opportunity to leave in search of other occupations in the area. The island fulfilled the promise, and Tegreman, the King of the Indians there, was friendly. They planted an experimental crop of tobacco which was a success; by 1623, therefore, Warner was certain enough of his scheme to want a backer to finance equipment and supplies for its further development, and to trade the tobacco for him.

In 1625 there were new arrivals in St. Christopher. A French privateer put in at the island for repair after an unsuccessful encounter with a Spanish galleon. One of its officers was Pierre D'Esnambuc who had been a freebooter in Caribbean waters for ten years. He saw the possibilities of the island and proposed to Warner that the two European groups might live together for their mutual defence against Carib attacks from neighbouring islands. Early in 1626 D'Esnambuc also set sail for Europe in search of backing for his enterprise.

In England, Warner found a wealthy supporter in the merchant, Ralph Merrifield. Together they secured a royal charter permitting Warner and Merrifield to plant and trade not only in St. Christopher, but also in Nevis and Montserrat. Warner received an appointment as governor of the newly established colony. In France, D'Esnambuc obtained similar advantages from a different source. In 1623 the government of France passed into the hands of the great Cardinal-

Minister, Richelieu, who was determined to make France a power in Europe. He was very ready to entertain ideas for challenging Spain's unrivalled prosperity in the Spanish American Empire, and D'Esnambuc's modest plan for a colony in St. Christopher seemed the beginning of such a challenge. Richelieu was the largest shareholder in the Company of St. Christopher which was formed to back D'Esnambuc's colony and any other islands 'not possessed by any Christian prince'. D'Esnambuc was also appointed governor of his colony. So, side by side the English and French colonists embarked on tobacco planting and faced the early hardships involved.

This was the beginning of a phase in which the small islands were in quick succession claimed in the names of the European rulers of their claimants. In 1625, John Powell, the commander of a merchant ship returning from a trading voyage to Brazil, landed in Barbados and laid claim to the island in the name of the King of England. On his return to England, the owners of the ship, the Anglo-Dutch firm of Courteen, were prepared to finance a settlement under Powell in Barbados, so good seemed the prospects for colonisation. Powell returned with eighty men in 1627; two years later there were about 1,700 people in the island.

Nevis was settled from St. Kitts in 1628, and Antigua and Montserrat in 1632. Between 1630 and 1640 the Dutch established themselves in Curaçao, Saba, St. Martin and St. Eustatius, all of which they used as depots for their trade with the French and English settlers. Dutch traders brought equipment and supplies to the struggling colonies and found a ready European market for the tobacco produced. In years when storms spoilt the crop, the Dutch were prepared to give credit until a new crop restored the colonists' finances. When the profits to be gained from tobacco declined, it was on Dutch advice that a change of crop was considered.

French enterprise was a little slower than the English because France in 1635 had joined in the exhausting Thirty Years War which dragged on in Europe from 1618 until 1648. Nevertheless, Cardinal Richelieu still saw colonisation as an important part of his attack on Spain, and in 1635 he organised further help for Governor D'Esnambuc in a Company of the Isles of America. This was like the Dutch West India Company in that it was organised and supported by the government with the help of private shareholders. In France the merchant class was smaller and less powerful than in England. The French Government had in fact claimed North America from 1524,

calling it New France, but French merchants did not show much enthusiasm for raising capital for settlement. It was left to French
statesmen to encourage and put government money into colonisation,
and many French settlers were transported across the Atlantic by
national companies.

In 1635, the directors of the Company of the Isles of America made
an arrangement with two adventurers, L'Olive and Duplessis, who
had surveyed Martinique, Guadeloupe and Dominica on a voyage
from St. Christopher. They were granted the right of colonising any
of these islands, the status of governor and promises of settlers and
financial support. They were daunted by the rugged mountains of
Dominica and returned to settle Martinique and Guadeloupe.
D'Esnambuc was appointed governor-general of the three colonies
now claimed in the name of France.

The fact that these claims could be made, despite the strength of
the Spanish American Empire, was due to the activity of Dutch
fleets which continued to attack Spanish shipping as a retaliation for
Spanish warfare against the Dutch in Europe. One part of the wasteful Thirty Years War was a Spanish attempt to take from Holland
the independence established for twelve years in the truce of 1609.
On their own soil the Dutch were suffering violence and bloodshed;
at sea they took their revenge.

In 1628, a Dutch fleet achieved what every pirate had dreamed of;
it captured the whole Plate Fleet off Cuba, bringing to the Dutch
West India Company 200,000 lb. of silver, 135 lb. of gold and quantities of pearls, indigo, cochineal, sugar, logwood and hides. The
Spanish never achieved such a rich annual cargo again. It was a
blow to their prosperity, but even more to their prestige. It was followed up in the sixteen-thirties by the Dutch capture of the rich
sugar-planting area round Pernambuco in Portuguese Brazil. As Portugal was ruled by Spain from 1580 to 1640, it was the Spanish who
lost valuable revenue.

The government in Madrid was then in the hands of incompetent
self-seeking rulers, but they did make one last effort against the
Dutch. In 1640, eighty-six ships and twelve hundred men were sent
to South America, only to be destroyed in the four-day naval battle
of Itamaraca along the coast of Brazil. The Spanish Empire was left
virtually at the mercy of its enemies. After this battle even the annual
convoy system broke down. The Spanish settlers never knew when
the fleet would arrive and themselves became as dependent on the

Dutch traders for slaves and manufactured goods as the other European settlers were.

By these continued attacks the Dutch fleets practically immobilised the Spanish in the Caribbean while the French and English colonies were facing their first difficulties. There were Spanish attacks on the islands; one drove D'Esnambuc from St. Christopher for a time. But they were sporadic and not followed up. None permanently expelled any of the new colonists.

FURTHER READING

Sources of West Indian History, People of the Caribbean, pp. 4–9, Economic Life, pp. 32–4, Government and Politics, pp. 89–91.

Williams, *Documents of West Indian History*, Chapter VII, The International Struggle for the Caribbean.

Carter, Digby and Murray, *History of the West Indian Peoples*, III, Chapter 12, the French and English Corsairs.

Parry and Sherlock, *A Short History of the West Indies*, Chapter III, The Challenge to Spain.

Chapter IV, The Settlement of the Outer Islands, pp. 45–56.

Jesse, *Outlines of St. Lucia's History*, Chapter II.

Ottley, *History of Tobago*, Chapters I–II.

QUESTIONS TO CONSIDER

1. Which of the methods given in this chapter do you think would be most likely to threaten the wealth of Spain?
2. Do you agree that 'the Dutch became the foster-fathers' of the early West Indian colonies? What other help did they have?
3. How was your territory first settled?
4. What would you consider to be the most immediate problems of the settlers?

The Colonists

THE EARLY SETTLERS

There was no shortage of people for the new colonies. The English had experience of transporting emigrants to new territories from the time of the Virginia settlement in 1609, and there were plenty of people who would take risks in the hope of bettering themselves. Neither France nor England could employ all their people and the number of indigent beggars was increasing alarmingly. 'Every man hath enough to do to shift for his own maintenance,' explained one English writer, 'so that the greatest part are driven to extremities, and many do get their living by other men's losses; witness our extortioners, thieves, unnecessary ale-sellers, beggars.' These he felt might perhaps prove profitable members 'in the New Found Land'. The growing number of paupers was a reason for encouraging emigration even before the colonies proved their worth as profitable concerns.

The English Government did not seek to direct the activities of colonists until their success had been proved. Nor, on the other hand, were they discouraged. England had become a maritime nation and if colonial trade could be developed it would encourage shipping, so necessary for defence. The government, therefore, maintained a general interest without much interference, and without giving material support. Royal patents were granted to companies and new territories were taken in the name of the King; beyond that, to begin with, there was little communication between colonists and royal officials.

English settlers were financed by joint-stock companies. Private investors bought shares valued at £12 10s. each, which was the estimated cost of 'planting' a settler. The company so formed was given a royal charter granting the monopoly of a geographical area where no person outside the company was allowed to trade. Private enterprise companies of this sort backed settlements in Virginia in 1609 and New England in 1627 as well as in the West Indian islands.

We have already seen that merchants like Merrifield and Courteen had not yet come to the fore in France, and it needed government encouragement and finance to secure backing for the French colonies. In the West Indies, however, the situation was similar for both groups of colonists. The supply of workers could best be maintained by employing indentured servants who contracted to serve their masters, usually for five years, before they became free settlers themselves. The able-bodied beggars, thieves and extortioners were no doubt among their number; debtors and others with personal reasons for escaping their past would seize such an opportunity. There were also respectable young people with no prospects in England, France or Ireland, whose spirit of adventure led them into this enterprise. The long war years had disrupted many families in France, leaving men ready to make a new start abroad. Whoever they were, they came out in their numbers.

Migration from island to island became increasingly common as new opportunity offered. Some islands such as Antigua, Nevis and Montserrat were taken over and populated from older colonies. In some cases the wandering life was a substitute for the hard work of the settler, and the more restless migrants were obvious recruits for piracy.

The first settlers were pioneers who cut down timber to build and to clear the land for planting the tobacco which was their first choice of crop. Richard Ligon, first historian of Barbados and himself an early settler, reported on the first tasks. 'The woods were so thick,' he wrote, 'and most of the trees so large and massive as they were not to be fallen with so few hands; and when they were laid along, the branches were so thick and boisterous as required more help, and these strong and active men, to lop and remove them off the ground. At the time we came first there we found both Potatoes, Maize and Bonavists planted between the boughs, the trees lying along the ground; so far short was the ground then of being cleared.' This was in 1647, twenty years after the first settlement was made. The earliest colonists lived on potatoes, plantains and maize, which 'with the Hogs flesh they found, served only to keep life and soul together'. Until transatlantic communication improved, supplies from Europe came very irregularly and slowly. In any case, a profitable crop for sale on the European markets was necessary to put the colonists in the way of trade at all.

The pamphlet writers were ready with descriptions of the easy life and good profits the colonies would yield. Everyone knew about the riches of the Spanish Main, and tall stories were told about the islands. 'All the prisoners are fettered in gold,' proclaimed the hero of one English play, 'and for rubies and diamonds, they go forth on holidays and gather them by the sea-shore.' The ports of London, Bristol, Liverpool, Dieppe, Havre and St. Malo were dangerous ground for the gullible, for there were plenty of agents to tempt people to migrate with promises of wealth and ease. Kidnapping increased as the facts became better known and recruits were harder to find.

The difficulties and hardships had to be revealed by experience. Emigrants arrived in the West Indies after a journey lasting between four and six weeks, in small vessels where the cabin passengers might be sleeping in cubby holes 6 feet by 3 feet, liable to be flooded in heavy weather. Working-class emigrants were crowded between decks and battened down during storms. 'They would not lie down,' reported one observer, 'but sat supporting their little ones who must otherwise have been drowned. No victuals could be dressed, nor fire got on so that all they had to subsist on was some raw potatoes and a very small proportion of mouldy biscuit.' This would normally be supplemented with bacon, salt beef and herring, with some bread and oatmeal. Cabin class passengers usually took their own supplies of eggs, butter, wine and other luxuries. The Atlantic crossing did not prepare the settlers for the rigours of a tropical climate where, as a new arrival noted, 'it is strange to see lusty young men, in appearance well and in three or four days in the grave, snatched away in a moment with fevers, agues, fluxes and dropsies'.

Even those who came out to stake a claim in the land and become estate owners had a hard life. Food and supplies were short until trade developed. Their houses were primitive by European standards, large, wooden structures, open to the rafters and sparsely furnished. There was little social life in a barely established colony, and violent quarrels broke out between neighbours. They faced also the danger of rebellion, both from indentured servants and, soon, from slaves.

CHOICE OF CROP

The success of the whole adventure depended on the colonists finding a profitable crop. They knew that the islands had no mineral wealth and that their future lay in the development of some tropical crop. There was little official debate or planning on the matter; the choice came largely through the trial and error of individual groups of colonists who had to make a decision for themselves.

There was a wide choice between the various things that would grow in the West Indies. It included sugar, tobacco, coffee, cotton, cacao, fruit, ground provisions, corn, dyes and, perhaps, timber. Some of these had to be ruled out at once because the slowness and irregularity of transatlantic shipping made it impossible to export perishable goods. For instance, tropical fruit and vegetables were unsuitable.

There was also another important consideration. In the seventeenth century ships were small so that it was not profitable to export bulky, relatively cheap goods, such as corn. In general, trade between distant places was confined to high-priced luxury goods which found their way only into the homes of the wealthy. For example, Eastern merchants had introduced tea into Europe and in the sixteen-sixties it was selling for about sixty shillings a pound; this was the basis of the Dutch trade in India. The West Indies needed as profitable a crop as tea was proving for the Eastern merchants.

Of the list of products which the West Indian colonist might most easily produce, six commodities could find markets among the relatively well-to-do people of Europe; cacao, coffee, cotton, dyes, sugar and tobacco. Of these tobacco, cotton and sugar offered the greatest inducements. Coffee and cacao were served in the 'coffee-houses' of Europe, but from the late seventeenth century onwards, they had to face an ever-growing competition from tea. Cotton and dyes, of which indigo and logwood were the West Indian exports, were purchased by cloth-makers rather than by individual shoppers, and the market remained small until after the inventions of the middle and late eighteenth century which enabled English factories to spin and weave cloth in great quantity.

Tobacco was highly profitable and was the choice of the earliest European colonists. People had long been used to smoking herbs for their medicinal effects. Tobacco smoking or the taking of snuff however became a fashion, indulged in for pleasure or for display. Smoking soon became a habit, and so created a sure market for tobacco. By 1628 Barbados and St. Kitts had already exported 100,000 lb. of tobacco.

The use of sugar also became habitual. In the Middle Ages, Europeans had sweetened their food and drink with honey. When sugar first became available it was used as an expensive alternative to honey, but, as the drinking of coffee and tea grew in popularity and the drinking of ales and wines declined, the demand for sugar rapidly increased.

Of these two precious export crops, West Indians quite soon discovered that their greater profits would come from sugar. Tobacco could be grown in Virginia in greater bulk than anywhere in the West Indies. With a profitable alternative, there was no point in maintaining competition. So, although tobacco was grown at first in St. Kitts, Barbados and Martinique, by the middle of the seventeenth century colonists began to abandon it for sugar-cane. By this time, the English West Indian colonists had sent home about one million pounds of tobacco compared with three and a half million produced in Virginia. The French were disturbed by the same competition and had been ordered to plant a tobacco crop only every second year because there was a glut on the market and only low prices could be obtained. In these circumstances, alternative crops were essential for both French and English colonists; those who could do so made attempts to get into the sugar market. In general only those who, for one reason or another, found it impossible to produce sugar profitably, chose to cultivate any other crop.

EUROPEAN INTEREST

The degree of interest of the European countries in their colonies was determined by the amount of wealth to be derived from them; profit was the original incentive for colonisation. We have seen that the Dutch West India Company was directed by the Dutch Government, who already knew from experience in the East Indies what profits could be expected from colonial trade; they would not farm out control to individuals as the French and English did.

It would seem that the French companies, organised by the government, should have been equally controlled from France, but the great difference was that French colonists traded with the Dutch and so in practice were more independent of control from France than the Dutch colonists whose company furnished their supplies. In fact, although Richelieu appointed the directors of both the St. Christopher and the Isles of America Companies, and the governor-general of the French islands, he had no more effective control than the English King who was making little attempt to exercise any.

D'Esnambuc, as first governor-general, was occupied with ensuring the survival of the first French West Indian settlement in its pioneer-

ing stages, and had to make the kind of day-to-day emergency decisions which were certainly not controlled across the Atlantic. De
Poincy, his successor in the office, was even more independent in his
methods, using a form of arbitrary justice which went as far as the
imprisonment of L'Olive, the Governor of Guadeloupe, on one
occasion.

Difficulties did arise between the governors and the governor-
general in the French islands. Headstrong and ruthless, they were
nearly all anxious to develop their own islands profitably, even at the
expense of the others. Their powers were strengthened in 1645 when
an arrangement was made for law cases to be tried in the colonies
instead of going to France for judgment. The governors, with the
assistance of councils of their own choosing, were made supreme
judges in their own islands. In the quarrels about lands and rights
which were always flaring up between planters, the governors could
lay down the law and use force to secure it. Even visits of investigation by individual directors of the Company of the Isles of America
or, on occasion, by royal officials did little to control the French
planters, who were trying to develop their new land profitably and
who did not accept readily any limitations on their activities from
France.

In 1648 the French governors reached the height of their independence, for the Company of the Isles of America failed. The directors sold the islands to the governors who ruled them, and let them
conduct their affairs to suit themselves. De Poincy continued in St.
Kitts; a highly individual ex-director of the company, Houël, ruled
Guadeloupe despotically for many years, and du Parquet who was a
rather better governor in Martinique sent out small groups of
settlers to St. Lucia and Grenada. They all increased the Dutch trading connection considerably while they developed their early sugar.
The Dutch advised them, provided them with equipment and sold
their produce.

The English Government was not indifferent and the Crown kept
the right of appointment to office. The previously unknown men who
first settled the islands and their merchant backers were not allowed
to own them. At first the King granted the islands to chosen noble-
men who were given the title of Lord Proprietor. In 1627 the Earl of
Carlisle was made Lord Proprietor of most of the Caribbean islands
then colonised, with the right to tax them and to raise duties on their
produce. He held this position until he died a bankrupt, despite the

money that had passed through his hands. His son, in 1647, leased the islands to Francis, Lord Willoughby, on condition that half the revenue would go to the payment of his creditors. These men were the lords proprietor who held the developing English territories for thirty-six years before they came under direct control by the Crown.

The proprietors were primarily concerned with the profits they could make from the islands. Carlisle's patent allowed him, without rendering any account for ten years, to collect customs on the West Indian trade, both in England and the island ports. He is said to have made £9,000 a year on the tobacco imports in English ports alone. In addition, taxes were levied from the planters for payment to the proprietor and the governor. A poll-tax of 40 lb. of tobacco a head became a regular payment in Barbados. Additional sums were levied for the Established Church, the Captain of the Train Bands of Militia, and, in the Leeward Islands, for defence against Carib attacks. The leasing of land was also an occasion for raising further revenue. These practices eventually led to objections from the colonists.

A place for expressing such objections soon came into existence. The English Crown delegated control to the lord proprietor, but he did not have absolute power. Proprietors appointed governors of the islands who in their turn appointed their own councils of ten or so leading planters. But Carlisle's original charter also said that laws were to be made 'with the Consent, Assent and Approbation of the freeholders of the said Province, or the greater part of them thereunto to be called'. So, in addition to the governor's council there was also an assembly of men elected by the freeholders. At first in most territories, they sat together for business, but later they became separate bodies. The islands were also divided into parishes with vestries to run them. Courts of law were established. The judges were the more prominent settlers and very seldom trained in law. The Council and the Assembly were regarded by the settlers as the equivalents of the House of Lords and the House of Commons in England. They soon claimed for them the same powers and privileges as the English Houses and so came into conflict, first with the proprietors and later with the home government.

By the middle of the seventeenth century it was clear that European colonisation of the West Indies had come to stay and that a profitable crop had been chosen for production. For the first decade, while the young sugar industry was being developed, the French and

English colonies made their advances with the aid of the Dutch traders as they had done previously, and their dependence on the Dutch was closer than ever. So colonies, started by English and French money, were bringing comparatively little profit to England or France. This certainly stirred the two governments into action, because colonies were now worth closer attention and control.

FURTHER READING

Sources of West Indian History, Economic Life, pp. 38-9.

Williams, *Documents of West Indian History*, Chapter VIII, The Early Organisation of the Non-Spanish Colonies, pp. 267-281.

Sherlock, *West Indian Story*. Chapter 9, White Bondservants, Chapter 10, England in the Caribbean, Chapter 11, Tobacco Patch and Sugar Plantation.

Carter, Digby and Murray, *History of the West Indian Peoples*, III, Chapter 15, The Character of the Earliest British Settlements.

Hoyos, *Our Common Heritage*, Henry Hawley.

QUESTIONS TO CONSIDER

1. Do you agree that 'the success of the whole adventure depended on the colonists finding a new crop'?
2. Which do you consider the most important reason for the choice of sugar?
3. Why were Negro slaves introduced into the West Indies?
4. What action would you expect the English and French Governments to take when their colonies were 'worth closer attention and control'?

CHAPTER FIVE

Planters and Rulers

SUGAR REVOLUTION

The change from tobacco to sugar planting was revolutionary. Tobacco cultivation is intensive and demands great care and attention to each plant; cane cultivation is extensive and the planter is concerned about the state of a field of cane rather than about individual plants. Tobacco growing requires no great expenditure on buildings and machinery; sugar must be processed where the cane is grown, therefore a much greater outlay in buildings, livestock and machinery is required. Tobacco was grown on small holdings; sugar-cane was an estate crop and the manufacture of sugar was expensive. A colonist and his family with the occasional help of friends and neighbours could profitably produce tobacco on a small family holding, but the production of sugar for export demanded much land, much capital equipment and large gangs of skilled and unskilled labour.

A change of such magnitude could be neither immediate nor easy. And, as the historian Ligon tells us, the Barbadians, and those in other islands who were doing the same thing, could not simply switch over from one staple crop to another without much trial and error. 'At the time we landed on this Island, which was in the beginning of September, 1647,' he wrote of Barbados, 'we were informed, partly by those Planters we found there, and partly by our own observations, that the great work of Sugar-making was but newly practised by the inhabitants there. Some of the most industrious men, having gotten Plants from *Pernambuco*, a place in Brazil, and made trial of them at the Barbados; and finding them to grow, they planted more and more, as they grew and multiplied upon the place, till they had such a considerable number as they were worth the while to set up a very small *Ingenio* (factory) and so made trial what Sugar could be made upon that soil. But, the secrets of the work being not well understood, the Sugars they made were very inconsiderable, and little worth, for two or three years. But they, finding their errors by their daily practice, began a little to mend; and, by new directions from Brazil, sometimes by strangers, and now and then by their own people, who . . . were content sometimes to make a voyage thither to improve their knowledge in a thing they so much desired.' The experience of Dutch Guiana and Brazil were much called on. This enterprise did not solve all problems, however, and much had to be learnt by developing skills in practice. The early sugar, being moist and badly cured, was not fit for sale in Europe, but by the time of Ligon's departure in 1650, he found it 'much better'd'.

Not only did planters need the special skills of sugar manufacture, they also needed more land and the buildings and equipment to make sugar. This called for money or credit. In Barbados and the Leeward Islands the more prosperous planters bought up the land of their less successful rivals. The process of enlarging estates for sugar became a costly business because these are small islands anyhow and, as the demand for land increased, so the prices asked increased. Ligon quotes the case of Major Hilliard's estate of five hundred acres which could have been purchased for £400 before sugar was produced but afterwards half the acreage was sold for £7,000. As skills improved the planters learnt an intensified plan of sugar production which put every available acre of land into cane growing. This was possible on the small, flat islands; in the mountains of Montserrat sugar could not be as profitably grown.

The French colonists were slower to produce sugar generally, although they were aware of its possibilities as early as the English. De Poincy agreed with Thomas Warner to restrict the production of tobacco in St. Christopher when prices were jeopardised by a glut on the European markets. He personally then experimented with a sugar estate which did well. The Company of the Isles of America recommended cotton as a substitute for tobacco at first, but themselves sent out a Dutchman who understood sugar cultivation to try it in Martinique. M. Houël, the strong Governor of Guadeloupe, cultivated sugar on his own while his fellow planters continued with tobacco. Gradually sugar was seen to be the most profitable crop and the French embarked on its cultivation as extensively as the English, also using the expert help of the Dutch refugees from Brazil.

SERVANTS AND SLAVES

Sugar production on estates needed a large number of workers. The simplest solution might have been for the owners of sugar estates to employ local people, but even in Barbados, already the most densely populated island, the number of people willing to labour for wages was insufficient. Those who had no land of their own, or who were losing their land to more prosperous neighbours, were not attracted to the idea of field-work. They generally sought occupations as town-workers, inn-keepers, clerks, skilled craftsmen, fishermen or even as small-scale cultivators of their own patch of land. Many left the islands in search of new and better opportunities. The independent cultivator, however small, can decide when he wants to leave his work and take a rest in the shade. The habit of independence is hard to lose and European immigrants were certainly reluctant to act as hired labourers in other people's fields.

Recruiting labourers for the colonies had become increasingly difficult in Europe. It was one thing to go out as a planter to stake a claim on the land with a view to becoming a property owner. But the bulk of men were needed to work under a tropical sun on heavy tasks, indispensable if estates were to develop. The supply of voluntary immigrant workers dwindled as the facts of life in the colonies became better known. The Company of the Isles of America was unable to fulfil its promises to the colonists of Guadeloupe and Martinique to provide labourers for them. More and more the unfortunates, kidnapped in French and English ports and criminals sentenced to transportation, made up the supply of workers. A slight impetus to enforced immigration was given by riots and rebellions, such as the Civil War in England, when prisoners taken by government forces were sent to the West Indies. None of this made the prospect any more pleasing for the man who had any choice in the matter; it became a dreaded fate for a prisoner of the Parliament forces during the Civil War to be sent to Barbados, so far had the reputation of the West Indies declined for working Englishmen. Transportation was entirely inadequate to provide a labour force for estate work. For that purpose a more certain and enforceable scheme was demanded.

The new European settlers did not take long to follow the lead of their Spanish neighbours in importing African slaves. The slave trade was now well organised in the coastal ports of West Africa, and the Dutch were very soon sufficiently organised to supply the newly-colonised islands. Indentured servants soon found themselves working side by side in the field with Negro slaves.

Negroes were imported as slaves because labour was needed for the estates, because free people shunned wage-labour, because the number of Europeans who could be had as indentured servants and slaves was far too small, and because it was cheaper to acquire an African slave than a European labourer. We learn that the money which procured a white man's services for ten years could buy a Negro for life. The Europeans, being scarcer in supply, were more expensive, and, unlike the Africans, few were bound to the estates for life. Besides, a slave's children belonged to his owner as well, so that a supply of West Indian-born slaves could be looked for.

The Dutch brought over a thousand slaves with them from Brazil to help in the development of sugar in the French islands. For all countries concerned an extensive slave trade developed in the seventeenth and throughout the eighteenth centuries, completely changing the balance of the population in the islands. At its first settlement, Barbados, for instance, contained forty Englishmen and eight Negroes. Fifty years later there were said to be 21,000 Europeans and 32,473 Negroes, though this was probably an exaggeration.

TO EACH HIS OWN

As it became apparent that the colonists had made a successful choice of crop and that they were going to fulfil all hopes by becoming prosperous, the home countries became increasingly interested in them. The English and then the French Governments now tried to gain control in their colonies, particularly to demand the trade which they had previously allowed the Dutch to enjoy so freely. Although success had been dependent on the Dutch traders in marketing the sugar, the French and English Governments were now anxious to end an arrangement by which the home countries lost most of the profits.

The Navigation Act passed by the Commonwealth Government in England in 1651 led to a dismissal of the Dutch traders from the English islands; by law English trade was now to be confined to English shipping. This was confirmed in 1660 when England became a kingdom again; as a result two strenuous wars were fought between the Dutch and English, with the French assisting their old trading ally, the Dutch. In the course of the struggle almost every settlement in the Caribbean was attacked and the Dutch colony of New Netherlands in North America was seized by the English.

By the Treaty of Breda in 1667 the Dutch were awarded a newly settled English colony in Surinam in exchange for New Netherlands, renamed New York, but England was not forced to abandon the

Navigation Laws, which was what the Dutch had hoped for. This was a serious setback for Dutch trade. So much merchandise accumulated at St. Eustatius that the Dutch had to smuggle it into Antigua and Montserrat at very low prices. As one of the French governors observed, 'the Dutch will certainly be ruined as far as the islands are concerned if the policy of excluding them is strongly enforced, for they will be obliged to see their merchandise perish or send it back to Europe, and in addition they will be forced to send their vessels away without any cargo whatever'.

The French Government's gratitude to the Dutch did not last much longer than the English Government's, and the sequence of events was similar. The French islands were slower than the English to develop as sugar plantations, but as soon as they did, Louis XIV, the new strong ruler of France, was ready to challenge Dutch power. French trade was now confined to French shipping. War came between the French and the Dutch in 1672; during its course, the trade of Amsterdam came to a standstill. By the Treaty of Nymwegen in 1678, the Dutch had to acknowledge the right of France, like England, to monopolise the trade of her own colonies.

This meant the end of the Dutch as a leading European nation. Their strength had been based on their trading monopoly and their naval power. The first had now gone, and both the French and the English had outstripped them in the second. The change of fortune was reflected in the decline of the Dutch West India Company and the lack of interest shown in its affairs by the Dutch Government once it ceased to be a prosperous concern. In a succession of renewed Dutch West India Companies, government control was relaxed; indeed in Berbice in 1678, a form of proprietorship was introduced when Abraham van Peere was granted this territory on condition that he maintained its administration and defended it. This was a reversal of policy and certainly different from the increase of French and English interest in their colonies.

The fact was that their High Mightinesses of the States-General of Holland were still not particularly interested in the Dutch-American settlements, except as trading centres. If these failed as such, the Dutch still had much business in the East and would concentrate their attention there. Arrangements were made to defend Dutch West Indian colonies and to maintain essential law and order in the settlements. The success of both depended almost entirely on the individual commanders or governors who took charge from time to time. As company servants, they could confine their job to keeping trade as lively as possible. If, like Storm van Gravesande, they became sympathetic towards the neglected Dutch colonists, they had a big task appealing for funds and supplies which were always slow in coming. The local planters had no say in the policy of the colonies and only a nominal part to play in their administration.

ENGLISH PLANTERS AND PARLIAMENT

The imposition of trading restrictions by the European governments first revealed clearly how different their interests could be from those of their colonists in the West Indies. If it suited the home governments to confine trade to their own shipping, it was by no means necessarily in the interests of the colonists there. They were selling their sugar and receiving their goods through the wide markets worked by the Dutch. Restrictions on trade could well create selling difficulties and affect prices. The English colonists were the first to express their displeasure.

Barbados, after overcoming the first difficulties of introducing sugar, was the most prosperous English island in 1651. And Barbadians objected strongly to imperial legislation on their trading practices. The issue was made stronger by the fact that the Barbadian planters supported the King's cause in the Civil War in England; several refugees in fact came to the island to escape from the Parliamentary Government. The island was a stronghold for the royalists when Lord Willoughby arrived in 1650, having newly received the lease of the proprietorship of the English islands. His declaration for the King was warmly greeted and there seemed every chance that, as sub-proprietor, he could maintain a territory overseas against Cromwell's regime. Finally, Barbadians were flourishing because they had strong trading and financial connections with Holland, while war had upset English trade. For the Commonwealth Government, trying to organise a trade monopoly, this was a most provoking situation.

An expedition was organised to deal with the dissident colonists; they countered defiantly with the Barbadian Royalist Declaration of Independence of 1651. 'We will not alienate ourselves from those heroic virtues of true Englishmen,' it ran, 'to prostitute our freedom and privileges, to which we are born, to the will and opinion of any one; neither do we think our number so contemptible, nor our resolution so weak, to be forced or persuaded to so ignoble a submission.'

This statement was backed by a proclamation passed in the Council and Assembly of Barbados condemning the action of the Parliamentary Government as being against the freedom and the safety of the island. Barbadians furthermore should not be bound by the measures of a Parliament to which they sent no representatives.

When the force arrived the Barbadians had to capitulate, but the Articles of Surrender were much in their favour. They could no longer support the Royalist side, but the established government by Governor, Council and Assembly was confirmed; there was to be no taxation unless approved by the Assembly and there was to be liberty of conscience. It can easily be seen why the Barbadians regarded this as the charter of their island; it recognised the rights of English landed gentlemen abroad to represent their own interests, as their counterparts did in England. This was the stiffest resistance offered by the colonists to the new imperial trade policy. It no doubt earned them some respect in London and it certainly ensured their right to have a say in their own affairs, but it did not restore their freedom to trade with whom they wished. This could only be done illegally, as it certainly was.

CLAIMED BY THE CROWN

When the Commonwealth Government ended in England, a disputed claim to the proprietorship gave the Crown an opportunity to abolish it. The Barbadian Assembly, and some of the other Leeward Island Governments, by refusing many of Willoughby's financial requests, made it quite clear that they no longer welcomed his authority and they declared themselves ready to come under the Crown. In the event, they agreed to an export duty of $4\frac{1}{2}$ per cent payable to the Crown as part of the arrangement for the transfer of authority. The English Government in its turn was now able to assume more direct responsibility for the now profitable colonies.

Jamaica also became a direct concern of the English Government at this time, for she was the first English colony to be gained by conquest. Cromwell sent an expedition against Spanish Hispaniola, but ill-trained troops, assisted by the malcontents from the Barbadian plantations, the only English West Indians willing to join the expedition, were quite inadequate for the task. They managed, however, to take Jamaica, which had been neglected by the Spaniards and only had a total population of fifteen hundred people, mainly concerned with cattle-ranching.

Cromwell decided to take this second-best conquest seriously, **and** to develop Jamaica as a sugar island. It was larger than any other English West Indian island and it promised well. Colonists were invited from the other islands and favourable terms were offered them. The new English Government after the restoration of the King saw to it that colonists in Jamaica should be as certain of their rights and dignities as those in Barbados. By a royal proclamation in 1661, new settlers were promised that they should be 'free denizens of England and shall have the same privileges to all intents and purposes as our free-born subjects of England'.

The planters had taken the first steps to becoming the really influential people that they were to be in the eighteenth century. It was no longer a question of a proprietor offering a settler the adventure of finding himself a piece of land. It was now a case of the government tempting gentlemen, aware of their own importance, to invest in a new territory for the national good. Things had changed a lot in the thirty years since Warner had made a pioneer start in St. Kitts.

Lord Windsor was appointed Governor of Jamaica in 1661, with instructions to set up a Council and arrange for the election of an Assembly, as elsewhere in the English territories. He was to appoint justices and pass laws for the good of the colony, 'provided they be not repugnant to our laws of England, but agreeing thereto, as near as the condition of affairs will permit'. In later years when they wanted to claim their rights, the colonists liked to quote these phrases. It was a century in which civil war had seized England, a King had been executed and another was to be deposed. It is not surprising that men independent enough to become settlers of a new territory would be strong enough to demand rights against a government which did not even claim to be working for their interests.

The French Government also considered that it should regain control of its all but lost West Indian colonial trade. In 1663 Louis XIV's minister, Colbert, sent out the Marquis de Tracy with the commission of Lieutenant-Governor of all French lands in the Western hemisphere. He found that the governors were often unpopular with their fellow colonists, particularly the high-handed Houël in Guadeloupe. Heavy taxes had been raised, many colonists were in debt and governors had used rough justice and force to get their own way. In these circumstances the colonists were willing to be directed and financed again by a French company. In 1664 the West India Company was formed under government guidance as the previous French

50

companies had been. It was under this new arrangement that Colbert was able to make the regulations restricting French trade to French ships which finally ended the Dutch control of West Indian trade. In 1674 the French West India Company failed and the islands passed directly to the French Crown.

There were now two clear interests in every West Indian colony. Rulers in Europe had claimed their colonial empires and were anxious to organise the maximum profit from them for the home countries. Planters in the colonies were increasingly anxious to secure personal fortunes and to return to Europe to live in style and comfort, or to live a life of dignity and importance in the colonies themselves. There was future conflict in these ambitions.

FURTHER READING

Sources of West Indian History, People of the Caribbean, p. 10, Economic Life, pp. 34–8, 39–46, Government and Politics, pp. 92, 93, 101–2.
Williams, *Documents of West Indian History*, Chapter VIII, Early Organisation of the Non-Spanish Colonies, pp. 282–290.
Hoyos, *Our Common Heritage*, Francis Lord Willoughby.
Taylor, *The Capture of Jamaica*.

QUESTIONS TO CONSIDER

1. Which do you think was the greatest problem that had to be faced by colonists wishing to plant sugar for the first time?

2. Which of the consequences of introducing sugar mentioned in this chapter do you think made the greatest change in West Indian society?

3. How were the European governments able to claim more control of their colonies once they were seen to be profitable?

4. What do you think is meant by the last sentence of the chapter?

CHAPTER SIX

Settling Down

WAR BY BUCCANEER

The decline of the Dutch in the Caribbean left the English and French to take measures against the Spanish Empire themselves. Even after their defeat at Itamaraca in 1640, the Spanish Empire dominated the Caribbean; it included the largest islands and the mainland. Vera Cruz and Cartagena, with great silver mines, ranches and plantations in their hinterland, and Porto Bello, transit point for Peruvian treasure, were still the richest and busiest ports in the Caribbean, even when left undefended and uncertain of the arrival of the yearly convoy. So it was not altogether surprising that the Spanish Government still refused to recognise as legal the French and English settlements in the Caribbean. This recognition the French and English Governments determined to win. The first challenge to Spain's monopoly had been made by pirates like Le Clerc and Drake; France and England now turned, for the last time, to piracy as a policy to assert their rights against Spain.

From the earliest days pirates had flourished in the islands. Menéndez's measures for defence in the Caribbean had discouraged them for a time, but the convention of 'no peace beyond the line' still held, and there were fresh inducements. New settlements and the expansion of trade, together with the breakdown of the patrols, improved the prospects for piracy. Above all, amongst the settlers in the islands were men prepared to turn pirate.

Some of these adventurers were colonists who found the drudgery of planting in a virgin country unbearable. They took to wandering from island to island in search of an easier and freer way of living. Some joined pirate crews; some settled on the north-west coast of Hispaniola and the neighbouring island of Tortuga. The Spanish Government had cleared Spanish settlers from this area in 1605 in a desperate effort to cut down an illegal trade in hides which was being carried on with the Dutch. The adventurers found the woods full of wild swine and cattle; some became cow-killers. They had a method of broiling meat on a sort of grid held on four sticks, called *boucan*, which they sold to the pirates. Sellers and buyers came to be called *boucaniers*, and so the name buccaneer was applied generally to the lawless sea rovers.

Tortuga was an ideal hide-out for them. The northern coast of the island was completely inaccessible, and the one harbour on the south coast could be defended from the heights of a hill six hundred yards from the shore. In 1655 the French and English each took over a new base in the West Indies. The French Government took Tortuga as a base from which they could extend their influence in Hispaniola. Bertrand D'Ogeron was appointed first official Governor of Tortuga. He had failed as a sugar planter in Martinique and had done some business with the pirates. He did not attempt to found a planting settlement on Tortuga itself, but chose Port Margot on the north coast of Hispaniola opposite Tortuga; he later moved to Leogane in the south-west. Two thousand settlers were sent out from France, and by 1670 there was a flourishing French planting colony on Hispaniola, which the Spanish were powerless to dislodge; equally important, Tortuga remained a pirate base, now under French protection. The capture of Jamaica in 1655 by the ill-disciplined force sent out by Cromwell provided the pirates with another hide-out. The island had an excellent harbour and occupied a strategic position for raiding the Spanish Main. Pirates made Port Royal their headquarters, under English protection.

Both D'Ogeron in Hispaniola and the early governors in Jamaica were glad to have these sea rovers as a guarantee that the new colonies would not be attacked by locally raised Spanish forces; while the home governments, unable to afford special naval squadrons in the West Indies, were glad to use them in war. The buccaneers were trained seamen with knowledge of the winds, currents and shoals of the Caribbean; the French and English Governments provided them with commissions of 'reprisals', entitling them to attack every town and shipping for limited periods. As long as they had this commission they could legally sell their goods at Port Royal and Tortuga. The Governors of Jamaica and Hispaniola had no effective means of controlling the ruffians they used. Rewarded by the plunder they captured, the buccaneers were most inclined to fight where the booty was enticing. Their most spectacular feats are all associated with the cities of the Spanish Main, Maracaibo, Porto Bello, Panama, rich in bullion and tropical products. Here they fought to good purpose. These exploits made use of sudden attack and terror·ism. The risks were great, but the stakes were high. For success, organisation and an imposed discipline were necessary. There was a certain rough justice amongst thieves too. For instance, the bucca-neers had a compensation scheme. The loss of a right arm brought six hundred pieces of eight, of a left arm or a leg, five hundred pieces of eight, of both eyes, one thousand pieces of eight. The work de·manded that each buccaneer should be both reckless and brutal. Men risking their lives for plunder do not accept discipline readily and their leaders always had difficulty in organising expeditions.

Sir Henry Morgan was the most notorious English buccaneer leader. His origins were typical of the men he led. An indentured ser-vant from Bristol, he found life too hard in Barbados, so he wan-dered through the islands in search of better fortune. He finally arrived in Tortuga where he graduated in buccaneering before he moved on to Port Royal. Morgan used the buccaneer's utterly ruth-less methods of warfare to good effect. Short of men to storm a for-tress at Porto Bello, he sent the monks and nuns captured in the town up the scaling-ladders first, to take the brunt of the assault. When the citizens of Maracaibo abandoned the town and tried to hide them-selves and their goods from the raiders, Morgan hunted them out and tortured them to find out where the goods were hidden.

Morgan's most famous exploit taxed his control over the bucca-neers to the utmost; this was his capture of Panama in December 1670. With a party of fourteen hundred men, he set off across the Isthmus, following the Chagres River as far as he could, then march-ing overland. He intended his men to live off the country, but the Spaniards hid or destroyed all foodstuffs along the route. Fortun-ately for the buccaneers a barn full of maize and a herd of cattle were found to help them through the nine day march. Panama, with its eight monasteries, two churches, a hospital, two hundred warehouses and many magnificent houses belonging to the merchants, was a city worth defending, and capturing. The Spaniards fought before the city and mounted heavy guns in the streets. It was a furious battle followed by twenty-eight days of fire, pillage and violence before Morgan withdrew with £10,000 worth of spoils.

This was Morgan's last 'official' exploit. Even before the notorious buccaneer left for Panama, Modyford, the Governor of Jamaica, heard from England of the Treaty of Madrid whereby Spain in 1670 recognised England's legal right to 'have, hold and possess for ever

. . . all lands, regions, islands, colonies and dominions situated in the West Indies, or in any part of America, that the said King of Great Britain and his subjects at present hold and possess'. Both parties also agreed to 'abstain from all pillage, depredation, hurt, injury and any sort of molestation as well by land as by sea or in fresh waters in whatever part of the world . . . to revoke all commissions . . . of reprisals'. This would end all official sanction for piracy. Modyford was prepared to disobey the order for this one expedition. It was therefore the last of its kind, and the most spectacular.

The buccaneers had helped England to win recognition of their colonies from the Spaniards; the difficulty was now to suppress them. Morgan himself was sent to England to stand trial for the affair at Panama; there he was acquitted, became a national hero, was knighted and sent back to Jamaica as lieutenant-governor. This gave him a new status and offered an easy life on his ill-gotten fortune. Port Royal no longer provided an open harbour for the sea rovers; they were once more outlaws. From time to time they brought cargoes to Port Royal and got away with it, but trading with the pirates gradually became unpopular.

Buccaneering had held back the development of Jamaica. 'People have not married, built or settled as they would in time of peace— some for fear of being destroyed, others have got much suddenly by privateers' bargains and are gone,' wrote a French visitor. 'War carried away all free men, labourers and planters of provision,' he continued, 'which make work and victuals dear and scarce.' It was when the planting interest became strong enough to demand peace for trading purposes that English naval squadrons were sent out. The first arrived in 1685. These practically wiped out the English buccaneers. In 1692 Port Royal was destroyed by earthquake.

The French buccaneers had a rather longer life. In the Treaty of Nymwegen, 1678, the Spanish refused to give St. Domingue, the French settlement on Hispaniola, the recognition they had extended to the English colonies in 1670, and so French 'official' buccaneering continued. But the convention of 'no peace beyond the line' was no longer acceptable to other nations. Spain's protests were supported by the Dutch and by the newly converted English. By the Treaty of Ratisbon in 1684, therefore, the French Government officially abandoned their buccaneers, agreeing that 'all hostilities shall cease on both sides . . . within Europe and without, both on this side and beyond the line'.

The final suppression of the French buccaneers actually took some time. One of the leaders, Laurens de Graff, was taken into the government service like Morgan, but the real work was done by Du Casse, appointed Governor of St. Domingue in 1691. He used the buccaneers as paid seamen in further war against Spain and disbanded them at the end of the campaign in 1697, when by the Treaty of Ryswick, Spain finally recognised French rights in Hispaniola. War by buccaneer had served its purpose. France and England had established their claims in the Caribbean and Spain had been forced to recognise them.

MERCANTILE SYSTEM

While encouraging the buccaneers in their savage piracy to force Spain's recognition of the new English and French colonies, their respective governments were also making sure that each kept the profits of its own colonies by enforcing navigation laws. The pattern of trade developed from these laws is called the mercantile system. In this system, tropical and semi-tropical colonies would provide their home countries with foodstuffs which could not be produced in temperate climates, and with raw materials for manufacture. In return, the colonists would enjoy protection from their enemies, an assured market in the home country for their particular staple product and the benefit of trade in goods produced there. All foreigners were excluded from direct trade with the English and the French colonists, and colonial trade was to be conducted in the vessels of the mother country.

This mercantile system was a monopoly system intended to benefit both the mother countries and their new colonies. It would, however, only remain acceptable to both groups as long as each was content with the benefits to be gained. The real disadvantage to the colonists of this mercantile system was not only in the trading arrangement itself but that it was enforced by laws of European governments which the colonists had no direct power to alter if they proved unsatisfactory to them. For the Barbadian planters, for instance, there was cause for anxiety. With their Dutch buyers of sugar now excluded, all their produce had, legally, to be exported to England. But the English market for sugar, although it was growing, was not keeping pace with the colonists' rapidly increasing output, and prices were falling as supply outgrew demand, just as they had earlier done with tobacco. From the sixteen-sixties until the late sixteen-eighties, the price tended slowly to decline, although certainly not to the extent of discouraging sugar production; this increased steadily and by the beginning of the eighteenth century British trade with the West Indian islands was greater in value and quantity than with North American colonies.

The English were by no means the only people in the western world who were aware of the profits to be gained, reduced though they might be, by making sugar for export from their colonies. The Portuguese in Brazil, the Dutch in Surinam, the Spaniards in Puerto Rico, Cuba and Santo Domingo, and the French in the western half of Hispaniola, Martinique and Guadeloupe, were all sugar producers and they all tried to rope off their colonies and colonial trade from foreign interference. They all supplied their home markets, and competed only in those European countries which had no sugar colonies of their own.

This system inevitably benefited merchants as much as planters. As sugar became a prosperous industry, the merchants who sold it and who supplied the planters with their requirements from Europe enjoyed a rapidly increasing business. There were the merchants who disposed of the sugar on its arrival in Europe; these became a wealthy and influential group. Other independent merchants worked on this side of the Atlantic. There were also factors, or commission agents, who received goods from merchant houses in Europe and sold them in the West Indies on commission for their owners.

Merchants, from the beginning of settlement, particularly in the English islands, financed the estates. Sometimes they lent money to intending planters at high rates of interest. This put a heavy burden on the planter until he had repaid his loan. Another method was to go into partnership. One partner would come to the colony to organise and manage the estate while the other remained behind, generally as agent for the sale of the produce in the home country. In this way planter and merchant shared the actual profits of the estate, and the risk of losses.

Fortunes could be made in trade in the West Indies as well as in planting. This has been well demonstrated in *A West India Fortune* by Professor Richard Pares, which describes the rise of the Pinney family. Among the prisoners listed for shipment to Barbados after a rebellion in the West of England in 1685 was a young man named Azariah Pinney. By some unexplained means Azariah escaped transportation as a rebel, but he was forced to leave England and went to

Nevis to seek his fortune. He began his career there as a factor, selling lace and other goods for his father in England. As his business developed, he entered into trade on his own account as a merchant, and before the end of the century he was buying land. Today, on approaching Charlestown one can still see the ruins of Mountravers Great House where succeeding members of the Pinney family lived. This pattern of progress was common in all the islands, though all did not do as well as the Pinney family.

RISE OF THE PLANTOCRACY

Planters and merchants connected with the sugar trade were by the end of the seventeenth century largely people of substance and power. Wherever West Indian opinion was given a hearing, it was their voices that were heard. The landless, whether white or coloured, and the ever-increasing number of Negro slaves played no part in government except as recipients of the laws. This was the European pattern of the time; property and capital were necessary for membership of the ruling classes, and government was the privilege of a small influential group everywhere.

We have seen that the Spanish Government built up a rigid system of appointments and control which theoretically left little power in the hands of their colonists. The French system, developed by Louis XIV and his minister Colbert after the formation of the West India Company in 1664, had a similar purpose. By the time that the islands were taken directly under royal government ten years later, the machinery of French government in the colonies was well established. Governors were maintained chiefly for military duties and to enforce the trade restrictions. Intendants were appointed to look after public works, law and order, and, no doubt, were instructed to watch the governor in each island. Instructions of this kind were given to different officials so that distant home governments could have some check on the activities of those they employed and paid to run their colonies.

There were councils in each French island, mainly composed of lawyers, the landed gentry and representatives of the garrisons; they advised, but could not make laws. The French colonies, therefore, were really ruled by civil servants advised by an island council whose members could look for promotion to noble rank if the colony was run to the profit of the home government. The governor-general, now in Martinique, was supposed to oversee the West Indian governors aided by a Superior Council of limited powers. The whole machinery was supervised in France by the *Conseil d'Etat*, which framed laws for the French colonies and directed their trade.

On the whole the system suited Colbert's avowed intention of turning the colonies into one of the main sources of French wealth. The governors in fact, perhaps because the need for defence was so great, insisted on superior authority so that their relationship with the intendant who was supposed to be on an equal footing, was not so difficult as it might have been. The island advisory councils later sought a part in making their own laws. While the colonists were still building up their sugar industry, they only wanted security to do it; they had known the consequences of bad government under some of the independent governors earlier and were prepared for a time to accept closer control, and protection, from France.

Governors in English islands had a far more difficult task. Appointed by the English Government, they had to work with councils and assemblies who, unlike the French councils, made some of their own laws. Governors were regularly asked by these bodies to forward for confirmation in England laws that they knew would not be approved. When the Assembly was displeased it refused to vote the annual revenue, and the governor, who was responsible for paying for the maintenance of the militia, courts of justice, the clergy and so on, was frequently embarrassed.

The Jamaican Assembly was particularly given to using this weapon. The Lords of Trade, who handled West Indian business for the English Government in London, tried to reduce this difficulty over money by persuading the Jamaican Assembly to pass a permanent Revenue Bill to ensure that there would be a public income each year. This was long resisted because the annual Revenue Bill was such a good weapon. In extreme cases revenue could be withheld altogether. More frequently the annual Revenue Bill provided a way of passing laws which the Lords of Trade might object to. By 'tacking' them to the Revenue Bill the Assembly in effect forced their Lordships in England to pass those laws, or not get the money. The Lords of Trade did not succeed in getting a permanent Revenue Bill until 1704, and then only for twenty-one years, on condition that the new Board of Trade should continue for the same period all Jamaican laws that had been confirmed by 1684. This measure was itself a major example of 'tacking'.

The heyday of the Jamaican Assembly was in the eighteenth

century; the seventeenth-century representatives, however, had already devised the tactics for often getting their own way. A wealthy and influential planter class was a formidable group to control. As they returned with their fortunes to England, they were able to watch their own interests at home and also act as agents to planters still in the West Indies. The authority of the Crown through the Board of Trade was constantly challenged.

This was not confined to Jamaica or Barbados. The Governors of the Leeward Islands found themselves faced with the same tactics and the same attitudes from the planters of the four separate Assemblies of St. Kitts, Antigua, Montserrat and Nevis. Sir William Stapleton in the sixteen-seventies first tried the experiment of calling a General Assembly of the Leeward Islands, with representatives from each. This idea for a federation of the Leewards was not well liked by the representatives, who tried to excuse themselves from attendance, and resisted the idea of the same laws for each island with a request, in 1683, for confirmation of their separate laws. The General Assembly continued to meet until 1711, but as it had no financial powers it then died, apart from a single meeting in 1798 to protest about a resolution on slavery passed by the English Government. It was not until 1871 that the Leeward Islands had a common legislature once again.

SHAPING WEST INDIAN SOCIETIES

The affairs dealt with by the governments in all the colonies show what was regarded as important in the early days of colonisation. Apart from the criminal laws, which were a reflection of their European counterparts, there were laws establishing and providing for such institutions as law courts and justice, the militia, the clergy and various officials, particularly for the administration of customs and taxes. The methods by which land was to be allocated were also discussed from time to time.

Religion was also a subject for legislation. Toleration was a principle of the English and Dutch Governments for their West Indian colonies. Indeed Montserrat was a refuge for Irish Catholics unwanted in Virginia. The need for settlers here was more important than religious conformity. The instructions to a new Governor of Nevis in 1670 stated that 'we are still content to give all possible encouragement to persons of different judgment and opinions in matters of religion, to transport themselves with their stock'. The oath of allegiance was only to be compulsory for members of Council in the

English islands. The governor alone was bound to profess the established religion. In a century of bitter religious wars and savage discrimination in Europe, this was a remarkable degree of toleration for European territories abroad.

It was not, however, always appreciated by the assemblies. The Barbadians were anxious to place restrictions on the Quakers, many of whom had been transported in 1665 to Barbados, Jamaica and Nevis. They were not popular because they attempted to convert the slaves, and it was feared that a Christian might also want to be a free man. They could not be expelled, however, and could only be harried by punishment for refusing to do militia training, or to pay tithes to the clergy of the Church of England or to take oaths. Similarly, petitions were presented to both the Jamaican and the Barbadian Assemblies to expel the Jews whose competition in trade was much resented by English merchants. They were from time to time victimised by special taxation, but they could not be expelled.

The Spanish policy remained that the Catholic Church was part of the government directed from Spain; after 1650, religious missions in Trinidad, for instance, ruled the countryside with absolute, if paternal, power over their people. The French also introduced Catholicism into all their islands, but there was no great fanaticism about conversion policies. In 1685, toleration which had existed in France for eighty-six years was abandoned there; this was followed by a banning of Protestants and the expulsion of Jews from French colonies.

The *Code Noir* issued by Louis XIV ordered the expulsion of the Jews in its first article, the baptism and Christian instruction of slaves in its second, and the banning of all but Catholic religious practices in its third. The whole document of sixty regulations reveals what the French Government thought their colonies should be like now they were established slave societies. The provisions for religious practice included the right of Christian slaves to sacraments and to burial in consecrated ground. Overseers were to be Catholics. Slave marriages were to have the consent of the master but were not to be enforced by him. Other articles dealt with the general treatment of slaves in detail. They were to receive two sets of clothing. Their food was itemised for each week; it was to be two and a half measures of cassava meal or three cassavas weighing at least two and a half pounds, with two pounds of salt beef or three pounds of fish. Children under ten were to receive half quantity. There were penalties for the masters who failed to provide these requirements, and slaves could appeal to officials in cases of neglect or maltreatment. On the other hand, cruel physical punishment and often death were to be the penalties for offences by slaves; assault and theft were very heavily punished. Finally there were rules about marriages between Europeans and slaves and the position of their children.

The separate English West Indian assemblies did not propose any such codes for their islands, and they certainly did not legislate for the conversion of slaves. It is doubtful whether in practice many French planters fulfilled more than the letter of the law. The *Code* shows rather what problems had to be dealt with once the slave society was accepted as the normal one in the West Indies. By the end of the seventeenth century West Indian history becomes the story of settled communities organising themselves, and being organised in varying degrees, to grow a crop profitable to planters, merchants and the governments of the imperial countries. To do this a slave society seemed the only existing answer to the need for plentiful labour. The slave trade was to provide the main addition to the population in the eighteenth century.

FURTHER READING

Sources of West Indian History, People of the Caribbean, p. 14. Economic Life, pp. 46–9, Religion and Education, pp. 143–6, Slavery and its Abolition, pp. 167–9.

Parry and Sherlock, *A Short History of the West Indies*, Chapter VI.

Black, *History of Jamaica*, Chapter I, The Buccaneers.

Roberts, *Sir Henry Morgan*.

Taylor, *Buccaneer Bay*.

Hoyos, *Our Common Heritage*, Christopher Codrington.

Ottley, *Spanish Trinidad*, Chapters VII–IX.

QUESTIONS TO CONSIDER

1. What part do you think that the buccaneers played in establishing the French and English colonies?

2. What differences and similarities can you discover between the English and French methods of colonisation?

3. What laws were passed in your territory in the last quarter of the seventeenth century?

4. What quarrels can you foresee between the assemblies in the English islands and the English Government in the eighteenth century?

CHAPTER SEVEN

The Slave Trade

THE FIRST TRADERS

The sugar estate depended on slave labour. The Spaniards in Hispaniola imported slaves for their estates as early as 1510 and later used them on the mainland. Other European colonists followed their example; as sugar cultivation spread, slaves were needed in increasing numbers to develop the West Indian islands. This led to a great expansion of the slave trade in Africa. For more than three hundred years people from many parts of the continent were exported as slave labour. In the West Indies, although confined by the slave system, these people created a new way of life for themselves.

The first slave traders were the Portuguese; the Treaty of Tordesillas, which had divided the world between Spain and Portugal, gave Portugal exclusive trading rights with Africa. While they were supplying only a European market the Portuguese traded chiefly in gold, ivory, palm-oil and dye-woods; Negro slaves were only a novelty for the rich. With the opening of a transatlantic market, the Portuguese were faced with a serious demand for slaves. Under the stimulus of supplying labour for the Spanish Empire as well as for their own colony of Brazil, they rapidly extended their trade in Africa. Portuguese traders were to be found on the Senegal and Gambia Rivers, the Cape Verde Islands, the Gold Coast, at Benin on the Niger Delta, on the islands of Fernando Po and Sao Thomé and farther south on the Congo at Cabenda, Loanda and Loango.

The Portuguese tried to defend their monopoly of the African trade by building forts at the important trading centres. These forts were commanded by a governor, helped by a factor who bought the slaves and by a priest who helped to make contact with the African slave traders. The forts also had a small European garrison. As trade expanded, undefended trading posts were set up in the surrounding country where traders supplied imported goods in exchange for further supplies of slaves; these trading posts were called factories. Ships' captains traded under the guns of the fort while they bought the slaves and sold their trade goods at the governor's price. In return the forts served to protect the traders in case of trouble with the surrounding tribes.

The forts never did succeed in maintaining the Portuguese monopoly. Slave trading could be carried on along thousands of miles of coast where there was every opportunity for interlopers to pick up a cargo. Furthermore, the governors at the forts were often very much concerned with trading on their own account and did not object to selling slaves to interlopers, any more than the Spanish settlers in the Indies objected to buying slaves from Hawkins. Hawkins was by no means the first interloper on the African coast. French and Dutch merchants sent ships to Africa from the middle of the sixteenth century, at the time when French privateers were attacking the Spanish monopoly in the Caribbean. But the Portuguese maintained their supremacy in the African trade until they faced the organised challenge of the Dutch.

THE NATIONAL COMPANIES

We have seen that a share in the African slave trade was one of the inducements to the Dutch Government to form the Dutch West India Company in 1621. This was during the period when Portugal was united with Spain; consequently, in their attacks on Spain the Dutch were in a position to attack the Portuguese, their old Eastern rivals, in West Africa. By 1642, all the trading forts on the Gold Coast, as well as Arguin and Goree, were in the hands of the Dutch. The Portuguese were left with Sao Thomé and Loanda.

The Dutch did not enjoy their predominance for long. When the market for slaves was increased with the spread of sugar cultivation, countries with no plantations to supply, like Sweden, Brandenburg and Denmark, saw that there was profit to be made in the slave trade. At the same time, France and England with their new settlements in the Caribbean were soon anxious to have their own supply of slaves without depending on the Dutch. This led to the formation of national companies to provide slaves for their own colonies.

The government of each country gave the members of their national company the sole right to trade on the African coast; in return for this privilege, the company was to maintain forts to defend the national interest in the trade. This meant that the company had to put up expensive buildings and supply armaments and garrisons. Such a combination of interests was not easily achieved. The problems of the English Royal African Company, founded in 1672, illustrate how difficult it was to make a success of the national companies.

By 1690 the Royal African Company were maintaining eight forts which were supposed to control English trade over a coastal area of 4,550 miles. The company claimed that the forts cost them £20,000 a year. Only traders with a licence from the company were supposed to trade in this vast area, and the licence might be worth as much as 40 per cent of the cost of the cargo. The company's monopoly roused opposition from many trading interests; planters in Barbados, who were supposed to buy only company slaves, said the price went up from £16 to £20 each between 1672 and 1675, and to £40 by 1690. The textile and iron industries in England complained that the company's monopoly limited the exports of textile and iron wares to Africa and led to high prices for the dye-stuffs and ivory for knife-handles brought back to England. The licensed traders to the coast complained bitterly. They claimed that the forts were no better than warehouses, incapable of standing up to an attack by two hundred men, that they were charged exorbitant prices for poor quality slaves and inferior stores and that they were expected to sell their trade goods at the governor's prices. They felt that they could trade much more satisfactorily with the Africans who brought their slaves and ivory out in small boats direct to the trading ship. As the demand for slaves increased in the eighteenth century, the Royal African Company played a smaller and smaller part in the trade until it died in 1750.

After that the independent traders to Africa joined together in a loose association called the Company of Merchants Trading to Africa. Anyone could become a member by paying £10 a year subscription for the privilege of trading in Africa. The association agreed to keep the forts on the coast in good repair, but this was not to be done at the expense of their company; the government gave a special grant towards keeping the forts in good condition.

Only two of the national companies left the business; the Brandenburger and Swedish sold out their interest to the Dutch and the Danish respectively. The other companies, of France, Denmark and Holland, continued their trade throughout the eighteenth century despite increasing competition from the independent traders.

The rivalry between France and England, which in the eighteenth century developed into wars in the West Indies, North America and

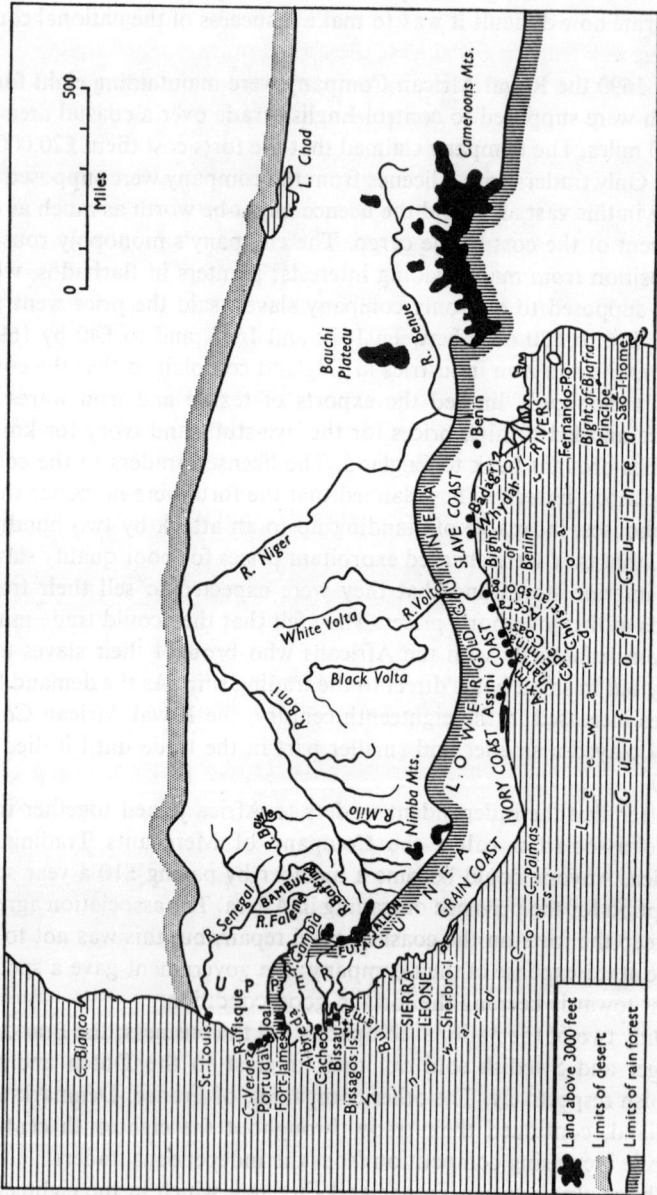

Fig. 4. The Slave Coast of Africa

India, led to an intense trade rivalry in Africa. English traders suspected the French of trying to turn the African chiefs against them to cut off their supplies of slaves; the French were worried by the number of English ships appearing off the coast. The issue was decided, not by war, but by the enterprise of the traders of London, Bristol and Liverpool. By 1785, British traders were shipping 38,000 slaves a year across the Atlantic compared with 20,000 sent by the French.

The number of slaves shipped in this trade can only be estimated, but there is no doubt that it steadily increased throughout the eighteenth century. The English slave trade to the West Indies lasted from 1651, when the navigation laws prevented further trade with the Dutch, until the abolition of the slave trade in 1808; it is estimated that 1,900,000 slaves arrived in the English islands during that period. The French trade lasted from the end of their business with the Dutch in 1664 until they abolished it in 1830; they imported about 1,650,000 slaves into the West Indies and their settlements in North America. The Dutch took 900,000 to the Guianas and their small West Indian islands.

These are the figures for arrivals after the hazards of the transatlantic crossing. But of course they do not include those who were killed during collection in Africa or who died on the long sea voyage. It is thought that during the whole European slave trade, a quarter of which was concentrated on the West Indies, no less than 20,000,000 Africans were sold out of Africa.

THE TRADE IN AFRICA

The national companies opened up the Senegal and Gambia rivers and the Gold Coast for slave trading, whilst the Portuguese dominated the Congo River and Angola. From these centres the slave trade in Africa spread. The independent traders found new areas to develop; they opened up the coast between Goree and Sherbro Island, the Slave Coast between the Volta and Badagri Rivers, and increased trade in the Niger delta. In all these new areas the ships' captains traded either directly with the African chiefs or through a factor.

Factors were in charge of trading posts where the slaves were brought, ready for shipment, by the African traders. Sometimes a member of a ship's crew was left to act as a factor. The slaves were kept in a rough prison called a barracoon until the ships arrived. Part of the slave factor's job was to keep on good terms with the local African ruler. Most of the African kingdoms, where the slave-trading posts were set up, covered only a small area, perhaps stretching only thirty miles inland. Sometimes small groups of kingdoms would acknowledge one chief as their supreme ruler. A trader living on the island of St. Ann, off Sierra Leone, described the organisation. 'These Kings,' he said, 'are headed by the King of Sherbro, who seems to have most power in these parts . . . his dominions reaching as far as Barras where every year he sends his canoe for duty. . . . These people that go by the names of Kings and princes are only so in title. Their substance consists of nothing more than a lace hat, a gown and silver-headed cane and a mat to sit down. . . . They are attended by a good many people when they go to see any white man, who follow them for the sake of what they can extort from us.' The King of Sherbro had to be given presents, or *dachy*, to win his co-operation.

Dahomey was the largest African kingdom that the traders dealt with. It stretched one hundred and fifty miles inland, and the slave port of Whydah was firmly controlled by the King. The slave factors lived beside the royal palace, and when the slave ships arrived the first business of the traders was to pay their respects to the King. The Kings of Dahomey were not satisfied with a little *dachy*. They had an elaborate system of taxes and licences for slaves bought at Whydah; the slave trade was an important source of revenue to them.

All over West Africa, domestic slavery was well established; people were born and lived as slaves within the tribe. They were used as permanent inferior household servants or by merchants for carrying head-loads through the forests. The slaves who made up the supply to the European slave traders, however, were said to be criminals and prisoners of war.

The so-called prisoners of war collected by the small coastal tribes were the result of raids carried out on neighbours within a radius of twenty or thirty miles. John Bowman, who had worked as first mate on a slaver, was during the seventeen-seventies left in charge of a small trading post on the River Scassus, between the River Gambia and the Windward Coast. According to his account the 'war men' used to go out once or twice every eight or ten days. It was their regular method of getting slaves, he believed, because they always came to the factory before setting out and demanded powder, ball, flints and small shot, as well as rum and tobacco. Once, anxious to know how they obtained the slaves, he joined the party. After a day's journey they came to a small river where they stayed until dark. Mr. Bowman at this point prevailed upon the King's son to leave him a guard of four men while the war men went on to what he took to be a nearby town. In half an hour he heard the war-cry and in about half an hour more the party returned leading about twenty-five men, women and children, some of whom were still at the breast. The town was in flames. When the party re-crossed the river it was just daylight and they reached Scassus about midday. The prisoners were carried to different parts of the town. They were usually led in with strings about their necks, and some had their hands tied. He never saw any slaves there who had been convicted of crimes.

The 'prisoners and criminals' could not be supplied by the coastal tribes alone. The slave trade in the end extended up to six hundred miles inland. Mungo Park, one of the first explorers of the African interior, during his travels in 1796 and 1797, described how one African merchant, two hundred miles inland at Kamalia on the head-waters of the River Gambia, gradually accumulated slaves to take to the coast. Some of them were captured in petty local wars, but most of them came by caravan 'from the inland countries of which many are unknown even by name to the Europeans'. One group included some who had spent three years in irons while they were bartered from market to market for gold dust. African slave merchants from Kano, six hundred miles inland, made regular journeys to the Gold Coast forts; they travelled by way of Ashanti territory to avoid hostile Dahomey, over a route of eighteen hundred miles. The Ashanti, a powerful inland kingdom, charged tolls on slaves on their way to the coast. Prices increased as the slaves were taken farther from their homes and the chance of escape decreased; many middlemen thus made their profit.

The journey to the coast was made by slave coffle. Two slaves were fastened together by chains round the leg and each group of four secured by a rope. Sometimes a heavy Y-shaped stick was fastened with the fork round the neck and the stem resting on the shoulder of the slave behind. The coffle was well guarded by free men. Each slave had to carry provisions, and often domestic slaves went with them to carry back the goods received in exchange. Of the slaves who left Kano yearly, two-thirds returned with goods. The coffle which Mungo Park travelled with had seventy-three slaves for sale and thirty-eight free men and domestic slaves travelling with them.

Every night the coffle had to negotiate for accommodation in the towns. Sometimes they would repay hospitality by entertaining the townsfolk with an account of their adventures on the way. Often the slaves were put up for the night in the homes of the people. The arrival and departure of the coffle was an accepted event in the life of the town and a little crowd would gather to see them set off. Sometimes they were given warning of an impending raid on the caravan. Mungo Park spent a night hiding in a cotton field so that his coffle could avoid such a rumoured attack.

On the coast, at the fort or barracoon, the slaves were prepared for sale. Often their bodies were completely shaved to remove signs of age, and oiled and polished to give a good appearance. The wary buyer insisted on seeing them move about vigorously before settling a price. The price of slaves fluctuated according to the number of ships on the coast at any time. As the slave trade developed, there was a steady rise in prices. European goods were luxuries and therefore commanded a high price, but, as the demand for slaves was apparently insatiable, African traders learnt to make a good bargain in return. When the Portuguese first started trading, a good horse bought fifteen slaves; but along the Gold Coast and Whydah by the end of the seventeenth century, the Africans demanded part payment in their own currency, cowrie shells, and would only take certain European goods. Brass basins were acceptable to cut into armlets; iron bars were taken to be worked by local craftsmen, and there was a steady demand for good quality cloth, carefully tested with lime juice to make sure the dye was fast, and some brandy, handkerchiefs and lace hats for *brawta*.

Three English slavers, loading at Whydah in the sixteen-nineties, paid in cowrie shells and the goods mentioned above to the value of about £3 15s. per slave. Just over a century later, the *Enterprise*, a Liverpool ship on her maiden voyage to the Coast, bought entirely in British manufactures. The price per male slave at Bonny included 96 yards of different types of cloth, 52 handkerchiefs, 1 large brass pan, 2 muskets, 25 kegs of powder, 100 flints, 2 bags of shot, 20 knives, 4 iron pots, 4 hats, 4 caps, 4 cutlasses, 6 bunches of beads and 14 gallons of brandy.

THE ATLANTIC PASSAGE

The African who lived as a domestic slave in his own country had a place in a society he knew and understood; the African who was sold to the Coast for shipment to America had no idea what was going to happen to him. The journey across the Atlantic was a one-way traffic; no African could know what lay beyond and he had no prospect of return. Some thought white men were cannibals; some could not believe Barbados had solid ground underfoot like Africa. The Captain of the *Hannibal*, picking up his cargo at Whydah, remarked that 'they had a more dreadful apprehension of Barbados than we can have of hell; though,' he was constrained to add, 'they live much better there than in their own country; but, home is home.' Slave captains were not likely to indulge in sympathy if there was no need for it, but many of them expressed their concern at the desperate efforts made by some of the slaves to escape. Sometimes the slaves awaiting shipment in the fort had the chance to rebel. But the most risky point was when the slaves were being taken out by canoe to a ship anchored off shore. Not many slave ports had adequate harbours and the ships had to anchor in the stream, loading the cargo from smaller boats. This was the last chance the slaves had to escape; some, rather than face the journey, jumped overboard in chains and drowned.

The quicker the slaver was loaded in Africa and made for the open sea, the healthier for crew and cargo alike. When the ships had to ply along the coast picking up small groups of slaves, months might be spent loading the cargo. Then, with the full complement of slaves aboard, the ship had to take in fresh provisions for the Atlantic crossing. The Dutch ship, *St. Jan*, for instance, arrived off the Slave Coast on 8 March, 1659; by the end of June, the slave cargo was complete, but the ship did not set out for Caracas until 17 August, having spent time 'hauling wood and water' and going to Annabon to purchase 'one hundred half tierces of beans, twelve hogs, five thousand cocoa nuts, five thousand sweet oranges, besides some other stores'. Even at the height of the slave trade, the Liverpool ship *Enterprise* spent three months off the coast, arriving at Bonny on 23 September, leaving for Cuba on 6 December. The journey from the coast to the Caribbean took from five to eight weeks, and quite often an equal time, or longer, was spent on board off the African coast. The West Coast of Africa was notoriously unhealthy until the beginning of this century; so, many slaves must have started the journey to the Indies very unfit after their prolonged stay on board.

When the ship was at sea the slaves were usually fed on deck and, though the crew mounted guard, one or two desperate ones would make their escape overboard. 'He put his head down under water,' said a ship's surgeon describing a slave drowning, 'but lifted his hands up, and thus went down as if exulting that he had got away.' The ship's surgeon was also often called on to deal with those who went on hunger strike, hanged themselves or tried to cut their throats. But the loss in numbers from suicide was nothing compared with losses from disease. The suicides were only the most desperate of an unhappy cargo; there was little incentive for any of them to resist disease. Some ship's surgeons thought that 'melancholy' caused more deaths than anything else. The physical conditions of the voyage certainly encouraged sickness.

At the height of the British slave trade, a naval officer went to Liverpool to collect statistics about the size of the ships and the number of slaves to be carried in them. The *Brookes*, one ship he measured, had a hold 5 feet 8 inches deep. In this case, not only was the floor of the hold packed with four lines of slaves, but platforms or shelves 6 feet wide were built off the side of the ship to fit in another layer of slaves. Since the total height of the hold was 5 feet 8 inches, the distance between floor and platform was only 2 feet 7 inches. If space 6 foot by 1 foot 4 inches was allowed for every male slave and the hold and quarter-deck packed in this way, the *Brookes* would carry four hundred and fifty-one slaves. In fact, the ship owners acknowledged that the usual cargo was about six hundred.

In these conditions epidemics were inevitable. Smallpox, dysentery, and the blinding eye disease, ophthalmia, were the most frequent scourges. 'The Negroes are so incident to small-pox,' wrote one captain, 'that few ships that carry them escape without it . . . but though we had 100 at a time sick of it . . . yet we lost not a dozen by it. . . . But what the small-pox spared, the flux (dysentery) swept off.' The slaves in the hold suffered greater hardship than the ship's crew, but losses among the sailors were also high; and there were sailors who deserted in the West Indies and were to be seen about the wharves 'in a sickly debilitated state . . . their legs swelled to the size of their thighs and in an ulcerated state all over'.

It is difficult to say how many slaves died on the Middle Passage. During thirty years of the eighteenth century, French slave ships from Nantes lost 13 per cent of their cargoes. Six per cent of all slaves shipped over the whole period of the trade is a conservative estimate. The average loss, however, gives no idea of the varying fortunes of individual ships. The *Albion* arrived in Barbados with three hundred out of a total cargo of five hundred and fifty, the rest had been carried off by dysentery. The *St. Jan*, a leaky Dutch vessel, sold ninety slaves in the Indies out of an original cargo of two hundred and nineteen.

Other ships were more fortunate; the epidemics did not take such a strong hold and losses would be confined to one or two a day.

Of course, conditions on slave ships varied. Some captains allowed the slaves out twice a day; one noted how he encouraged them to dance in the evening to keep up their spirits. Some took the men out of irons after a few days, while others, short of crew, kept them in irons all the time. Some ship's doctors tried to do their duty; others preferred not to try. Some captains indulged in brutality to slaves and crew alike, while others tried to take an interest in their welfare. But slavers were always overcrowded and insanitary. Liverpool ships were not expected to survive more than eight trips to the Coast.

The captains of the slave ships were not usually much concerned about the morality of the trade, but they had to deal at first hand with their human cargo and sometimes this prompted a feeling of sympathy. The captain of the *Hannibal*, for instance, was not a brutal or ignorant man. He could not be persuaded to amputate rebellious slaves as an example to the rest, for the 'poor creatures who, excepting their want of Christianity and true religion, (their misfortune more than fault), are as much the works of God's hands and no doubt as dear to Him as ourselves; nor can I imagine why they should be despised for their colour, being what they cannot help, and the effect of the climate it has pleased God to appoint them.' The captain wrote this at the beginning of the voyage. By the end of the journey he was writing in quite different terms. As the captain of a slaver he was concerned with profit first and foremost. On this trip he had bad luck; of the seven hundred slaves loaded, three hundred and twenty died. As he watched the profits dwindle, his humane attitude to the cargo disappeared. He wrote in disgust, 'after all our pains and care to give them their messes in due order and season, keeping their lodges as clean and sweet as possible, and enduring so much misery and stench so long among a parcel of creatures nastier than swine . . . to be defeated by their mortality!'

SALE IN THE WEST INDIES

When a slave-ship arrived in the West Indies, the cargo was advertised in the local newspaper or by placards. The number of slaves for sale, their age, sex and country of origin were all detailed. The workers of each African nation had a special reputation. The Mandingoes, for instance, from the area east of Sierra Leone, showed very gentle dispositions; sometimes they could write Arabic and repeat parts of the Koran. They were not well suited for field-work. The Koromantyn or Gold Coast slaves were distinguished by 'activity, courage and stubbornness'. Tacky, leader of a slave rebellion in Jamaica in 1760, was a Koromantyn for instance. Slaves from Whydah, called Papaws, were particularly popular, since they worked hard like the Koromantyn, but submitted to discipline. The Eboes from the Bight of Benin, on the other hand, became so despondent with their situation that they were likely to commit suicide.

The actual sale was held on board the ship or on the wharf, with the men collected at one end and the women at the other. Bryan Edwards, a famous planter and author, described the way the slaves behaved during the sale. 'They display on being brought to the market,' he wrote, 'very few signs of lamentation for their past, or apprehension for their future condition; but wearied out with confinement at sea, commonly express great eagerness to be sold; presenting themselves when the buyers are few, with cheerfulness and alacrity for selection and appearing mortified and disappointed when refused.' The buyer was supposed to avoid breaking up families; this frequently occurred nevertheless.

The planter's first concern after completing his purchases was to issue a suit of coarse osnaburg, a cheap linen, to the slaves who had arrived naked. They were also given a knife, a hat and handkerchiefs before being taken to the plantation. For the first few months the slaves were seasoned, that is, left to adjust to the change of climate and the new country. This was often done by distributing new slaves among those already on the plantation and letting the old hands look after them. This practice was heavily criticised in England, sometimes by the planters themselves, as putting too great a strain on the resident slaves by expecting them to support newcomers. Bryan Edwards maintained, however, that the system worked very well because the new slaves were virtually adopted by the people who took them in while they got their huts built and provision ground started, before being sent out to the fields.

ATTITUDES TO THE SLAVE TRADE

For three hundred years the churches accepted the slave trade. It was argued, firstly, that the slaves were slaves in Africa already and, secondly, that by coming into a Christian society they would have an opportunity for conversion. The attitude of the Catholic clergy in Africa is well demonstrated by the views of Brother Luis Brandaon of the Jesuit College at Loanda, Angola, who was asked in 1610 to express an opinion on whether the slaves were legally captured in Africa. He admitted that it would be hard to distinguish which of the slaves were legally captured and which not, 'but the traders who take them away from here do not know of this fact, and so buy these negroes with a clear conscience and sell them out there with a clear conscience'. His conclusive argument in favour of the trade was that 'to lose so many souls as sail from here because some, impossible to recognise, have been captured illegally, does not seem to be doing much service to God'. In this argument slaves were regarded rather as souls to be saved than as people to be protected.

What tended to happen in practice was that the actual fate of the slaves' souls became less important to the churchmen than the business of the slave trade. So we find the Portuguese Catholic priest at Cabenda licensing an English ship to collect slaves, although he complained that 'the English carried the slaves to Barbados, to the heretics', where, he was sure, 'the poor wretches would never be instructed in the Christian faith'. The only Protestant group to question the trade were some of the Quakers, and we have seen how unpopular they were.

Eventually, it was laymen, not churchmen, who began an organised protest against the slave trade. In 1787 and 1788 societies were formed in England and France respectively to abolish the trade. The members of these societies did not accept the idea that teaching the slaves Christianity justified the trade. They emphasised that it was morally wrong for Christians to traffic in men at all, and that it was inhuman to subject fellow creatures to the actual conditions of the slave-ships. They set to work to convince the public. The fight to end the slave trade had begun, but not before the trade had provided the bulk of the West Indian population as labourers for the most profitable cultivation in the world in the eighteenth century.

FURTHER READING

Sources of West Indian History, Economic Life, pp. 35–8, 49–53, Slavery and its Abolition, pp. 162–6.

Williams, *Documents of West Indian History*, Chapter V, Negro Slavery and the Slave Trade, pp. 151–163.

Carter, Digby and Murray, *History of the West Indian Peoples*, III, Chapter 10, African Homes of the West Indian Negroes, Chapter 11, West African Society.

Williams, *History of the People of Trinidad and Tobago*, Chapter IV.

QUESTIONS TO CONSIDER

1. How much did the development of your territory depend upon the introduction of slaves?
2. What changes did the European slave trade bring to life in West Africa?
3. What arguments can you find for and against the slave trade?
4. What forms of resistance do you expect that the slaves showed to their condition of life?

PART II

ESTABLISHING THE SOCIETY

CHAPTER EIGHT

The Sugar Estate

ESTATE ORGANISATION

The eighteenth century was the time when the British West Indian islands came to be called 'the jewel in England's crown'. The other European countries with West Indian possessions valued them just as highly. Sugar was established as 'king', and he was a very wealthy monarch. The profits of a West Indian sugar estate were generally much greater than those of any other cultivation in either America or Europe. For this reason European nations went to war to defend their possessions abroad. As so much was at stake, the wars were frequent and bitter. In our area small islands changed ownership many times. But more slavers than warships crossed the Atlantic and it is the rise and fall of the plantation system that is the key to West Indian history in the eighteenth century.

In describing life on a plantation, then, we are properly describing West Indian life as it was lived here when sugar was king. To understand the working of the plantation and the problems of all its members, from its owner to its newest-born slave child, is to understand the most characteristic part of West Indian history in its most prosperous period. The best account of sugar estates in the eighteenth century is given in Bryan Edwards's *History of the West Indies*, first published in 1793. Bryan Edwards was a Jamaica planter and knew that island best, but his description is useful as a general guide to all of them.

The estate-land usually consisted of cane-land, provision-grounds and woodlands. The greater the area of cane-land, the better, of course. A planter liked to have at least two hundred to three hundred acres planted in cane, though this was not generally possible in the smaller islands. There they were limited by lack of available land. The provision-grounds were used by the estate slaves for growing root-crops and vegetables for food. Where woodlands existed, they were used for supplies of lumber, logs and firewood. Pasture was sometimes available for cattle.

The cane-fields were of two main kinds, plant canes and ratoons. Plant canes were, as their name indicates, newly planted. Ratoons were the new stalks growing out of cane-roots left in the ground after a crop had been cut. Ratoons were classified according to the number of successive years in which they were cultivated; so there were first ratoons, being the first crop out of previously established roots, second ratoons, third ratoons, and so on, even, on a few estates, up to fifteenth and twentieth ratoons. Ratooning was less expensive than planting, but, unless the planter took care, successive ratoon crops could have a greatly diminishing sugar content.

On each estate there were the factory buildings. The general process of sugar manufacture from the cane may be seen from the essential parts of a factory. They were the mill, the boiling-house and the curing-house. On some estates there was also a still-house for the distillation of rum. Around the factory yard were many other buildings and sheds. There were workshops for the skilled wheelwrights, carpenters, coopers, blacksmiths and masons. There was a hospital room for sick slaves and a small gaol for slaves in punishment. There were sheds for livestock and the sheds where the cane trash, *bagasse* or *megasse* as it was variously called, was stored for use as fuel, as well as lock-ups in which other stores were kept.

Not too far from the factory buildings were the small houses occupied by the managers and supervisors of the estate. These people ranged in status from the overseer through book-keepers, who were not accountants or ledger-clerks but supervisors of field work, down to a number of skilled craftsmen and unskilled white subordinate staff. The estate owner, or his attorney, if either of them were resident, usually lived a little apart, in grander style in the estate greathouse.

Set apart from the estate buildings were the slave quarters. They might be individual small huts with thatched roofs, or long barracks. Here lived the majority of the people on any estate. The number of slaves required depended, roughly, on the number of acres of cane-land to be cultivated and, although labour requirements varied according to soil and other conditions, a population of one adult slave per acre was generally thought sufficient. Bryan Edwards's estimate of 'stock' required to keep three hundred acres in sugar production included 'two hundred and fifty negroes, eighty steers, and sixty mules'. For the eighteenth-century planter, the slaves were the most important part of the estate's 'stock', and in the rendering of accounts they were normally classified with the estate animals. The animals were kept for two main purposes—turning the mill and hauling carts; they also provided the estate with manure. In islands where streams and rivers were strong enough, water-mills were used and animals were needed only for haulage. But in the Leewards and Barbados, where rivers are non-existent and the few streams are small and capricious, the planters relied on wind and animal power to turn their mills. Where a reliable water-mill was impossible, it was the best practice to have at least one cattle-mill and one windmill. Of the three types, the water-mill was most reliable and also the most expensive to set up, the windmill was the cheapest but also the least dependable.

THE SUGAR CROP

The cultivation of the sugar crop was a systematic and patient piece of farming. First, the land was prepared for planting by burning and clearing grass and shrub then the labourers would mark it off in lines for the cane-holes which were dug about 2,700 to the acre. When this was done, several cane-tops were placed at the bottom of each hole and lightly covered with earth. As the canes grew, more earth was banked around them. Plant canes took about fifteen months and ratoons about twelve months to mature. During this time the rows would be weeded three or four times and the dry trash removed from the cane-stalks. When the canes matured they were cut by workers using machetes, cutlasses or bills, bound together in bundles and loaded on to cattle wains for transport to the factory.

Standing in the yard of one of these old factories, it is easy to let the imagination slip back and to find ourselves in the noise and bustle of a day in crop-season two hundred years ago. Along the estate roads, narrow, unpaved and scarred by terrible ruts, the dust rises as oxen drag the wains in from the fields to the factory. In the fields, gangs of men and women are cutting, bundling and loading the canes. They work steadily and some are singing, but not far from each group stands a man with a whip and occasionally it flashes across the back of one of the workers. All these people are slaves, including the man with the whip, who is called the driver of the gang. The drivers have been given power over their fellow slaves and because individuals behave differently, some abuse their authority, some use it justly, and others try to escape using it. Nor do all the cane-cutters behave alike. A few are sullen and rebellious; the majority appear much as people on the same work today; a few others are clearly terrified of the drivers.

A few hundred yards away, moving to and fro, is a European. He is one of the estate book-keepers. Wherever he goes the drivers become more alert and a few of them seek his approval by shouting at the cutters and perhaps flicking their whips at them. But the book-keeper, too, is an individual with his particular character and beliefs and he may chastise the driver for being too zealous or, on the other hand, he may praise him for being so watchful of his master's interest.

The carts laden, the oxen pull hard but reluctantly out of the field where the cane-tops lie, on to the dry dusty road to the heat of the factory yard. Long whips crack, the oxen moan and bellow, the carts creak and jolt so that some of the canes fall off into the roadway. Round the last bend a laden cart comes into the yard and, while the wainman stretches his legs or attends to the harness, other slaves unload the bundles of cane in high heaps around the mill house. The empty cart turns, the oxen find it lighter against their tugging and it bumps and rattles back to the field for another load.

SUGAR FACTORY

As we pass through any of the West Indian territories today, we can see ruins of old estate houses and factory buildings, especially in the islands earliest colonised, such as Barbados, Martinique, Guadeloupe and the Leewards. By the shapes and positions of the brick towers we can tell whether they were the mill-house towers or the boiling-house chimneys. In some cases the remains of the boiling-house are enough to give quite a clear picture of the process of manufacture; indeed, people who live in Nevis can see at New River a factory which produces sugar almost exactly as it was produced two hundred years ago. There are very few such old factories still in operation, and all have undergone some change. At New River, for instance, the mill is no longer driven by the wind but by a late nineteenth-century steam-engine. This factory, and others like it, cannot produce the semi-refined crystals which are made in the large modern factories. They produce raw muscovado sugar for local consumption such as was exported in the eighteenth century.

As the canes were crushed through the mill the juice from them was conveyed by gutters into the first receptacles, the syphons; the trash was removed and stored for use as fuel for the boilers. In the syphons the juice was clarified by heating it with a small quantity of lime. The clarified juice was then skimmed or ladled into successive copper boilers, each smaller than the previous one, and hung over a hotter fire. There were usually three such coppers, the last, smallest and hottest of which was the teache. By the time the juice was boiled down in the teache it was reduced by evaporation to a thick syrup which would stretch between thumb and forefinger. At this stage the boiling was over.

The sticky mass was then run off into shallow wooden troughs to cool before it was potted into hogsheads in the curing-house. In curing, the sugar was simply left for about three weeks in the hogsheads, which were perforated at the bottom, allowing the molasses to drip out. In the curing-house the floor was made of crossed beams so that the dripping molasses could fall into cisterns beneath to be recovered and re-boiled. On the upper section the hogsheads of crystallised sugar were sealed and rolled out on to carts for the first stage of their journey to Europe. But not all the sugar reached the markets in Europe. Crude methods of manufacture and curing meant that the sugar still contained a proportion of molasses, some of which leaked from the hogsheads during the long transatlantic voyage. The eighteenth-century hogshead of sugar commonly weighed 14 cwt. when it left the estate, but anything from 10 to 25 per cent less by the time it arrived in Europe.

When rum was made, as it was in all estates of any size, the skimmings from the first boiling of the cane juice were used as a fermenting mixture with a roughly equal quantity of molasses. This was left for a week's fermentation and then distilled twice to make proof rum.

Crop time therefore meant a scene of industry in the factory and its yard as well as in the fields. There were slave-labourers about the factory who unloaded the wains and kept feeding the canes to the mill. Others were busy moving moist trash from mill to trash-house, others moving dry trash from the trash-house to the fires under the great copper boilers. If it was an animal-driven mill, others were leading the animals round the mill-circuit or preparing relays of fresh mules to take over the work.

Within the factory, too, there were slave-labourers rolling hogsheads, scurrying out to yell at the fireman to stoke up under the big copper, cleaning out the cooling troughs, shovelling the cooled sugar. There were also the skilled slaves in the factory, such as the slave who added the lime to the juice and watched the process of clarification, the slaves who ladled the boiling syrup from one copper to the next, the slave who stood by the teache testing the readiness of the sugar for cooling by stretching the syrup between his thumb and forefinger. These were all skilled people whose competence was of great importance.

Outside, the wheelwrights and blacksmiths were kept constantly busy as damaged wains were dragged in from some accident on the rutted roads. The carpenters stood ready to repair the wooden gutters along which the juice flowed from mill-house to boiling-house, or hammered out the staves which the coopers encircled with metal hoops to make the hogsheads.

There was no relief. The work went on at night by the light of lamps and torches. The factory overseer organised shifts of slaves and animals to keep the factory working, and unconcernedly turned his eye away as the slaves chewed cane or took long draughts of juice as it came from the mill. Sugar is a fuel which keeps the human body going. Only in the fields did the darkness bring quiet. During the day enough cane was cut to feed the mills all night and from dusk till dawn the field workers took their rest, unless their additional labour was needed in the factory. This was the pattern of activity during the six months of crop season every year.

SLAVES ON THE ESTATE

The crop season over, the estate became a quieter place. In the fields the gangs were still at work digging cane-holes, weeding or trashing ratoons, or applying manure. The work was hard but the pace less feverish. There were fewer labourers about the factory, but the white tradesmen and their skilled slave assistants were engaged in maintenance work or in building. On the road, gangs of labourers filled up the pot-holes, and repaired fences. This was the time of planting, cultivation, repair and maintenance. It was the dull, or off, season. But estate workers were not allowed to idle; some kind of occupation was found for every slave for as much of the working day as possible. Lack of work allows more time for leisurely meeting and chatter. Slave-owners did not like their slaves to indulge in much idle conversation because they were afraid that discontented workers might use such opportunities to incite their fellow slaves to open rebellion, or disobedience, or to delay the processes of cultivation and manufacture by 'working slow'.

Eighteenth-century West Indian society was not a happy society. On every estate, the slaves far outnumbered the free people and the slave-owners were always alert for rebellion and resistance. This is not to say that the slave-owners were always waiting for a chance to intimidate their slaves or the slaves to retaliate. Not all slave-owners were cruel and not all slaves were spirited enough to strike back. Furthermore, by our present-day standards, the eighteenth century was in many respects a cruel period both in Europe and Africa, the areas from which the West Indian population came. The treatment of criminals in Europe was harsh; many petty offences were punishable by death, and the use of the lash in the armies and on naval vessels was as brutal as on the estates in the West Indies. Those slaves who had recently come from Africa would also remember the harshness of their treatment in the slave coffles and at the trading stations.

The root of the fear where slave-worked plantations flourished, as in the West Indies and the southern states of America, was in the system of slavery itself. On the estate, the resident owner or manager was in full and complete authority with hardly any effective restraints on his behaviour. There is not a man in the world who can carry such unlimited authority over his fellow creatures without abusing it. Among the eighteenth-century planters, as among any other group of people, a few were men of high principles, a few were rogues, and the majority were something in between these two extremes. The abuse of power was common, though few individual planters set out deliberately to mistreat their slaves, except in moments of fear and anger. At such times careless acts of violence were numerous, and it was precisely this sort of behaviour which might have been checked if the masters, instead of having unchecked authority, had been restrained by fear of certain legal or social punishment as the consequence of such conduct.

Both in French and Spanish territories codes of slave law existed and there were officials to supervise the treatment of slaves. The Dutch too had an official for this purpose. For the English islands there was no code and only occasionally was there a Protector of Slaves. Each had different laws and these were the business of the local assembly who obviously would not be anxious to restrict their own powers as slave-owners. In practice, the French and Spanish law, imposed from Europe, was avoided wherever possible. There were no police to supervise what happened on the estates and only one official to whom slaves could lay their complaints. If the official decided to take their case to a court of law (for the slaves could not plead for themselves) slave-owners and masters sat as judge and jury.

Like most people, the slave disliked hard work and violence, but he was probably less constantly disturbed by these things than by the knowledge that he was powerless to avoid them. The estate slave knew that he lived in fact at the whim of his master. In consequence, the masters feared the wrath of their slaves who might feel that they had nothing to lose by resorting to violence themselves; the slaves for their part feared the sudden passions of their masters.

THE ESTATE HIERARCHY

The estate population was not simply divided into masters and slaves. Within each of these groups there were social classes. Thus the resident owner or the attorney was a step above the overseer, who in turn occupied a more exalted position than the book-keepers and looked down on the white tradesmen and other white estate employees. Because of the great numerical superiority of the slaves, there were in some English islands regulations called Deficiency Laws by which slave-owners were required to employ one white person for every twenty or so slaves in their possession. These laws were not always observed; it was cheaper for some planters to pay the annual fine for not obeying the law than to hire a white man. In Jamaica by the end of the eighteenth century, the Deficiency Laws were recognised as a source of revenue to the government rather than as an effective means of increasing the white population. In Barbados, where there was a proportionately large number of whites, descendants of the earliest indentured labourers, it was easier for planters to find white employees; descendants of the Barbadian 'deficiency men' are still to be found in that island as poor white peasant cultivators. Between the estate owner or attorney and the deficiency man, though they were both white and free, a great social gulf existed. Other distinctions in white West Indian society were created between the creoles, born in the West Indies, and the immigrant whites. In islands such as Grenada, St. Vincent, St. Lucia, Dominica, which changed hands often, there were also national differences between the Europeans. The adjustment had to be made between English and French in these islands; later, in Trinidad, it was to be the English, French and Spanish who maintained distinctions, even though they were by then creole families.

Similarly, among the slaves there were social groupings based on place of birth, and on colour, for not all slaves were black. For newly imported slaves, their previous rank and occupation in Africa were important considerations. Also taken into account were the wealth and social standing of the slave's owner, and the nature of the slave's occupation. A skilled slave was a person of some prestige among his fellows. A domestic slave gained social stature from the comparatively easy nature of his work and his close association with the master. The field slave was in the lowest social group, unless he could show some other claim to prestige, such as powers of healing or powers of obeah, or employment as a driver. But even within each of these groups there was a hierarchy. Among the domestic slaves it was most pronounced, as it is even today in the homes of the very wealthy where the butler and the cook lord it over the laundry woman and the cleaner.

Reading the arguments which, from the late eighteenth century until emancipation, were offered for and against the practice of slavery, we get two quite different pictures of life on the West Indian sugar estates. The abolitionists, painting the scene in harsh and cruel colours, emphasised the brutal planter and the cowed and beaten creature from whom he extracted labour by the lash of the whip. The defenders of slavery drew a different picture of wise paternal masters who valued their slaves because they were expensive to buy and maintain, and who tried by divers humane and friendly acts to improve the conditions of slave existence. In fact, the lives of the majority of slaves were spent in a continuous round of hard, enforced labour broken at intervals by some festive occasion such as Christmas, the end of crop-taking, the birthday of a master, or the marriage of his child. On these occasions there would be extra portions of imported salted beef or fish and a share-out of rum, and there would be dancing and singing in the light of flares and lanterns in the mill-yard or outside the great-house, or even inside for domestic slaves at Christmas. But normally the routine of labour was interrupted only by the Sunday morning visit to market where the slaves gossiped and bought and sold the vegetables, fruit and other small produce raised by them on the estate provision-grounds.

It was a life from which few could really expect to escape. To be sold might mean a harder master, to run away meant severe punishment if caught, to achieve legal freedom was practically impossible. Nevertheless, slaves did run away, particularly in areas where they could hide easily. The Bush Negroes in Guiana made use of up-

country regions and settled by the rivers where rapids made it dangerous to pursue them. More aggressive were the Maroons or
Cimaroons, of the mountainous islands of Jamaica, Dominica, St.
Vincent and St. Lucia, who lived 'bush' lives and were prepared to
raid estates from time to time.

The Jamaican Maroons in particular were a community to be
reckoned and bargained with. They were numerous, having started
as a sizeable group which escaped from the Spanish during the British
capture of Jamaica. They had settled the inaccessible mountain
country and made a refuge for slaves escaping from the estates.

The military were posted to keep the Maroons in this territory, and
were provided with dogs to catch raiders who tried to slip through
the defences to the estates. In 1734 Indians with skill in tracking and
knowledge of bush fighting were imported from the Mosquito Coast
to assist the troops. In 1738 the British military actually entered into
a treaty with the Maroon chief, Cudjoe. By this the Maroons were
guaranteed their freedom in their chosen territory, on condition that
they gave up runaway slaves and helped in defence should Jamaica
ever be invaded by enemies. This kept the Maroons separate and
peaceful for a time, but they remained a body who could give trouble
if provoked. Their big rising in 1795 at the same time as the greatest
Negro revolution of all, in St. Domingue, will be discussed later.

The Maroons disturbed the peace but did not directly affect estate
discipline. There were rebellions on the estates but they were punished by such cruel deaths, burning, hanging and breaking on the
wheel, that it was some time before they spread. In Jamaica, however, there were at least twelve slave rebellions during the eighteenth
century; one in 1760 spread to several estates, and sixty Europeans
and four hundred Negroes were killed before order was restored. In
Barbados in 1804, a thousand Negroes died before a rebellion was
quelled.

Even so, there was no great retaliation on the part of the slaves
when it is recalled that they greatly outnumbered the Europeans on
all estates, in all islands. It can only be concluded that the system of
arbitrary discipline, if not outright viciousness, succeeded in quelling
the spirit of most slaves who, knowing their lack of protection outside the estate, submitted to the system. Mutiny as such was rare
because its suppression was brutal. It was possible, however, to
calculate the minimum of work which could be achieved without
retaliation, and deliberate carelessness with tools and property could

damage the work of any estate. Individual slaves were also goaded to desperate measures such as suicide and infanticide. As well as being an unhappy life, it was a wasteful and crude system which ultimately held the seeds of its own failure in the long years ahead.

FURTHER READING

Sources of West Indian History, People of the Caribbean, pp. 15–16, Slavery and its Abolition 169–77.

Ragatz, *The Fall of the Planter Class in the British Caribbean*, Chapter 1, Caribbean Society in the Eighteenth Century, pp. 1–18.

Roberts, *The French in the West Indies*, Chapter XIV, The Code Noir.

Black, *History of Jamaica*, Chapter VIII, The Maroons.

Black, *Tales of Old Jamaica*, Three Fingered Jack.

QUESTIONS TO CONSIDER

1. Why did the West Indian colonies become the most valuable colonies to European countries in the eighteenth century?

2. In what ways was a sugar estate almost a self-contained township?

3. You know that the French islands had a *Code Noir* from 1685; British islands also passed laws to regulate the life of the slaves. What rules do you think they would contain to improve the slaves' position? Try to discover if you have worked out some of the actual provisions. (*Sources of West Indian History*, pp. 167–9.)

4. What risks might a plantation owner run of not securing a profit on his sugar? Can you think of any that are not discussed in this chapter?

CHAPTER NINE

Wars, Trade and Empire Building

THE NEW RIVALS

Whatever uncertainties the planters may have felt about the safety of life on their estates or the length of time that sugar production might be profitable, they were quite certain in the eighteenth century that it was a way of life that promised much wealth. They ran their estates to make profits quickly so that they could live in comfort and ease here or, in ever increasing numbers, return to Europe to live among the landed aristocracy there, leaving agents or attorneys to manage their properties in the West Indies. In the eighteenth century the West Indies were not a popular resort. The interests of the planters in the area were therefore limited to the profits that could be made from sugar production. To that extent they were concerned to defend their territory from attack.

Earlier colonists had had to make their way in the smaller islands against attacks from Carib Indians; and the danger of sporadic raids from the Spanish only died by the end of the seventeenth century. The Spanish for their part had had to defend themselves against buccaneer warfare. Raids and sudden attacks were expected in all West Indian colonies, so defence was organised here from the beginning of settlement. Forts were built to guard the coasts and all free men were armed and partly trained in militia groups.

By the end of the seventeenth century, as we have seen, Spain had recognised the rights of the English and French to their West Indian islands; the way was clear for a new rivalry, this time between the English and French. This development had been inevitable ever since both nations had restricted their colonial trade to their own shipping and ports. As sources of wealth for their European owners, the colonies became as important a cause of European war in the eighteenth century as quarrels in Europe itself. Commerce, colonies and power in Europe were vitally connected, and any limitation of trading rights or any blow to a colony was a method of keeping the rival down.

The West Indian islands were the cause of much bitter fighting because they were until the end of the eighteenth century the most prosperous of English and French oversea possessions. Fighting, however, also took place in North America and India in jealous attempts to increase empires. The excuse for the wars was usually some European quarrel, but the reason for their bitterness and widespread fighting was the rival struggle for trade and colonies. Since the warfare was now the concern of European governments, they directed it; more and more the colonists found themselves pawns in a game which they could do little to control.

The wars of the Spanish Succession (1702–13), Captain Jenkins's Ear (1739–48) and the Seven Years War (1756–63) were all concerned with this rivalry. The Treaties of Utrecht, Aix-la-Chapelle and Paris, which respectively followed these three wars, all included important matters concerned with colonies and the many changes of ownership. This was also true of the Treaties of Versailles (1783) and Vienna (1815) which followed the War of American Independence and the French Napoleonic War respectively. It took over a century for the English and French to settle their claims; by then the West Indian colonies were no longer in the first flush of their prosperity.

WARS OF EMPIRE

Trade as a benefit of empire was earliest apparent in the English islands of Barbados and the Leewards, where exports to England rose steadily in the first twenty years of the eighteenth century. In 1699, 21,300 tons of sugar were sent to England from these islands. In 1720 the sugar exports amounted to 49,740 tons; that is, in twenty years they more than doubled.

During eleven of these years, England was engaged in war with France and Spain about the succession to the Spanish throne. In fact both the English and the Dutch were fighting desperately to prevent a union of the Spanish and the French crowns. This would have been a great menace to them in Europe; in North America and the Caribbean it might well have brought English and Dutch trade to a standstill.

In 1713 England followed victory in the war with gains at the treaty table. By taking Nova Scotia, the English established their right to Newfoundland and they forced France to acknowledge the rights of the English Hudson Bay Company in North America. In the Caribbean, they were granted the French settlement in St. Kitts, which now became a wholly English island. Finally the English were granted the *asiento* for thirty years to trade in slaves with the Spanish Empire, and the right to send one ship a year with goods to trade at the great annual fair at Porto Bello.

The French defeat was by no means crushing and in fact served as a spur to their government to make much greater efforts in the colonies. Martinique and Guadeloupe had by 1714 developed into successful sugar islands. According to the trade restrictions colonial sugars had to go to their home countries, but the stage had now been reached when they were producing more than could be used in England and France alone, so both countries were now in a position to re-export surplus sugar to other European countries and to their own colonists in North America. In this competition France increasingly in the eighteenth century did better than England; for, in 1714, there was still French West Indian territory to develop. After the war, the French settlement in Hispaniola, St. Domingue, was made into a separate colony, no longer nominally in subjection to the governor-general in Martinique. From this point, small beginnings in sugar-planting were developed fast and France's youngest West Indian colony entered upon three-quarters of a century of great prosperity.

French sugar production in St. Domingue, Martinique and Guadeloupe went ahead by leaps and bounds just when the soil of Barbados and the smaller English sugar islands showed signs of deteriorating under its longer use. The French planters had an abundance of fertile, untouched land at their disposal in St. Domingue and were producing increasing quantities of sugar at low cost. Even with the production of Jamaica, exports of sugar to England did not increase at the same rate as those to France.

The French were equally active in North America and India. They penetrated along the Mississippi River and tried to close in the thirteen English American colonies on the eastern seaboard. New Orleans was founded in 1717. In India the French trading port of Pondicherry was built up to rival the English East India Company's stations at Bombay, Calcutta and Madras. A naval dockyard was set up on the French island of Mauritius. There was no mistaking French ambitions. The merchant marine which had numbered eleven hundred ships in 1713 had grown to eighteen hundred by 1735, and cargo to and from the West Indies was a very considerable proportion of its business.

A TRADE WAR

The English privileges in Spanish American trade won in 1713 proved by no means an unmixed blessing. The authorities knew well that in practice it was going to be extremely difficult to tell a legal trading ship from the host of illegal traders plying the Caribbean waters in ever-increasing number. Spanish 'coast guards' were multiplied to meet this situation and were largely manned by the tough, experienced seamen who had formerly had to deal with the buccaneers. They insisted on searching every English ship they came across, and occasionally they seized a legal slave-ship. It was then practically impossible to get compensation from Spain.

The Spanish authorities were not entirely to blame for this attitude, for their English counterparts were not above pressing some very dubious claims against the Spanish Government. An embarrassed British ambassador in Madrid expostulated, 'Are the oaths of fellows that forswear themselves in every custom-house, in every port they come to, to be taken without any further enquiry or examination, what should we say to a bawling Spaniard who made a derelict of his ship in Jamaica and afterwards swore blood and murder before the Mayor of Bilbao?'

Yet it was on such a claim that England again went to war in 1739. When Captain Jenkins swore that his ship had been illegally searched by the Spanish and his ear chopped off in the foray, members of the British Government showed much sympathy with his case on little more evidence than the sight of an ear pickled for their inspection. The ensuing war lasted nine years and the French joined in before it was finished.

The British Government were hardly concerned to send armies, navies and money simply as retaliation for Captain Jenkins's ear. They were, however, prepared to use the excuse to attack practices that threatened English trade. Despite the *asiento* and favourable arrangements for the annual trade-ship, the English had not in fact the monopoly of trade with the Spanish Main. By using merchants in Cadiz as their agents for transporting their goods across the Atlantic, the French had also found a way of selling a good many of their products in the wealthy Spanish American market.

This threatened the British trade, and especially that part of it which was growing up in the Caribbean itself. Merchants in the British islands had a definite interest in Spanish trade. Jamaica had

93

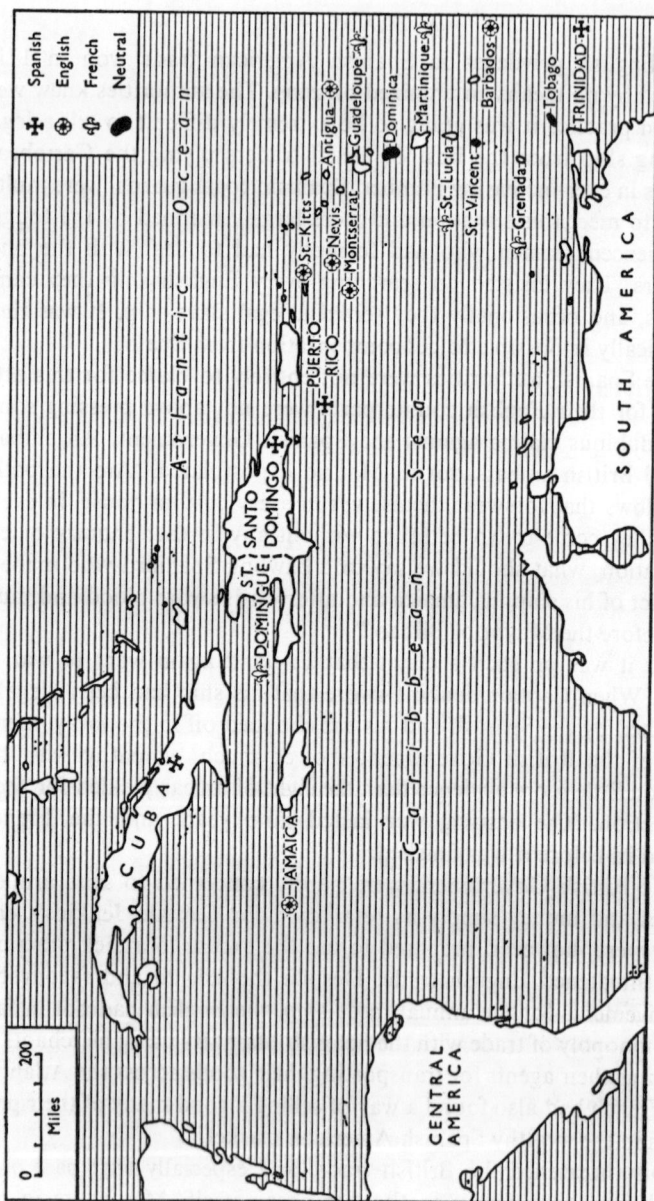

Fig. 5. The West Indies in 1756

become a trade depot for slaves and manufactured goods for the Spanish islands, and many Jamaican merchants had a slaver in the trade themselves. The Spanish islands by this time were as dependent on British supplies as they had formerly been on Dutch. Even during the war, the Governor of Havana wanted Jamaica to send him two thousand slaves, flour, rice, pulse beans, sheet-lead, tin, pictures, linseed oil, window-glasses, household furniture, looking-glasses, diamonds and sail-cloth. Everything except the sail-cloth, which counted as war material, was sent.

By 1744 the French had joined in the war which had long ceased to be concerned with Jenkins's ear. As Governor Trelawney of Jamaica said, 'Unless French Hispaniola is ruined during the war they will, upon the peace, ruin our sugar colonies by the quantity they will make and the low price they can afford to sell it at.' The rivalry was now unmistakable.

THE SEVEN YEARS WAR, 1756–1763

In the next stages of the struggle the focus moved from the Caribbean to the other parts of the world where the English and the French were competing for mastery. The North American colonies were becoming increasingly important and consequently became the scene of one of the most critical phases of the next war. In England's thirteen seaboard colonies, the population was rapidly increasing and creating a larger market every year for English manufactures, while the European population in the Caribbean islands was nearly static. North America had vast resources, unexploited land and raw materials, while the islands had apparently reached the peak of their productivity.

In the Caribbean, which was still the scene of fighting, the motive was defence of existing interests. More British and French capital was still invested in the West Indies than in any other part of the world. The islands were well worth defending. There was also another use for them. Even if a particular small island was not wanted for further sugar cultivation, it could be used as a pawn in the diplomatic game at the treaty table. It could be exchanged for territories in other parts of the world. During the Seven Years War the British took French islands for just this purpose. When Spain joined the war on the side of the French, victories against the Spanish Empire were used in the same way.

This practice sometimes had disadvantages. When the British

captured the French colonies of Guadeloupe and Martinique, the French planters there, who had been unable to export their sugar during the fighting, shipped the accumulated stocks straight to the London market. This shipment increased the quantity of sugar for sale in London and brought the prices down immediately, to the loss of the British planters in the West Indies.

There were other calculations to be made and these are best illus‑ trated by the decisions over the 'neutral islands' of Tobago, St. Lucia, St. Vincent and Dominica, which were held neither by the British nor the French in 1756. St. Vincent and Dominica were still in the hands of the Caribs. St. Lucia and Tobago had a few scattered settlements of Frenchmen who supplied some hardwood and ground provisions to other islands and grew some cocoa and cotton. None of these settlers had enough capital to cultivate sugar on large estates. At various times the governors of Barbados and Martinique were invited by their respective home governments to settle these islands for strategic reasons. St. Lucia, for instance, was occupied by a force from Martinique when France entered the War of Jenkins's Ear in 1744. The treaty of 1748, however, left the islands still un‑ allotted. The British colonists were afraid that if these islands were opened to settlement the white populations of the older islands would be greatly reduced; and this was at a time when the slave populations on the British plantations already greatly outnumbered the whites. On the other hand, if war was to continue in the Caribbean, the islands had also to be considered as points of defence and attack. St. Lucia, for instance, had a first-class harbour and was the only island from which French activities at Fort Royal in Martinique could be supervised.

During the Seven Years War, the neutral islands were occupied by the French and later captured by the British. Their strategic value by the time of the treaty in 1763 was held to outweigh the dangers of depopulating the older colonies as a means of settling the new. St. Vincent, Tobago and Dominica were kept by Britain, as was Grenada, an older settled colony, which had also been taken from the French in the war. The other Caribbean gains were ex‑ changed for advantages in North America. Guadeloupe was re‑ turned to the French in return for Canada, which now became British. The island of St. Lucia and a victory over Spain at Havana were used to bargain for the right bank of the Mississippi to ensure navigation rights on the river to British American colonists. At the end of the Seven Years War Britain had succeeded in asserting herself over France in every theatre of war—in North America, the Caribbean, India and West Africa.

GARRISONS AND MILITIA

These wars between European nations brought a new population to the West Indies in the military and naval establishments which grew up in the British and French islands. Governors had now to deal with generals and admirals who had independent schemes of defence for their islands; the partnership was not always easy. Militia forces were still organised; every free man was supposed to do duty. But in a serious invasion, the militia would be far too small for efficient defence. Furthermore, in their councils and assemblies, the planters made it quite clear that they were not prepared to spend much money on defence. They considered this to be the responsibility of the home country which had initiated the wars. Particularly in the British islands, they entered into prolonged and bitter argument on the subject; it was in fact one of the major points of disagreement between the West Indian assemblies and the British Government. Garrisons and guns were expected from Europe for the forts, which alone the local governments were prepared to supply.

Land defence was on the whole very inefficiently conducted, and there was little military experience amongst the planters. Governor Robinson of Barbados, for instance, ordered guns from England heavier than any that had ever been cast. Expensive guns when they arrived would be left unmounted, or hired out at a profit to privateers, as they often were in the French islands. The forts that were provided often proved very vulnerable to attack from the sea. Basse-Terre in Guadeloupe and Fort Royal in Martinique were easily reduced. Port Royal's defences in Jamaica were never put to the test, but the naval commanders had no faith in its power to defend Kingston harbour and employed instead the method of setting ships broadside across the narrows.

It was difficult to find enough professional soldiers to supply these forts with garrisons. Large armies were not maintained by many European countries in peacetime and soldiers for oversea service were hard to find. When a company heard it was detailed for oversea service, many men deserted, fearing that they would never see home again. They were justified in dreading the West India service, since a battalion was not expected to survive more than two years.

Yellow fever, malaria and dysentery took a greater toll of soldiers' lives than the enemy.

In wartime, special troops were sent out, combined with naval forces, to take enemy islands or important towns. This sort of expedition used the same tactics on a large scale as the buccaneers had done, but it was very costly in man-power. The buccaneers were thoroughly acclimatised to the tropics and could survive even in the jungles of Panama. But raw recruits from Europe brought over on crowded transports had even less chance of survival than the men on garrison duty.

A big venture of this sort was an English expedition sent under Admiral Vernon in 1741 to take Cartagena, the Spanish stronghold on the Main. Thirteen thousand troops were sent out; six hundred fell as casualties before the town, which was much more thoroughly defended than the commanders had anticipated. But most casualties were caused by malaria and yellow fever which spread through the transports. There was no medical attention, nor even enough orderlies to keep the hospital ships clean. Two months later only one thousand seven hundred men reached Jamaica fit for duty, and there for the next month they continued to die at the rate of a hundred a week. By the end of the year only three hundred men were left fit for duty. The campaign provided a perfect example of how not to wage war in the tropics; but the lesson was not finally learnt until the end of the century when Britain again tried to transport an army and maintain it in St. Domingue. The enormous losses from sickness once again finally forced a British withdrawal.

THE NAVIES

The real defence of the islands depended on sea power. 'All turns on mastery of the sea,' said Christopher Codrington, Governor of the Leeward Islands, 'if we have it, our islands are safe however thinly peopled; if the French have it, we cannot raise enough men in all the islands to hold one of them.'

France and England developed two different systems of naval defence. The British practice was to keep two squadrons stationed in the West Indies; Port Royal, Jamaica, was first established as a naval base, since it was well placed for attacks on ships from the Spanish Main. But Port Royal could not serve to defend the Leeward Islands, which were open to attack from Martinique, and where an enemy fleet from Europe would first be sighted. So, in 1743, English Harbour in Antigua was established as a naval base to serve the Leeward Islands, leaving only Barbados in an exposed position. The squadrons stayed in the West Indies during the winter and early summer, leaving in July for the North American service to avoid the hurricane season.

The French did not keep permanent squadrons in the Caribbean, preferring to send out a freshly equipped fleet every spring; this also went on to North America in July. This system meant that the French ships were in better condition than the British. Wooden ships deteriorated very quickly and the naval bases of Port Royal and English Harbour, useful though they were for victualling and naval stores, did not have the facilities for doing elaborate repairs; English Harbour could not even take the largest ships. For anything more than routine repairs the British ships had to return home. The French method also had its disadvantages; the fleet was frequently delayed in putting to sea and the ships of the line were often so over-loaded with stores for their six or seven months' tour of duty that the lowest level of guns were put out of action.

These systems of naval defence only operated fully in wartime. In 1756, for instance, when the Seven Years War started, there were only two frigates and two ships of the line in the Leeward Islands. The British Admiralty decided that wartime strength would demand eight ships of the line and eleven frigates in Jamaica, and eight of the line with eight frigates in the Leeward Islands.

The duties of the naval squadrons were to attack the enemy's trade, to intercept and destroy their forces and to give convoy protection against enemy naval ships. The business of convoying trade vessels caused constant quarrels between the merchants and planters and the navy. The merchants complained that not enough care was taken of vessels sent to the West Indies; the navy annually provided only two convoys to leave the West Indies with sugar, and this caused trouble between the Leeward Islands and Barbados. Barbadian sugar was ready for export two months later than the Leewards crop, so no naval commander could please both places.

The British naval squadrons in wartime had to deal with the French privateers which lay in wait for the merchantmen. The privateers were not as active or important as the buccaneers had been, but they enjoyed many of the same advantages; they used small, fast ships and changed their headquarters so frequently that the regular naval ships could not keep up with them.

But in many ways the most serious wartime problem for the

Key to symbols: ✠ = Spanish (S), ⊕ = English (E), ⚜ = French (F), ⛨ = Dutch (D). Contested cells shown with two codes.

Year	Cuba	St. Kitts	Barbados	Nevis	Antigua	Montserrat	St. Lucia	Jamaica	Virgins	St. Domingue	Dominica	Grenada	St. Vincent	Tobago	Martinique	Guadeloupe	Trinidad	Demerara	Essequibo	Berbice
1623	S	E						S		S							S	D	D	D
1624	S	E	E					S		S							S	D	D	D
1625	S	E/F	E					S		S							S	D	D	D
1628	S	E/F	E	E				S		S							S	D	D	D
1632	S	E/F	E	E	E	E		S		S							S	D	D	D
1639	S	E/F	E	E	E	E	E	S		S							S	D	D	D
1641	S	E/F	E	E	E	E	E	S	DUTCH BUCCANEERS	S							S	D	D	D
1650	S	E/F	E	E	E	E	F	S		S		F			F	F	S	D	D	D
1655	S	E/F	E	E	E	E	F	E		S		F			F	F	S	D	D	D
1664	S	E/F	E	E	E	E	E	E		S		F			F	F	S	D	D	D
1666	S	E/F	E	E	E	E	F	E		S		F			F	F	S	D	D	D
1713	S	E	E	E	E	E	F	E	E	S/F		F			F	F	S	D	D	D
1759	S	E	E	E	E	E	F	E	E	S/F	E	F			F	F	S	D	D	D
1762	S	E	E	E	E	E	F	E	E	S/F	E	E			F	F	S	D	D	D
1763	S	E	E	E	E	E	F	E	E	S/F	E	E	E	E	F	F	S	D	D	D
1778	S	E	E	E	E	E	E	E	E	S/F	E	E	E	F	F	F	S	D	D	D
1779	S	E	E	E	E	E	E	E	E	S/F	F	F	F	F	F	F	S	D	D	D
1780	S	E	E	E	E	E	E	E	E	S/F	F	F	F	F	F	F	S	D	D	D
1782	S	F	E	E	E	E	E	E	E	S/F	F	F	F	F	F	F	S	D	D	D
1783	S	E	E	E	E	E	F	E	E	S/F	E	E	E	E	F	F	S	D	D	D
1793	S	E	E	E	E	E	F	E	E	S/F	E	E	E	E	F	F	S	D	D	D
1794	S	E	E	E	E	E	F	E	E	S/F	E	E	E	E	E	F	S	D	D	D
1794	S	E	E	E	E	E	F	E	E	S/F	E	E	E	E	E	F	S	D	D	D
1795	S	E	E	E	E	E	F	E	E	S/F	F	F	F	E	E	F	S	D	D	D
1796	S	E	E	E	E	E	F	E		F	E	E	E	E	E	F	S	D	D	D
1797	S	E	E	E	E	E	F	E		F	E	E	E	E	E	F	S	D	D	D
1801	S	E	E	E	E	E	F	E		F	E	E	E	E	E	F	S	D	D	D
1802	S	E	E	E	E	E	F	E		F	E	E	E	F	F	F	S	D	D	D
1803	S	E	E	E	E	E	F	E		F	E	E	E	E	F	F	E	E	E	E
1804	S	E	E	E	E	E	E	E			E	E	E	E	F	F	E	E	E	E
1807	S	E	E	E	E	E	E	E			E	E	E	E	F	F	E	E	E	E
1808	S	E	E	E	E	E	E	E	HAITI		E	E	E	E	F	F	E	E	E	E
1809	S	E	E	E	E	E	E	E	HAITI		E	E	E	E	E	F	E	E	E	E
1810	S	E	E	E	E	E	E	E			E	E	E	E	E	E	E	E	E	E
1814	S	E	E	E	E	E	E	E	E		E	E	E	E	F	F	E	E	E	E

✠ Spanish   ⊕ English   ⚜ French   ⛨ Dutch

Fig. 6. Ownership of West Indian Colonies

British was provided by their American colonists, who insisted on carrying on their trade with the French islands. The French planters bought their plantation supplies from the British colonists in America and, in return, supplied molasses for the rum distillers of New England. An attempt to stop the trade in 1733, by the Molasses Act, discussed later, was never put into effective operation. While the British Government could afford to ignore this trade connection in time of peace, in time of war it amounted to little less than treason. The Prime Minister, during the Seven Years War, declared that this trade 'principally if not alone enabled the French to sustain, and protract, this long and expensive war'. It was practically impossible for the naval squadrons to put an end to this trade being carried on by the American colonists under the British flag. In the next war, the Americans won their independence from the British and so became free to trade with whom they pleased.

The British and the French were not reluctant to seize land under cover of any war. The French considerably added to British difficulties in the War of American Independence, for instance, when nearly all the small Caribbean islands were re-occupied by their forces. But they were returned at the treaty of 1783, except that Tobago passed temporarily to the French. In the French Revolutionary and Napoleonic Wars from 1792 to 1815, the last exchanges of territory between the two powers in the Caribbean took place. This was not so much a matter of empire building as a final settlement of the English and French West Indian claims. We leave you to work out the facts of further captures in war and losses and gains at the treaty table from the chart on the opposite page.

FURTHER READING

Sources of West Indian History, People of the Caribbean, pp. 11–14, Economic Life, pp. 57–9.

Parry and Sherlock, *A Short History of the West Indies*, Chapter VIII, Commerce and War, 1739–63.

Jesse, *Outlines of St. Lucia's History*, Chapter III.

Ottley, *History of Tobago*, Chapters III–VI.

QUESTIONS TO CONSIDER

1. Why did the wars of the eighteenth century come to be called wars of empire?

2. What part did the small islands play in these wars?

3. Which do you consider the most efficient method of defence in the West Indian islands in the eighteenth century?

4. Do you think that the British or the French colonies were likely to be the most prosperous communities in the West Indies after 1763?

CHAPTER TEN

Resistance and Revolution

PLANTERS' PRIDE

Clearly if the European powers were very concerned with their Caribbean possessions in the eighteenth century, European planters in the area were no less so. Their interests, however, were not identical. We have seen that they differed over the use of the 'neutral islands'. The planters saw them as unwelcome competitors for people and, later, for markets; while the European governments saw them as strategic points for naval warfare. Remember also that the assemblies were very reluctant to provide men and money for the defence of their own islands.

When such differences of interest brought conflict between the colonists and the home government, the form of government in the British islands aggravated it. The governor, the council and the assembly together made the laws; but it was seldom that all three worked together smoothly. The governors were the servants of the home government and when they carried out their instructions, they clashed with the assembly members, who were determined to rule with as little interference from the British Government as possible.

The character of the eighteenth-century governors was another reason why relations between governors and assemblies were not cordial. We learn of governors, such as Hamilton in Jamaica in 1716, being removed at the petition of the colonists. Others had an even less peaceful end of office. In 1710, for instance, Governor Parke of the Leeward Islands so roused the people of Antigua that they attacked Government House and killed him; the British Government did not even try to bring his murderers to trial. Six years later, Parke's successor was sent to gaol in England for maladministration. The eighteenth-century governors had usually secured a lucrative post by the bribery which was common in the appointment to most government posts at the time. People of this type in the colonies were usually the least successful. The more influential could secure a profitable place in Europe, and there is little doubt that most governors were only biding their time until they could do better for themselves at home.

Other officers of the home government who came out here were equally provoking to the planting interest. Registrars, legal officers, customs men, were all appointed in England on the same basis of graft and favour. These officials, moreover, increasingly farmed out their duties to deputies and did not come to the West Indies to supervise their work. They demanded high returns for this patronage and the deputies could only pay out of fees raised in the West Indies, so that the financial drain on the colony was as large as they dared make it. Not only did this touch the colonists' pockets, but it also touched their pride. Public officials were not selected locally; they were sent from England and there was an absence of lucrative employment in public service for the white residents here. This was to become an increasing cause of resentment.

The holders of the highest offices sat in the councils, together with the richest planters, and generally they both supported the governors. For this reason the assemblies saw them as enemies to be attacked. So the powers of the council were gradually weakened until the office of councillor was large in dignity but small in power. The assemblies, which had already asserted themselves in the seventeenth century, thus became more and more the source of West Indian protest. As an institution they were hated and feared by governors, military leaders and civil servants, who had to live cheek by jowl with their vigilant and outspoken critics in the assemblies.

The constant argument with the mother country as to the rights of the assembly went on throughout the eighteenth century and indeed throughout more than half of the nineteenth century until most of the assemblies voted themselves out of existence. The fight for a permanent revenue bill in Jamaica was partly resolved in 1728. In that year both sides made a concession and gained a point in return. The British Government agreed to confirm all existing laws of the island. In return, the assembly agreed to make a permanent vote of £8,000 a year to the British Government. If this seems like a declaration of peace, it was hardly so. Only existing laws were acknowledged, all future laws were still scrutinised in England, so that there was no guarantee of their being confirmed. As often as they could, the assemblies avoided submitting their laws for scrutiny by the British Government. They delayed sending them or made laws valid only for short periods, renewing them if necessary. The practice of sending a law of short duration to England, long after it had been passed, meant that it had often expired before the British Government could use its powers of scrutiny. This effectively reduced their chance of disallowing colonial laws which were against imperial interests or contrary to English law.

When they could not get their own way, the assemblies adjourned and refused to do business, not even to vote the money already agreed on for the expenses of government. No amount of persuasion and cajoling from distracted governors could alter their resolve. In Jamaica this particular practice was applied to the maintenance of the military establishment. After the war which ended triumphantly for England in 1713, the Jamaicans were asked both to finance some new white immigration to the island and to support two regiments, as they had done during wartime. In a memorial to the British Government some of the assemblymen expressed a marked preference for one proposal rather than the other. 'As to their refusal to subsidise the soldiers there,' their memorial ran, 'Jamaica has been the only of H.M. colonies that supplied the Army with additional subsistence wherein above £150,000 hath been expended by the said island, during and since the late war; which provision whilst there was an immediate danger by the war was cheerfully raised by the Assembly of Jamaica by several Acts, but on the conclusion of peace a number of white people to settle in the island was in justice to themselves to be the further care of the Assembly.' Therefore, they concluded, they would rather not accept the charge of the regiments. The governor dismissed the assembly and, on another occasion, the assembly adjourned itself. The upshot was that the money was not voted. This particular issue was one that the assemblies would always argue about; the planters continued to maintain that the defence of colonies was the business of the mother country.

Despite the angry quarrels, the bitterness and the inefficiency, not to mention occasional violence, the system was highly regarded by the colonists. In 1763, when the new territories which had been the 'neutral islands' became British the British government hesitated to grant them the same form of government as the older colonies, until they realised that Englishmen would not go to the new colonies unless they were granted the same system of representation in assemblies as existed in the others. An interesting and famous case arose from this decision. Before the form of government was decided, the King ordered that the new colonies should pay the same 4½ per cent duty on goods exported as Barbados and the Leewards had agreed to. This order was renewed after he had given instructions for an assembly to be called. In Grenada one independent-minded planter, named Campbell, challenged this and took his case to court in England. Campbell claimed that the tax was illegal because it was imposed by the Crown after the King had granted law-making authority to the new assembly. 'We therefore thought,' claimed the contestant, 'that the King had immediately and irrevocably granted to all who were and should become inhabitants, or who had or should acquire property in the island of Grenada, that the subordinate legislation over the island should be exercised by an Assembly with the consent of the Governor in Council.' As a consequence, Campbell argued, laws for Grenada could no longer be made merely by royal order. Lord Mansfield, the Lord Chief Justice of England, gave his verdict for Campbell. The immediate result was that Grenada did not pay the 4½ per cent export duty; but a further consequence was that the colonies captured by the British in the Napoleonic Wars were not granted an elected assembly.

THE INTEREST AT HOME

Not all the protest was made in the West Indies. As the number of absentee proprietors increased, so did the West Indian lobby in England. They came to have a strong influence in the British House of Commons and they kept closely in touch with events in the West Indies through agents sent to England by the West Indian assemblies.

There were remarkable examples of how this lobby sometimes successfully influenced British Government policy. In the seventeen-thirties, the Barbadian planters and the Leeward Island legislatures appealed for restrictions on the trade which was developing between North America and the French and Dutch colonies in the West Indies. This was really an attempt to prevent the French from getting advantages in trade. The American colonists certainly did not favour heavy import duties on molasses proposed for them by the West Indian planters, and their argument against these duties was later to be a battle-cry. 'It is divesting them,' said the agent for New York, 'of their rights and privileges as the King's natural born subjects and Englishmen in levying subsidies upon them against their consent when they have no representatives in Parliament.' This protest, shortened into 'no taxation without representation', became the colonists' slogan against interference from the mother country.

On this occasion two sets of colonists were attacking each other's interests and it was a case of which could win the support of the British Parliament. This was easily done by the West Indian lobby. As the American Benjamin Franklin realised, 'the West Indies vastly outweigh us of the Northern colonies'. A heavy duty on all molasses imported into America was imposed by the Molasses Act of 1733 and was re-imposed, though at a reduced rate, by the Sugar Act of 1764. This was still one of the main grievances of the Americans when their resentment lit up into rebellion in 1776.

The peace treaty at the end of the Seven Years War was another occasion on which the West Indian lobby sought to protect their own interests. Guadeloupe and Martinique were returned to the French in exchange for the relatively undeveloped territory of Canada. This was a British move to stop the French from closing in the seaboard British North American colonies and it suited the West Indian interest because sugar from Guadeloupe and Martinique would no longer rival sugar from the British islands on the London market. On the other hand, the West Indian lobby did not object to the acquisition of the 'neutral islands' as strategic positions to hold in time of war because they had not yet become sugar producers.

The nabobs, who startled London with their extravagance, their large houses, their entertainment, their liveried servants and their equipages, were those who had made money in the tropical East and the tropical West. They entered into London society. In the eighteenth century it was a short step from aristocratic drawing-rooms and country houses to a seat in the House of Commons, if a man had the money to buy it. Writing to his son in 1767 Lord Chesterfield lamented that he had been unable to buy him a seat in Parliament for £2,500 because the borough-jobber to whom he had offered the money had laughed at him and said that 'there was no such thing as a borough to be had now for the rich East and West Indians had secured them all at the rate of £3,000 at least, but many at £4,000, and two or three that he knew at £5,000'. There were in the latter half of the eighteenth century always about thirty 'West Indians' in the House of Commons and some of them were very active members indeed.

THE AMERICAN REVOLUTION

All the British colonists across the Atlantic shared the same objections to the attitude of the British Government. The thirteen

American colonies had similar representative assemblies to the West Indian islands and they could all object to the interference with their freedom to make laws and to taxation without representation, whether it was in their favour or not. The Stamp Act of 1765, which brought in a tax on newspapers and legal documents, annoyed many West Indians as much as it did the Americans; there were riots here too. Both groups of colonists objected to paying for their own defence, and defence seemed less urgent since the defeat of the French in the Seven Years War. This was more easily felt in North America, however, as the French settlements, which had hemmed in the British colonists along the eastern seaboard, were no longer there. Americans could now think themselves capable of their own defence; but the small white populations of the West Indian islands could not hope to challenge the might of a European army, unless they enlisted the slaves on their side, and this was as yet unthinkable. So, whereas in the north resentment turned to riots, raids and finally war against Britain, West Indian resentment hardly went beyond grumbling and deadlocks in the assemblies.

The Jamaican Assembly indeed championed the rights of the American colonists to the extent of addressing a memorial to King George III, *Relative to the present State of American Affairs*. In this the King was assured that Jamaicans had no intention of resisting the British Government, but they claimed that no section of His Majesty's subjects could legislate for another section, and no law was binding without the assent of the representatives of the people to whom it applied. Laws, furthermore, should not be injurious to those concerned. It was then declared that any colonial people who did not receive equal rights with Englishmen were thereby released from any dependence on the mother country. The King was therefore recommended to reconcile the differences between his British and his American subjects. This form of reasoning was notoriously misunderstood by the British authorities, and by 1775 the reconciliation point was past. The colonists in North America had resorted to armed resistance and in the following year declared their independence.

The West Indians suffered inevitably in the ensuing War of American Independence. In 1778, the old enemy, France and a year later Spain, joined the fighting as an occasion for another attack on Britain. It was certainly an opportunity to seize the small islands, lost in the previous war, and there were captures and recaptures for a period of four years. Even more distressing for those living in the

British islands was the stoppage of imports from America. The grave shortage of American flour and salt fish at some periods of the war led to a real danger of starvation amongst the slaves, and prices were prohibitive when shipments did get through. Attempts were made to find substitute foods, and the ackee and the mango were first brought to the West Indies during this war.

The British navy was not able both to support the war effort on the mainland and tackle the French and Spanish fleets in the Caribbean. Dominica, St. Vincent and Grenada were all recaptured, and St. Kitts taken, by the French. Jamaica, now the wealthiest of the British West Indian islands, was next threatened.

It was this threat against Jamaica which led to the biggest eighteenth-century naval battle in West Indian waters. During the war the British had made only one capture, St. Lucia. This, however, had great strategic value, as it was possible from there to supervise the activities of the French fleet in Fort Royal in the neighbouring island of Martinique. When, in February 1782, the French fleet left harbour for a rendezvous with the Spanish fleet in readiness for a joint attack on Jamaica, the commander of the British squadron, Admiral Rodney, was in a position to catch them and defeat them at the Saints, a small group of rocky islands near Dominica. Jamaica was saved from invasion, and five French ships were captured, including the flagship with the French Admiral de Grasse aboard; some escaped, however, to fight for the American colonists. This naval victory gave Britain sufficient advantage by the end of the war to recover Grenada, St. Vincent, St. Kitts, Montserrat, Nevis and Dominica at the peace treaty in 1783.

The British West Indies, however, had suffered badly from the war and were to suffer more from its outcome. A new independent nation stood in the place of the thirteen separate colonies on the North American mainland; it now became for the British a foreign country unable to trade directly with their colonies. This will be more fully discussed later, but it can already be seen how this would continue to threaten the vital estate supplies which had been missed by the British plantations during the war.

FRENCH PLANTOCRACY

The largest French colony, St. Domingue, had been relatively untroubled by the war. The planters of St. Domingue soon produced cheaper sugar than the British, and France became a more formidable

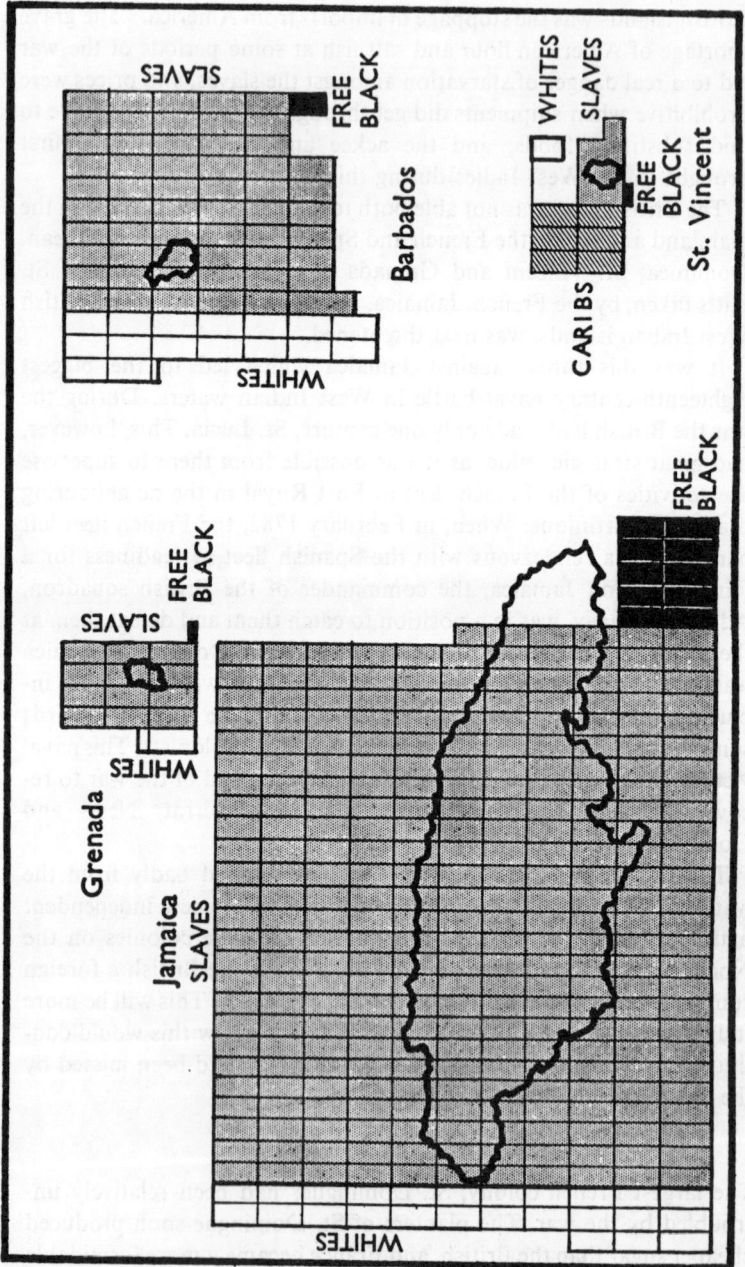

Fig. 7 (a). Population of the English Islands in the West Indies in the middle of the Eighteenth Century. 1 unit = 1,000 people
N.B. 'Free Black' means Free Black and Coloured people

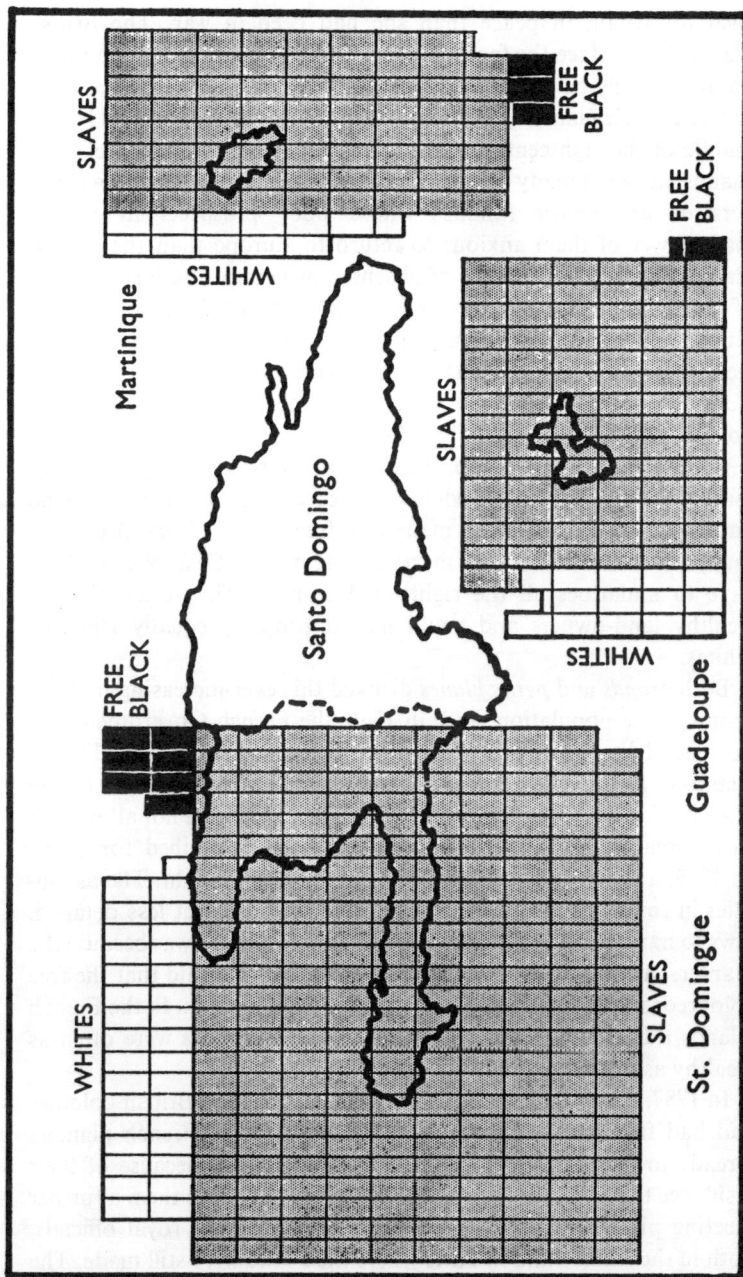

Fig. 7 (b). Population of the French Islands in the West Indies in the Middle of the Eighteenth Century. 1 unit = 1,000 people
N.B. 'Free Black' means Free Black and coloured people

rival to Britain in peace than she had been in war. The British planter had to face the fact that West Indian sugar production might not indefinitely be an easy road to wealth.

The French planters, like the British, were well established by the middle of the eighteenth century. The increasing prosperity of their islands attracted ready colonists and many of them were young members of aristocratic families whose poor prospects in France made fewer of them anxious to return to Europe than the British planters were. The number of absentee owners of the large colony of St. Domingue was comparable with that of Jamaica, but in Guadeloupe and Martinique most planters were resident. These were the *grands blancs* and they were sharply divided from the *petits blancs* or poor whites, who were, as in the British islands, smallholders, shopkeepers or simply idlers.

In the French islands, too, there was an ever-increasing number of mulattoes, the offspring of white and Negro parents. The master who had a son by a slave often made him free. *Petits blancs* also made many slave women free by marrying them. The *Code Noir* of 1685 gave to mulattoes all the rights of free men. They often became wealthy land-owners and could inherit property equally with the whites.

Both *grands* and *petits blancs* disliked this ever-increasing mulatto group in the population, and, in 1766, the French Government was persuaded by the advice of planters in the councils of the French islands to restrict the rights of coloured people. They could no longer have legal posts or be officers in the militia. They were not allowed to carry firearms and even their garments were prescribed for them. In 1779, a curfew was imposed to keep them in at night. The assemblies in some of the British islands passed similar, but less detailed, laws to harry their free coloured populations. All this was because the planters, already uneasy about their slaves, were afraid that the free coloureds might in an emergency join forces with them. In the French islands there was jealousy too because the mulattoes were often as wealthy as the white planters.

In 1787, the French islands were granted what the British colonies had had from the start, an elected assembly. The French planters already in fact had great influence in their islands because of their residence there. The coming of the assembly only gave them a further meeting place for making their views known to the royal officials, both in the islands and in Paris where their laws were still made. The

French West Indian assemblies were not themselves law-making bodies, but the laws of the French Government for their colonies had now to be approved by the assemblies before they could come into operation in the West Indies. The French planters had now become as much of a plantocracy as those of the British islands. Both were now demanding rights from their home countries. They had the same crops, similar trade restrictions and all were slave societies. Both French and British planters, therefore, in the last quarter of the eighteenth century were demanding their own freedom from European control on the one hand, while, on the other, their prosperity depended on the restrictions of freedom to others. It was an explosive situation.

REVOLTS IN THE FRENCH ISLANDS

The explosion came in the French islands and was fired by the much larger explosion in France itself. The outbreak of the French Revolution in 1789, with its watchwords of fraternity, liberty and equality, seemed an opportunity for different French colonial groups to seek remedies for old grievances. The French planters demanded, and won, some representation in the National Assembly in Paris. In 1791 the free coloured in St. Domingue demanded the right to vote.

The decree of the National Assembly in May 1791 which gave them that right was just what the whites most feared. They stoutly resisted, but the mulattoes had armed themselves and were prepared to fight for their new-won rights. Their leader, Ogé, was captured and cruelly put to death on the wheel, which served to inflame the mulattoes even more. They had shown their hand; they could expect no mercy if they withdrew now.

Both whites and mulattoes, however, were taken by surprise in August when they found that a slave rebellion had broken out in the northern plain of the island. The constant fear of all planters had become a reality. Slaves were murdering whites and systematically setting fire to cane-fields and houses. In different parts of the island, different groups fought each other with the utmost cruelty and violence. It was estimated that in two months two thousand whites were killed, and ten thousand Negroes were killed, died of starvation on ruined estates or were executed.

The revolt continued in the north for two years, and troops sent out by the French Revolutionary Government added to the bloodshed, without suppressing the rebellion. The slaves were organised under two leaders from British islands, Boukman from Jamaica and Christophe, who may have been either from St. Kitts or Grenada. They made every use of differences between whites and mulattoes and the incompetence of French troops, unfamiliar with the territory, to spread the area of violence.

In the other French islands where there was a longer-standing resident planter class, there was less trouble. The planters of Guadeloupe and Martinique, however, were not well disposed towards the new revolutionary Jacobin Government in France although they also sent representatives to the new assembly in Paris in the early days of the revolution. In 1792 the Jacobins sent commissioners to both islands to rally support for the revolutionary government from those most discontented with their lot, the *petits blancs* and the free coloured. The governors, who had been appointed by the King, were forced to submit. When the British and Spanish declared war in 1792, the planters were readier to support the British in the Caribbean than their own government. This enabled the British in 1794 to take Guadeloupe, Martinique and St. Lucia, with the support of the planters themselves who in return enjoyed access to the British markets for their sugar and appreciated the short prosperity that followed.

This was not to last for long. A new Jacobin commissioner, Victor Hugues, soon appeared in the Caribbean with a fleet. He was prepared to use the most formidable weapon of all by encouraging slave risings. St. Lucia and Guadeloupe were quickly recaptured after Hugues declared immediate emancipation of the slaves and encouraged them to rise against both the British and the French planters. He also sent agents into Jamaica and St. Vincent to incite the Maroons of the former and the Caribs of the latter to attack their British masters. In 1795, there were risings of both groups, which kept the British soldiers occupied in those islands.

In Grenada, the circumstances were different. The French planters were ready to turn against the British, because they had suffered from religious and social discrimination under British government for a long period. Here a coloured planter, Julien Fédon, led the revolt assisted by all the French planters and their slaves. There was nearly a year of internal warfare before the British suppressed this rising. Again their forces were occupied in one of their own islands, as Victor Hugues had planned that they should be.

In 1792 both the British and the Spanish had sent expeditions to St. Domingue, ostensibly to rescue the white population from their rebellious slaves. In fact it was part of the general attack on France; the British had every intention of taking at least part of St. Domingue for themselves. The expedition which set out from Jamaica was disastrous. It was never reinforced, as the Maroon War effectively alarmed the Jamaican Government and occupied the garrison there. More devastating were the old enemies of yellow fever and dysentery. Between 1794 and 1798, nearly one hundred thousand British soldiers and sailors were lost in the West Indies, the greater part in St. Domingue.

The final expulsion of the British was effected by the most remarkable Negro leader of the rebellion. Toussaint L'Ouverture was a slave from a plantation on the northern plain who had seized his opportunity in the disorders there to attach himself, first to the Spanish army as a mercenary, and then to the French. In 1795, the Spanish made a separate peace with France, ceding their part of the island, Santo Domingo, to them. Toussaint now organised a Negro army against the other invaders, and by 1798 had expelled the British.

The revolt in St. Domingue was different from the risings in the smaller islands because it was not incited by any French Jacobin leader. St. Domingue produced its own leaders, both free mulattoes and Negro slaves, who understood for themselves how the revolutionary slogan, 'Liberty, Fraternity, Equality' might be applied to their society. For this reason, the Negro leaders have been called the Black Jacobins. Toussaint himself was a domestic slave who could read and who no doubt overheard many conversations about the ideas of the French Revolution as the free white organisers of his estate indignantly discussed them. For himself he conceived the idea that slaves too could be free, and that all freemen, of whatever colour, should participate in the government of their own country. But peace had first to be restored and not all Negro leaders were as clear about their motives as Toussaint. They were flushed by their success against both their old masters and other European invaders and they were anxious, after years of oppression, to enjoy power and, later, independence.

By 1800, Toussaint had restored an uneasy peace to St. Domingue, but not without cruelly murdering and mutilating ten thousand mulattoes. He was now effective ruler of the island and managed to get the ex-slaves back to work on the devastated estates. In 1801, he sent a constitution to France declaring the island's allegiance, but its independence in law. He proclaimed himself ruler for life. In France, in the meantime, another dictator had emerged in Napoleon Buona-parte, who would not tolerate this degree of independence in a colony. He sent a large French force to St. Domingue under General Le Clerc, who was eventually joined by some of the Negro leaders now jealous of Toussaint. Toussaint was taken by trickery and sent to France, where he died in prison. Le Clerc himself was to be defeated by the great killer of all European troops. He died of yellow fever, and his army dwindled, a prey to the same disease. The remnant sur-rendered to the British in Jamaica in 1803. The island was now free of French authority.

The African-born slave, Dessalines, emerged from the years of brutality and bloodshed to proclaim himself, in 1804, Emperor of the newly named Haiti, having conducted a final extermination of whites to secure his position. His successors three years later were, sig-nificantly, Christophe, an illiterate Negro ex-slave, who ruled the north, and Pétion, an educated mulatto, who ruled the south. Not until Christophe's death in 1820 was Haiti finally under one ruler and established as the first independent republic to emerge from the whole system of European colonies in the West Indies.

The Haitian Revolution was an achievement of violence and action. The revolution in other West Indian territories was to be less startling, but there also the pre-eminence of the planter was challenged and the status of the slave questioned. In the case of the British islands, the argument was largely conducted outside the West Indies.

FURTHER READING

Sources of West Indian History, Government and Politics, pp. 94–101, Economic Life, pp. 57–9.

P. C. Somervell, *A History of the United States*, Chapter II, The American Revolution, 1763–1783.

Carter, Digby, Murray, *History of the West Indian Peoples*, Book IV, Chapter 8, The Negro Revolution.

Hoyos, *Our Common Heritage*, Sir John Gay Alleyne.

Ottley, *Spanish Trinidad*, Chapters XX–XXI.

Jesse, *Outlines of St. Lucia's History*, Chapter IV.

QUESTIONS TO CONSIDER

1. How did the Assembly in the British islands achieve its full powers in the eighteenth century?

2. How did the issues defended by the West India interest in London help the British West Indian planters?

3. Do you agree that the American Revolution favoured the French more than the British?

4. How far do you think that the Haitian Revolution was part of the French Revolution?

CHAPTER ELEVEN

Reckoning and Decline

WHOSE MARKET?

The successful British West India sugar planter of the mid-eighteenth century was marked by his great wealth and the display with which he spent it. In 1771 a very popular play, *The West Indian*, was produced in London. The opening scene was a bustle of preparation for a planter's return to England. A servant philosophised, 'He's very rich, and that's sufficient. They say he has rum and sugar enough belonging to him, to make all the water in the Thames into punch.' By the [eighteen-twenties, the situation was recognisably different. 'There is an end of any use of colonial property in the way of sale or security', the Secretary of State was informed by the Society of Merchants. What were the reasons for this dramatic decline in sugar prosperity for English planters?

The first reason has been hinted at more than once already. It was simply that, by the second half of the eighteenth century, the French planters made sugar more cheaply than the British. This meant that, in the areas where they were competing for trade, the French obviously got it. By the late seventeen-eighties, the French in fact were in almost complete control of the European market, except of course in Great Britain. Furthermore, they continued to gain considerable trade with the American mainland once the thirteen colonies had won their independence from England.

What made the French sugar cheaper? In 1790, Mr. Long, an absentee Jamaica planter, was asked this question by the British Government. In his reply he discussed the advantages of St. Domingue which produced about three-quarters of the French sugar. In St. Domingue, he said, there were more resident planters and white inhabitants than in any of the British islands, and cheaper ship fares from France encouraged Frenchmen to emigrate to their colonies. Secondly, the French planters traded freely and directly with the Spaniards in Santo Domingo, the eastern part of the same island, and also with the Americans, receiving from them cheap and abundant lumber, flour and salt fish for estate supplies. Thirdly, he said, the French colonists produced a greater variety of export crops and this meant that, when the colonial taxes were levied, the burden did not fall only on the sugar planters. Fourthly, and most important, he claimed, was the far greater fertility of the St. Domingue soil. Thus, he concluded, 'the French planter, from this simple circumstance, if there were no other in his favour, must be well enabled to undersell the Jamaica planter at every market in Europe; nor is it in the power of the British planter by any possible exertion, to enter into competition with him. On the contrary, he is obliged to employ about five times the quantity of land and labour, and incur proportionately heavier expenses of every denomination, in order to obtain from FIVE AND A QUARTER ACRES the same quantity of sugar only which the Frenchman gathers from a single acre.'

This seemed to be a fairly conclusive answer, except that it had one major omission. The great advantage not noted by Mr Long was the simple fact that, by West Indian standards, St. Domingue is a very large island. This meant that the French planters had not only more fertile land, but also a far greater area of it.

NEW COLONIES AND EXPORTS

The re-export of sugar from Britain to Europe declined at the same period as the volume coming from the British West Indies increased with the added produce of Grenada and St. Vincent, Tobago and Dominica, the 'neutral islands' assigned to England by the settlement of 1763. The later acquisition of Trinidad, St. Lucia, Demerara and Berbice in the Napoleonic Wars added still further to the quantity of British West Indian sugar exported to Britain. The quantity produced, amounting to a glut on the British market in some years, eventually brought the prices down dramatically.

The increase in British sugar exports expected from the acquisition of new colonies was not immediately felt, as in fact only Grenada had sugar estates in 1763. But in all islands the cultivation of land was encouraged. It was decided that, where French inhabitants had settled, they were to remain in possession of their estates provided that none of them continued to hold more than five hundred acres, that they gave allegiance and paid rents to the Crown, since the land had been acquired by conquest, and provided that they lived on their estates for at least half of every year. Lands that had belonged to the Church under French rule were confiscated. After convenient sites

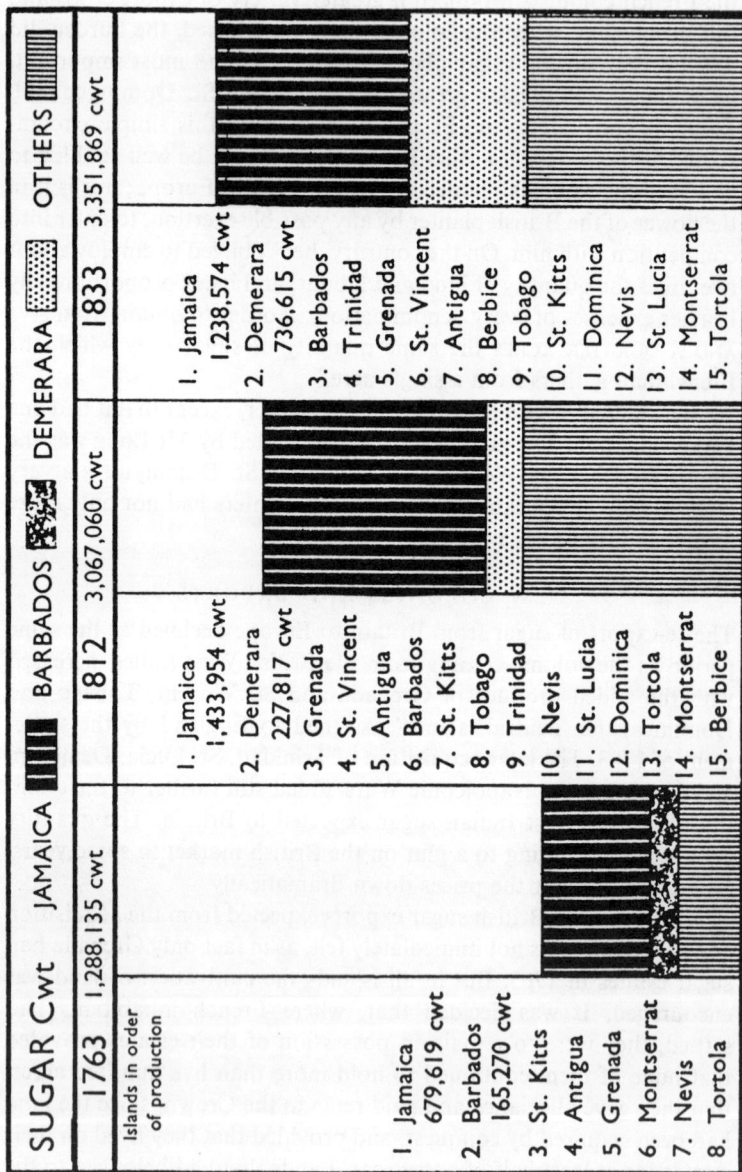

SUGAR Cwt ▦ JAMAICA ▨ BARBADOS ▒ DEMERARA ▥ OTHERS

1763 — 1,288,135 cwt

Islands in order of production

1. Jamaica 679,619 cwt
2. Barbados 165,270 cwt
3. St. Kitts
4. Antigua
5. Grenada
6. Montserrat
7. Nevis
8. Tortola

1812 — 3,067,060 cwt

1. Jamaica 1,433,954 cwt
2. Demerara 227,817 cwt
3. Grenada
4. St. Vincent
5. Antigua
6. Barbados
7. St. Kitts
8. Tobago
9. Trinidad
10. Nevis
11. St. Lucia
12. Dominica
13. Tortola
14. Montserrat
15. Berbice

1833 — 3,351,869 cwt

1. Jamaica 1,238,574 cwt
2. Demerara 736,615 cwt
3. Barbados
4. Trinidad
5. Grenada
6. St. Vincent
7. Antigua
8. Berbice
9. Tobago
10. St. Kitts
11. Dominica
12. Nevis
13. St. Lucia
14. Montserrat
15. Tortola

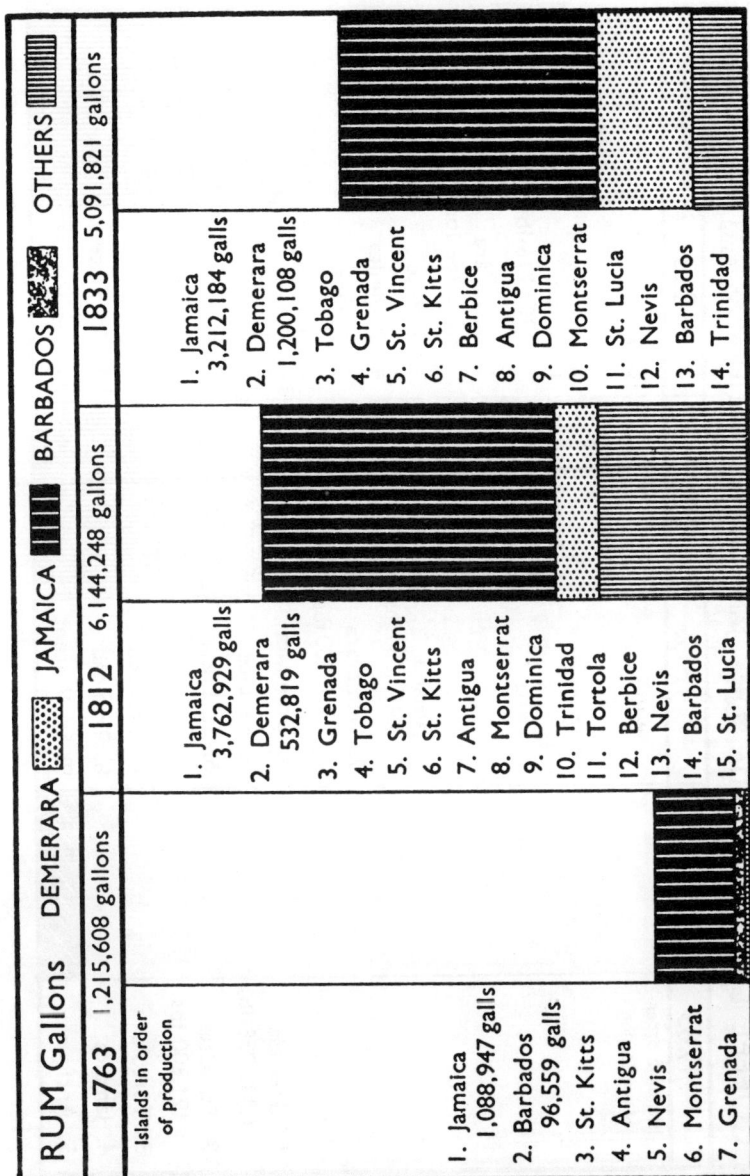

Fig. 8. Exports of Plantation Produce from the British West Indies in 1763, 1812 and 1833

RUM Gallons — DEMERARA · JAMAICA · BARBADOS · OTHERS

1763	1812	1833
1,215,608 gallons	6,144,248 gallons	5,091,821 gallons

Islands in order of production

1763
1. Jamaica 1,088,947 galls
2. Barbados 96,559 galls
3. St. Kitts
4. Antigua
5. Nevis
6. Montserrat
7. Grenada

1812
1. Jamaica 3,762,929 galls
2. Demerara 532,819 galls
3. Grenada
4. Tobago
5. St. Vincent
6. St. Kitts
7. Antigua
8. Montserrat
9. Dominica
10. Trinidad
11. Tortola
12. Berbice
13. Nevis
14. Barbados
15. St. Lucia

1833
1. Jamaica 3,212,184 galls
2. Demerara 1,200,108 galls
3. Tobago
4. Grenada
5. St. Vincent
6. St. Kitts
7. Berbice
8. Antigua
9. Dominica
10. Montserrat
11. St. Lucia
12. Nevis
13. Barbados
14. Trinidad

COFFEE Lbs   GRENADA   JAMAICA   DEMERARA   OTHERS

1763 1,621,198 lbs	**1812** 27,690,500 lbs	**1833** 28,517,813 lbs	

Islands in order of production

1763
1. Grenada 1,338,998 lbs
2. St. Kitts 121,300 lbs
3. Tortola
4. Jamaica
5. Antigua

1812
1. Jamaica 14,467,600 lbs
2. Demerara 7,710,500 lbs
3. Dominica
4. Berbice
5. St. Lucia
6. Barbados
7. Grenada
8. Trinidad
9. St. Vincent

1833
1. Jamaica 11,302,716 lbs
2. Demerara 4,260,766 lbs
3. Berbice
4. Dominica
5. Trinidad
6. St. Lucia
7. Barbados
8. Grenada
9. Antigua
10. St. Kitts
11. St. Vincent
12. Nevis

CACAO Lbs	TRINIDAD	JAMAICA	GRENADA	OTHERS

1763	1812	1833
242,842 lbs	456,720 lbs	2,120,527 lbs

Islands in order of production

1763

1. Grenada 196,300 lbs
2. Jamaica 33,100 lbs
3. Montserrat
4. Tortola
5. Antigua
6. St. Kitts
7. Barbados

1812

1. Trinidad 204,400 lbs
2. Grenada 87,200 lbs
3. St. Vincent
4. St. Lucia
5. Berbice
6. Jamaica
7. Dominica
8. Antigua

1833

1. Trinidad 1,755,144 lbs
2. Grenada 312,446 lbs
3. St. Lucia
4. Dominica
5. Barbados
6. St. Vincent
7. Jamaica
8. Demerara
9. Berbice

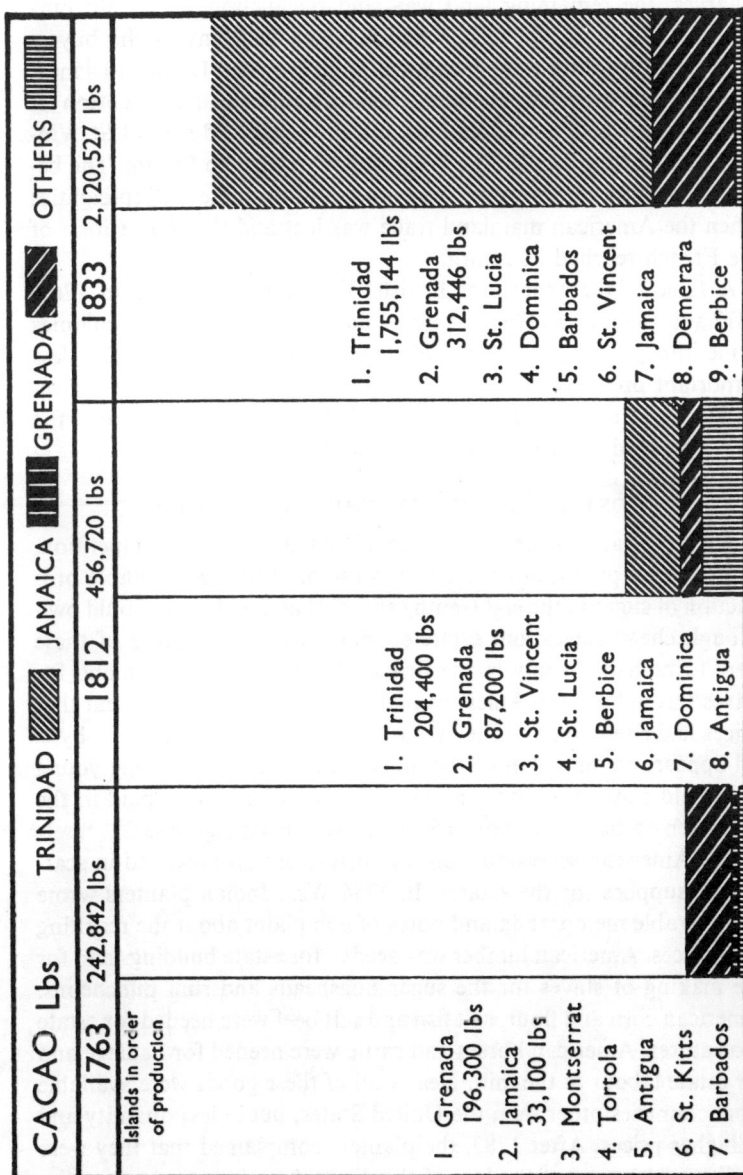

Fig. 8 (continued). Exports of Plantation Produce from the British West Indies in 1763, 1812 and 1833

123

had been set aside for public purposes and for urban areas and wharves, the remaining land was sold by auction to private purchasers to a limit of five hundred acres each. Many of the buyers were from the older-established and more crowded Leeward Islands, as had been expected. In time, therefore, the sugar and cotton of Grenada, the coffee of Dominica and the sugar and rum of St. Vincent and Tobago swelled the West Indian exports to Britain. The beginning of disaster, however, was not felt until the seventeen-eighties when the American mainland trade was lost and the competition of the French reached its zenith.

A table of the exports of British West Indian produce in 1763, 1812 and 1833 shows the increased volume of exports as new colonies came into production. After 1763, the Leeward Islands became less important producers than they had been and, by 1812, only the relatively large island of Jamaica was able to exceed the produce of the new mainland territories of Demerara and Berbice.

COST OF LIVING IN THE WEST INDIES

There were hazards for the planter other than those of competition, markets and prices, however. It was essential to the profitable production of sugar in the eighteenth century that the planter should own enough cheap slaves and estate supplies. By 1783, neither of these were to be had cheaply in the British West Indies. The demand for slaves throughout the Americas had increased to such an extent that prices had risen greatly. They varied according to the age, sex, physical appearance and skill of the individual slave, but a strong young male field slave, for whom about £35 would have been paid in the seventeen-forties, cost about £50 in the seventeen-eighties.

The American secession from the British Empire resulted in scarcity of supplies for the estates. In 1784 West Indian planters wrote innumerable memoranda and notes of complaint about the resulting high prices. American lumber was needed for estate buildings and for the making of staves for the sugar hogsheads and rum puncheons. American corn and flour, salt fish and salt beef were needed for estate food stores. American horses and cattle were needed for haulage and for estate labour at the mill. Nearly all of these goods were available from countries other than the United States, but in less quantity and at higher prices. After 1783, the planters complained that they were in distress because of the loss of the direct American trade. Supplies previously purchased from the Americans, they said, were now either unobtainable, or obtainable only at 'ruinous' prices. They objected to the rule that American produce must now reach them in British ships via an English port because of 'the heavy expense, uncertainty, and delay of such circuitous navigation'.

The prices for essential estate supplies just before and just after the American Revolution tell their own story:

Commodity	Pre-war prices	Post-war prices
BARBADOS		
LUMBER, per 1,000 ft. . . .	£4	£8
HORSES, each	£20	£30
HORNED CATTLE, each . . .	£5–£7 10s.	£10
RICE, per cwt. . . .	12s. 6d.	£1 10s.
INDIAN CORN, per bushel . .	2s. 6d.	3s. 9d.
BEEF, per barrel	£2 10s.	£3
LEEWARD ISLANDS		
OAK STAVES, per thousand . .	£5–£10	£12–£15
HORSES, each.	£16 10s.–£35	£30–£70
CATTLE, each	£16 10s.–£19 16s.	£20–£40
RICE, per cwt. . . .	18s.–24s.	38s.–41s. 3d.
INDIAN CORN, per bushel . .	4s.–8s.	8s. 3d.–10s.
BEEF, per barrel	£2 10s.–£4	£4–£6 12s.
JAMAICA		
OAK STAVES, per thousand . .	£6–£18	£10–£20
RICE, per cwt. . . .	13s. 9d.–£1	£2 2s.–£3 10s.
INDIAN CORN, per bushel . .	2s. 6d.–6s. 3d.	7s. 6d.
COMMON FLOUR, per cwt. . .	15s.–£1	£1–£2 10s.

Not all the West Indian sugar planters were equally affected. In Jamaica, for example, where there was more land space for food cultivation, more standing timber to be cut and a large number of 'pens' where cattle were reared, the effects were less harsh than in the smaller islands such as Antigua or Barbados. But Jamaica also had a much larger population and, as the price increases of essential supplies show, there was still reason for alarm.

The body of absentee West Indian planters and merchants involved in the West Indian trade in Britain tried to take direct action to remedy the problem. One idea was the importation of the breadfruit tree 'by any Commander of an East India ship, or other person', who should be rewarded with £100. In 1794 the thanks of the planters and merchants were recorded to 'Captain Bligh for his great care and attention to the great object of bringing the Breadfruit tree and many other useful plants to the West Indian Islands'. Bligh's importation of the breadfruit, which is a prolific bearer and requires no cultivation, provided cheap food for the slave population. This part of his career should be at least as well known as the mutiny on his ship, *The Bounty*.

AN ESTATE'S ACCOUNTS

One of the important things to remember in talking about the accounts of estates in the eighteenth and nineteenth centuries is that the flow of actual money across the Atlantic was extremely small. Planters, if they were careful, kept their own detailed accounts in their estate books, and the merchants in Britain, to whom they consigned most of the sugar they produced, kept strict accounts of all business they carried out on behalf of various planters. Let us take an imaginary estate to see just how the system worked.

Suppose Mr. Planter owned an estate which produced on an average about 300 hogsheads of sugar per year. Obviously he would have many expenses to meet before a crop of sugar was sold. There would be the costs of maintaining his slaves and his factory and buildings; there would be the cost of various supplies for the estate; there would be taxes and other local dues to be paid, and, of course, he would want to buy food and clothing and as many luxuries as possible for himself and his family. If he did not have enough money for his expenses before the crop was taken, he could obtain them on credit. Most of his supplies had to be paid for in England, some in America, and a few, such as free estate staff, taxes and other duties, were paid for here. The things he needed from Britain were obtained through the British merchant house with which he dealt, and the merchant would supply Mr. Planter on credit and eventually reimburse himself when he sold Mr. Planter's sugar. The things obtained from the American mainland were acquired through local merchants trading with American sea captains, who were usually willing to receive in exchange produce of the estate, especially rum and molasses.

In years when the sugar prices were high, the planter usually made enough money from the sale of his sugar crop to pay all these debts. The money itself did not necessarily come into his hands. The merchants in Britain would receive the sugar, sell it and then send an account to the planter something like this:

Receipts from the sale of 300 hogsheads of sugar . . .	£6,000
Expenses of shipping, insurance, warehousing, import duties and commissions to the merchant himself and others who handled the sugar	£2,000
CREDIT BALANCE	£4,000

Against this balance would be listed all the other expenses incurred by the merchant for the planter who might during the preceding months have ordered items of estate equipment or personal items such as a dress for his wife or a crate of wines. As far as payments to local merchants and local governments were concerned, these were usually met either by giving them the required quantities of produce, or by giving them credit notes on the planter's merchants in Great Britain, or by a straight payment of money; but the use of money was limited because coin was scarce.

The merchants in Britain, therefore, acted not only as the agent who sold the planter's sugar, but also in a way as his accountant and his banker and his buying agent. It was consequently all too easy when a planter suffered a series of poor crops, or when the price of sugar remained low for a number of years, for the planter to become heavily indebted to the merchant. These debts dogged the planters during the second half of the eighteenth century and throughout the nineteenth. Indeed, by 1850, merchants in Britain were extremely reluctant to allow any kind of credit to any but a few exceptional planters.

But most planters, and especially those in the 'older' colonies, were burdened with expenses which had really nothing to do either with the cultivation of their estates, or the manufacture of sugar, or the upkeep of themselves and their households. Before the seventeen-eighties, when sugar planting had been at its most profitable, many planters, expecting that it would always remain a highly profitable business, made binding arrangements by which they assigned to friends, relatives or charities, fixed annual sums of money to be paid out of the profits of their estates. As long as the profits remained high these annual charges could be met, but when profits declined, it became increasingly difficult for the planters to continue these payments. Also, many planters had from time to time borrowed large sums of money to enlarge or improve their estates or, as in the case of many Windward Island planters, to restore their estates after they had been damaged in warfare. These loans all had to be paid back with interest.

Now, when prices fell, the planter might be able to reduce some of his costs of making sugar. He could for example be more careful with his equipment and livestock. He could allow cane-fields to bear another crop of ratoons instead of re-planting them, and he might even try to introduce labour-saving methods and devices. But one thing that he could not do was to reduce his fixed annual commitments in the repayment of debts with their accumulated interest, or the promised annuities to relatives and charities.

Mr. Planter therefore at the end of each year might have been faced with the following list of expenses: (*a*) cost of production of sugar, rum and molasses; (*b*) cost of shipping and selling sugar, rum and molasses; (*c*) amounts due to merchants in Britain for equipment and supplies provided on credit; (*d*) amounts due to local merchants and local governments for taxes and goods and services obtained locally, or from America through local merchants; (*e*) payments of fixed sums due to relatives who had been given annuities in years past; (*f*) repayment of instalments and interest on any loans that he might have raised.

In difficult years he would have not only to face the problem of meeting his expenses, but also the fact that he had standing obligations and, if they were not met promptly, they would involve him in lawsuits. It is easy to see that a succession of poor crops or a consistent fall in the prices offered for sugar would bring about the ruin of any estate which was either overburdened with annuities or debts or which was badly managed. This was the plight of many West Indian properties during the late eighteenth and nineteenth centuries.

PRICES

In 1830, the British West India merchants declared without much exaggeration 'that many estates have not paid the expenses of their cultivation for the past year, without charging interest on the capital, or even interest on the debts with which the estate may be encumbered, or anything for the support of the families dependent upon them; and that a debt has actually been incurred by the proprietors, in consequence of the expenses exceeding the sale of the crop'. Even the more fortunate estates which had covered their expenses for the year had 'yielded so little net income, that, upon the whole, great distress has fallen upon the families of proprietors, and upon all connected with or dependent on the West Indian colonies'.

Prices would obviously make the difference between survival and ruin in these circumstances. A diagram of prices in every tenth year between 1730 and 1840 shows that prices tended on the whole to rise until some time between 1810 and 1820, but then a decline set in and they did not go up again until 1840. By 1831, according to the planters of the day, an average estate employing 242 slaves and produc-

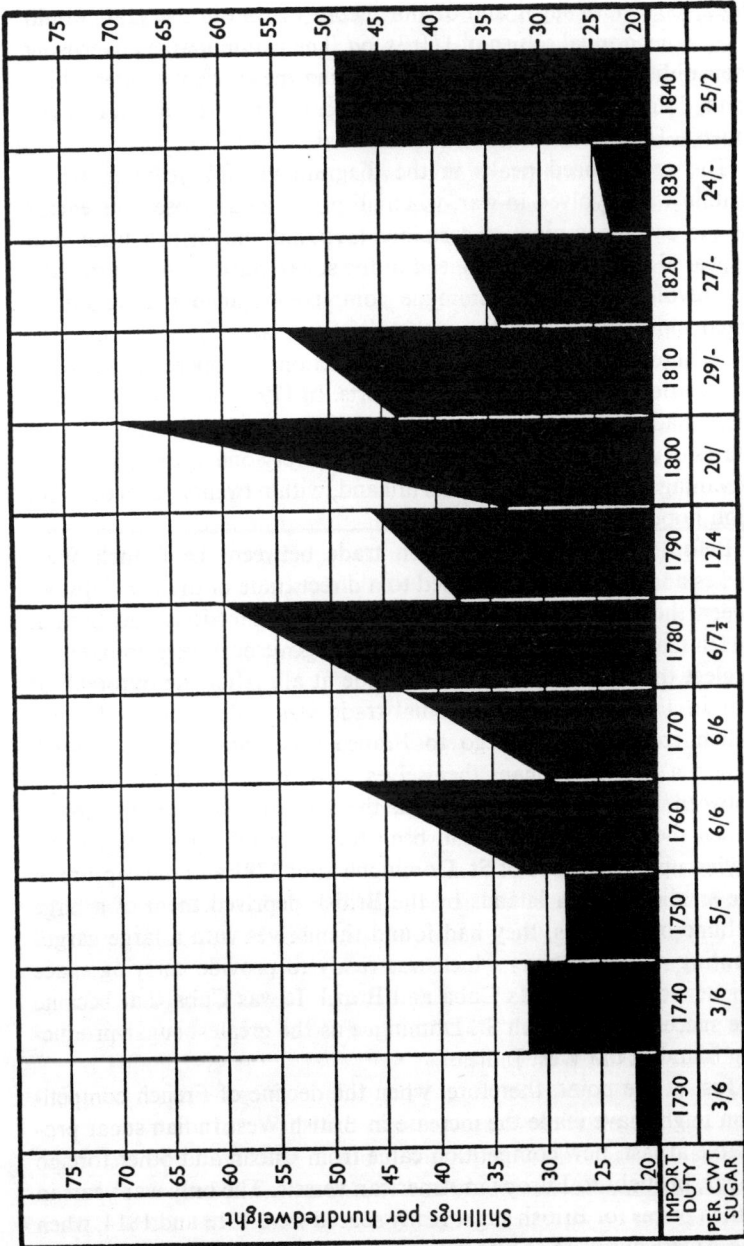

IMPORT DUTY	1730	1740	1750	1760	1770	1780	1790	1800	1810	1820	1830	1840
PER CWT SUGAR	3/6	3/6	5/-	6/6	6/6	6/7½	12/4	20/	29/-	27/-	24/-	25/2

Shillings per hundredweight

Fig. 9. Sugar Prices in London 1730–1840

ing 2,400 cwt. of sugar and 67 puncheons of rum in the year, would show a net annual return of £60 3s. 6d. The planters were advertising their difficulties, so they were not quoting the efficient estates which were doing better than this, but generally the reward was poor indeed. They had reason to be perturbed.

The pronounced peaks in the diagram are for years in which Britain was involved in war, when all prices tend to rise. The events of the seventeen-nineties certainly favoured the British trade and appeared to end the French lead in the sugar market. In that decade, the revolution in St. Domingue completely ruined that country's sugar industry. In 1793 the outbreak of war with France brought to the planters fears of invasion and destruction of property, but also the expectation of higher prices for exports. In 1794, the British Government had announced that a limited direct trade with the United States of America could be resumed. But every one of these apparent advantages carried a sting in its tail and, within twenty years of 1790, high hope had turned to despair.

Before the French Revolution trade between the French West Indies and Europe was confined to a direct trade in French ships between the islands and France. But when insurrections had broken out in many of the French colonies, their governors were prepared to neglect this rule just to maintain trade at all. After the outbreak of war in 1793, the French colonial trade was wide open, and sugar which could no longer go to France was transported to North America. The Americans themselves took over the triangular trade between the French West Indies, the United States and Europe, which the French marine had been forced to relinquish. When the drying up of the trade of St. Domingue after 1791 and the capture of the smaller French Islands by the British deprived them of a large volume of business, they had found themselves with a large cargo-hunting merchant navy which was ready to provide carrying space for new clients, such as Cuba and Brazil. It was Cuba that became the successor to French St. Domingue as the greatest sugar-producing island in the West Indies.

Just at the point, therefore, when the decline of French competition might have made the increase in British West Indian sugar profitable at last, new competition came from Cuban and other foreign sugar, brought to Europe in American vessels. The only war years in which prices for British sugar really soared were 1813 and 1814, when the Americans were at war with the British and their marine was engaged in fighting rather than trade. The flow of foreign sugar to Europe was temporarily reduced, and British sugar was sold extensively on the continent for the first time for many years. The London price soared to nearly 95s. per cwt., exclusive of duty, in comparison with the 40s. per cwt. average for the other war years.

After 1814, as the long war against France was ending, the collapse was sudden. The American marine became once more fully occupied in peacetime traffic; the French and other continental shippers resumed operations; foreign sugar again flowed freely into European ports; the glut of British sugar returned and was further increased by new supplies of East Indian sugar which had developed in the war years; and, as a final blow, the post-Napoleonic war period was one of great economic depression in Britain, so that all prices, including those offered for sugar, tended to decline.

THE PLANTOCRACY REDUCED

The final acquisition of Trinidad, St. Lucia, Demerara and Berbice by Britain at the peace treaty of 1815 increased the volume of British colonial sugar production and export. The planters of the Leewards, Barbados and Jamaica certainly did not welcome the expansion of the British Empire in the Caribbean. Nor did they relish the British acquisition of the sugar-producing island of Mauritius in the Indian Ocean, east of Madagascar, or the growing volume of sugar exports to Britain from British India. A flood of documents and memoranda from planters in the 'older' colonies argued that the products of the 'new' Caribbean territories and of Mauritius should only be allowed to enter Britain at a higher rate of import duty than that levied on older West Indian produce. The appeals were only partly and temporarily successful. The produce of the new Caribbean colonies was immediately admitted into Britain at the existing rates of duty on West Indian produce. Mauritian and East Indian products, however, were charged higher rates until 1825 and 1836 respectively, when they too were admitted on the same basis as West Indian produce.

Another consequence of the war was that the newest British acquisitions of Trinidad, St. Lucia and the two mainland colonies of Berbice and Demerara were all made Crown colonies, that is, they were not granted assemblies as the islands won in 1763 had been; Trinidad and St. Lucia retained their law-making bodies, the Illustrious Board of the *Cabildo* and the *Conseil Supérieur*, for only a short while after capture; then they were placed under governors who appointed their own councils and were answerable to the British Government. Trinidad and St. Lucia could not therefore under British rule make their own laws; they were governed by ordinances from England. The two mainland colonies were also subject to ordinances from England, but they were allowed to retain the law-making bodies which had existed under Dutch rule; Berbice and Demerara both had Courts of Policy, but Demerara also had the College of *Kiezers*, or Electors, and financial representatives. These bodies had not only helped to make laws, but had been partly elected, and had also been given a voice in taxation; they retained these rights until 1928. Yet their difference from St. Lucia and Trinidad did not make them like Jamaica or Barbados because the British Government remembered Lord Chief Justice Mansfield's judgment in 1774 in favour of the Grenada planter, Campbell, and retained the right to make laws for Trinidad, St. Lucia, Berbice and Demerara by Royal Order. So, the new colonies found themselves required, for instance, to better the position of their slaves by Amelioration Laws imposed by the British Government, who could only suggest that the old representative assemblies should pass the same laws. This again was the beginning of a limitation on the plantocracy which was to extend to nearly all the other colonies in the next half-century.

The decline of the wealthy plantocracy was therefore a gradual one. Efficient and more fortunate planters continued to make great wealth from sugar cultivation, but there was an ever-growing toll of failed estates and planters selling out to any available buyer. We shall see that this in the long run made for changes in social classes even before the social revolution of the emancipation of the slaves. The remaining planters did not give up their ambitions readily and continued long into the nineteenth century to seek a restoration of their former fortunes, but their influence as a political force in England was already declining.

FURTHER READING

Sources of West Indian History, Economic Life, pp. 59–68, Government and Politics, pp. 104–6.

QUESTIONS TO CONSIDER

1. Can you account in detail for the rise and fall of exports of British plantation produce shown on the chart on pages 120–3?

2. Which threat to the prosperity of British sugar mentioned in this chapter do you consider the most dangerous?

3. What internal hazards to the profits on sugar estates had the planter to face?

4. What attitudes do you anticipate that the planters would adopt towards proposals for the abolition of the slave trade, and later the emancipation of their slaves?

CHAPTER TWELVE

Church and Mission

OFFICIAL RELIGION

The discussion of West Indian society to this point has been mainly
concerned with planters, their European employees and their Negro
slaves on the estates. We can see that there were also many employees
of the imperial governments; the civil servants, particularly in the
French and Spanish territories, were numerous, consisting of law
officers, tax-collectors and customs men, as well as higher officials.
Garrisons and naval stations also swelled the ranks of Europeans for
more or less extended periods.

Another group were the priests and clergy of the official churches.
In the French and Spanish colonies, as we have seen, the Catholic
Church became the only form of religion tolerated by their governments in Europe. In the British islands, the established religion was
the Church of England, conducted in the West Indies by clergy appointed by the Bishop of London. Although the British West Indian
planters often wished it otherwise, they could not suppress other
forms of religion; their assemblies, however, continued to legislate
against Catholics, Jews, Quakers and the new Protestant missionary
groups which arrived in the latter part of the eighteenth century.

In the Spanish Empire, the Catholic Church continued as part of
the government machinery directed by the rulers of Spain. Bishops
were appointed and the whole hierarchy of the Church worked in
Spanish America, preaching, teaching at all levels from slave schools
to universities, ruling great estates in country areas and, above all,
seeing that orthodox views prevailed concerning both religion and
the authority of the Spanish Crown. They were as necessary to the
maintenance of Spanish domination as were the government officials.
For such a task the Church in Spanish America was fully organised
from the beginning of Spanish settlement.

The provisions of the *Code Noir* would suggest that the French
Government were equally concerned with the conversion of slaves in
their colonies and with the formation of fully Catholic populations.

134

This was certainly the intention of Cardinal Richelieu who, through his colonising companies, sent out missionaries with the slaves in the middle of the seventeenth century. The 1685 edict led to the departure of Jews and Protestants from the French territories, but those who remained by no means formed a devout Catholic society. The French Government continued to call for the conversion of the slaves. Missionaries were sent out to the French islands throughout the period of slavery, but they had achieved very little with the Negro population by 1848, when slaves were finally emancipated in the French colonies.

The Catholic missionaries made little headway with the mass of the people in the French colonies because of the unwavering opposition of the planters, and also of many of the government officials in the islands. Missionaries who attempted to instruct slaves found themselves removed or their property confiscated. Years of discouragement led to a decrease in their number, and by the end of the eighteenth century the conversion policy was a dead letter for the simple reason that there were nowhere near enough missionaries to effect it.

The reason for this opposition was that planters feared the consequences of religious instruction for slaves, who might thereby get new ideas about their worth as human beings and rebel against their servile condition. The Governor of Martinique, writing in 1764 to the Minister of Marine, who conducted the affairs of the colonies in Paris, put the matter directly. He explained that he had come out with every intention of encouraging humane treatment of slaves and their religious instruction, but he had changed his mind. 'Religious instruction could give to the negroes here an opening to other knowledge, to a kind of reason,' he wrote, 'the safety of the Whites, fewer in number, surrounded by these people on their estates and at their mercy, demands that they are kept in the profoundest ignorance.'

In fact, life was crude in both English and French islands. The slave society was demoralising for the owners as much as for the slaves. They more or less maintained the practice of religion themselves, but the religious spirit could hardly survive such a way of life. In any case, the clergy, Catholic or Anglican, were increasingly poor in quality and never enough to minister even to the whites, who mostly lived far apart in country areas. In Europe the Church was at a low ebb and clergy willing to go out to the colonies were not amongst the most devoted or well-equipped of this notoriously inadequate body.

Of course, some clergy of both denominations in the West Indies were respected for their sincerity, their good works or their learning. Others were gamblers and drinkers. Some were unfrocked priests, and many were absentees; laws had to be passed withholding their stipends if they were absent for unreasonable lengths of time. Others engaged in the same pursuits as the more prosperous Europeans and became planters, merchants or even, in one case, the commander of a privateer. They could gain scant respect from other Europeans in the West Indies and their churches, often handsome buildings, were left empty. It was an irreligious society, as was observed by a Methodist missionary in Antigua writing in 1799. 'I am in an enemy's country,' he declared, 'women and drink bear down all before them.'

In the circumstances, religious teaching for slaves was not to be expected, even when in some islands, despite protest from the slaves, the traditional Sunday market was changed to Saturday to enable it to take place. Furthermore, planters in British islands were as much afraid as their French counterparts of the effects of Christian teaching on their slaves. 'Within the last thirteen months,' wrote one rector in Jamaica, 'I have twice made known to the principal proprietors and attorneys in this parish my readiness to attend on such properties for the religious instruction of slaves as they would permit me to visit, but I have not been able to obtain the consent of more than two of them.'

Some clergy in any case shared the planters' view against the conversion of slaves, and this was sometimes extended to all coloured persons, although the hour of instruction on Sunday was intended for them too. The Lieutenant-Governor in Jamaica in 1811 complained that on several occasions clergy had refused to take services if there were no white people in the congregation. The Church of England remained predominantly the white man's church, but he usually gave it only a nominal allegiance.

The slaves had their own rituals and beliefs which had nothing to do with Christianity. Obeahmen were sometimes detected on the estates, put on trial and deported; some obeahmen hid in the bush and lived on the offerings brought by clients. Some planters believed that they frightened their victims to death, or even poisoned them if this failed. Mrs. Carmichael, a level-headed Scottish resident of the West Indies, doubted however whether there was any more harm in obeah in the West Indies than there was in witchcraft in Scotland; she reported that when one obeahman's hut was raided, nothing worse was found than a few cats' ears and some human hair. Slave-owners knew that there were special ceremonies at funerals and saw slaves wearing unfamiliar objects round their necks, but they had no real understanding of practices which were brought from Africa.

Two aspects of plantation life were particular obstacles to the development of Church membership amongst the slaves. In the first place, the Sunday market died hard; even when it was changed to Saturday, the tradition persisted and Sunday remained the slaves' day for their own concerns. Secondly, marriage amongst slaves was uncommon and was certainly not encouraged on the estates. Men and women changed partners without regard for permanent unions. The missionaries were the first people to face these problems in instructing the slaves and to regard them as matters of concern to the whole population.

FOUNDING OF MISSIONARY SOCIETIES

The missionaries who worked in the West Indies belonged to different denominations of Protestant Christianity. When the Protestant countries began to develop oversea empires, isolated attempts were made to provide money for missionary work. A Dutch minister first emphasised the need in 1590, but it was not until 1622, when the Dutch were dominating the East Indies, that a special establishment was set up in Leyden for the training of missionaries. In England, the Society for the Propagation of the Gospel was started in 1699 with £12,000 raised in a country-wide collection. The S.P.G. has made a special contribution in the West Indies with the money left by Christopher Codrington in 1710 to found a college in Barbados 'for use of the Mission in those parts'. This was easily the most effective activity of the Anglican Church in its least effective period in the West Indies.

These were small and conscientious endeavours; it was not until the religious revivals of the later eighteenth century in England that money and recruits were available for more extensive missionary work. The religious fervour that caused a group like the Pilgrim Fathers to uproot themselves from their homes to seek a place where they could pursue their own form of worship uninterrupted had not survived. Apathy reigned and the clergy made little attempt to touch the consciences of their congregations either in Europe or the West Indies. Above all, the mass of the people, whether the working men living lives of poverty and often squalor in England or the slaves cowed on the estates here, were not touched by Christian religious practices or teaching.

The indignant reaction to this situation was the foundation of new, nonconformist sects within the Protestant Church. They were mostly concerned to establish simpler forms of worship centred on the Bible, to encourage their followers to lead lives based on their fairly strict idea of Christian morality and to spread Christian teaching as widely as possible. In Germany, a group of families combined to found the United Brethren, or the Moravians as they came to be called. In England, John Wesley was forced out of the Anglican Church and formed his separate group of Methodists, who preached up and down both England and the settled parts of America. In his preaching activities Wesley is said to have covered 224,000 miles in his life and to have preached 40,000 sermons. He begged his hearers to acknowledge their sinful way of life and their need for conversion to practising Christianity. It was an active, vigorous gospel taken into the highways and byways to those people who were untouched by a passive Established Church. From this new enthusiastic movement came the volunteers who wanted to spend their lives preaching to the unconverted.

Wherever the converts turned, there was a field for their endeavours. It was early apparent that the vast mass of the English working classes were not the only problem. In America there was an equally compelling challenge; although long-established settlements had their church and preacher, new settlements were growing up without either. Thirdly, in most of the British colonies there was the continued flow of new arrivals from Africa, untouched by Christianity.

By the end of the eighteenth century, all the churches inspired by the religious revival had started missionary organisations. The Anglican Established Church itself had also been stung to some action in the field in 1794, when it set up the society for the Conversion and Religious Instruction and Education of the Negro Slaves in the British West Indian islands. The Baptist and Methodist Missionary Societies were founded. For all these, money was raised by their congregations in England and America. The societies had to support the missionaries until they were able to organise self-supporting churches in their new fields of endeavour. This took several decades in the West Indies, where the converted were likely to be slaves or free coloured people in humble circumstances.

The Moravians were the first comers. They established successful stations on the Danish island of St. Thomas and in St. Kitts in 1756, and in Antigua in 1774. By 1800 there were about 2,000 Moravians in St. Kitts and 7,000 in Antigua. In Jamaica they took over a plantation given to them by two absentee slave-owners; this proved a failure, as did efforts in Barbados and Tobago. The Moravians expected their missionaries to support themselves by doing manual work, so they had a particularly hard task in a society where Europeans did very little. Their main chance of success was to set up a station on the estate of a sympathetic owner so that the whole estate became something of a Moravian community, guided by the pastor; this was their characteristic method of development.

The original Baptist Church in Jamaica also had an early start. It was founded by two Negroes, George Lisle and Moses Baker, brought from America in 1783 by loyalist families who did not want to remain there after the British colonies had won their independence. They set up a brick church in Kingston to hold five hundred people and hired pack-horses to reach slaves on the estates. Imprisonment and persecution did not damp their ardour. In 1813, when they appealed to the Baptist Missionary Society for support, they had already established a small but vigorous Baptist community in Jamaica. The Methodist, Dr. Coke, who visited the area in 1789, and later wrote his *History of the West Indies*, preached at a number of towns in the islands. On his advice twelve Methodist missionaries were sent out.

It was not until after the Napoleonic Wars that missionaries came out in any number. Most missionary stations were set up between 1815 and 1830. The coming of the English Baptists in 1814 set the pace, and they and the Methodists proceeded in a similar manner. The Presbyterians, who had started in a small way in 1800, made their contribution between 1820 and 1830 on a smaller scale than the other denominations.

DIFFICULTIES OF MISSIONARY WORK

The main object of these missions was undoubtedly the conversion of the slaves to Christianity. It was an extraordinarily difficult task, even if it had received encouragement. The slaves lived in closed communities, which left them little chance of learning any new way of life other than the grinding labour of the estates. The African tribal customs which survived would not be readily given up for the little understood practices of Christianity. The differences in

139

language were yet another obstacle to the missionary. The field slave heard little English except the commands and curses of the book-keeper or the manager; he could learn enough words to answer questions, but not the kind of English which would help him to follow missionary teaching about Christianity. Whatever the goodwill of a devoted body of missionaries, the chances of rapidly overcoming these obstacles were slim.

In the event, a hard task was made infinitely harder by the opposition of most planters. To the organisers of missionary activity in England this seemed the major obstacle. Instructions to Anglican missionaries illustrate this apprehension. 'You must be careful,' they were told, 'to give no offence either to the Governor, to the Legislature, to the Planters, the Clergy or any other class of persons in the island.' They were to prove first of all that a man could be a good Christian and a good slave at the same time; for the only way to win the confidence of the ruling classes was to assure them that converted slaves would go on working as they had always done.

The attitude of the ruling class was one of the biggest difficulties the missionaries had to face. Some missionaries worked at the request of planters, chiefly absentees, such as the Dutchman who owned Le Resouvenir in Demerara where the ill-fated missionary John Smith worked. In Antigua and St. Kitts, this type of planter predominated. In Jamaica, Barbados and British Guiana, although the missionaries could work unmolested for years at a time, it was in an uneasy atmosphere of antagonism which could easily flare into open hostility, and even violence. It was the idea of brotherhood in Christian teaching which seemed so dangerous to the planters. The missionaries in the West Indies were to all intents and purposes saying for the first time that a European was the 'brother' of a Negro slave. This was certainly alarming to some. 'What will be the consequences', asked the Demerara *Royal Gazette*, 'when to that class of men is given the title "beloved brethren" as is actually done?'

Laws were passed to cut down the activities of missionaries, or sectaries as they were sometimes called. Licences to preach were sometimes required, and in most territories the law forbade religious services between sunset and sunrise, which very effectively prevented slaves from attending. Ministers could be imprisoned for keeping congregations beyond sunset. Such laws were not regularly enforced, but they provided the magistrates with reserve powers to use when they felt inclined.

By their sermons many missionaries tried to give the slaves a thorough grounding in the Bible. Verbal instruction was not enough, however. It was important that converts should have daily guidance in practising the Christian life from private prayer and Bible reading. Teaching the slaves to read was an important part of the missionary's job, and a very unpopular one with their critics. John Smith was interviewed by the Governor of Demerara. 'His Excellency frowned on me,' he reported, 'and asked me what I had come to do and how I proposed to instruct the negroes. I answered, "by teaching them to read: by teaching them Dr. Watts' catechisms; and by preaching the Gospel in a plain manner". To which he replied, "If you ever teach a negro to read and I hear of it I will banish you from the colony immediately." '

In spite of this, Sunday-schools for children were attached to most missions. Primers were sent out from London and catechisms and Bibles sold to the slaves. Many slaves who had never been to church learned to read from church-goers, and missionaries found slaves of all ages anxious to learn.

Even persuading the slaves to attend church on a Sunday interfered with the established routine. When the missionaries arrived, Sunday was firmly established as market day for the slaves to sell the produce from their provision grounds. In crop time the slaves were needed on the plantation itself. The missionaries had to emphasise the necessity of keeping the Lord's Day holy, not only as a part of Christian belief, but because it gave them their only opportunity to teach the slaves. 'The days of this week have passed away,' wrote Smith, 'and I have done almost nothing: the negroes are worked so hard they have no time to come to me . . . besides the smallness of the congregation we are much annoyed . . . by the noise of the cattle-mill grinding coffee, and often by the flogging of the negroes.'

The conflict between what the missionary taught and what the slave-masters demanded was summarised by an Anglican clergyman: 'the authority of the master which they must enforce and the law of God which they profess to teach must often draw the hesitating slave different ways. . . . God sets apart the Sabbath to recruit the body for labour, and improve the mind to futurity; the master . . . obliges the slave to toil on that day.' Some of the slaves in Demerara worked out a reasonable answer to this problem; if Sunday must be used in the service of the Lord, their Saturday should be given them for market day. But what the planters saw in this teaching was a direct challenge to their authority and a plain proof that the missionaries had come to upset the system of slavery.

The number of missionaries at work in the West Indies was never sufficient for the task before them. The Baptist missionary, William Knibb, illustrated this with a description of a week's work in the summer of 1830. 'Sabbath three services with the whole of the singing etc.', he began, 'Tues. to Ox. or Cambridge. On Wed. to Rio Bueno or Arcadia, 14 miles. Thurs. back to Falmouth, 14 miles, to preach in the evening. Sat. to Stewart Town, 18 miles or some other distant place, for the Sabbath. This every week with heavy experiences, correcting disorders in the church, baptisms etc. is too much for me. Connected with the stations are more than 5,000 persons, and I feel an awful responsibility. I long to establish a sabbath school, but I cannot; for now from 6 in the morning till 3 in the afternoon I have scarcely a moment's rest. In addition to this I have to take my turn in Westmoreland, which is 86 miles from the other extremity of my stations.' Even by this great effort, travelling by horseback in the heat of the day, he was only touching the fringes of the slave population. The majority of slaves were on the plantations and might have to walk several miles to the nearest church.

Knibb was particularly fortunate in fact in having a strong constitution. The West Indies provided early graves for many missionaries. Knibb's brother survived only a few months at Port Royal. Fatal fevers and agues interrupted missionary service more effectively than the magistrates, since it was always many months before a man could be replaced, and frequently the work lapsed for years at a time. At Port Royal a Methodist society founded in 1790 collapsed in 1796 with the death of the missionary; it was fifteen years before a Methodist from Kingston started preaching there again.

FRIENDS AND ENEMIES

The missionaries were energetic preachers and prided themselves on the numbers that came to hear them. Not all the congregation were church-members, however. Only church-members took communion and held 'tickets' which were renewed quarterly if there were no complaints about bad conduct. To become a church-member a slave was first put on probation as an 'inquirer'; if his conduct proved him converted, then he had to answer questions set by the missionary. John Smith described how he examined an inquirer. 'On these occasions,' he explained, 'I generally begin by asking them how many wives they have. Then I question them in Dr. Watts' first catechism. If they give satisfactory answers to these questions, profess to believe in Christ and be sorry for their sins, I do not refuse them.' The slave accepted as a church-member in the Baptist Church was then baptised in a nearby river.

The chapels built by the Wesleyans and Baptists were partly subsidised by money from England and the rest was provided on credit. The slaves, however, made a remarkable contribution themselves. Ticket-holders among the Baptists paid 6d. every quarter. Smith's congregation sent £26 to the parent society in London for missionary work elsewhere. In Spanish Town, Jamaica, slaves gave labour in their free time to build a chapel to hold some fourteen hundred people. The Methodist slaves paid 1½d. for collection at the Sunday service and 1s. 6d. a month for class meetings. The slaves were certainly making contributions to their churches.

While the missionary could feel satisfied with his work for individual slaves, it was impossible for him to feel satisfied with conditions in a slave society. Living on a plantation, Smith was constantly aware of the whip being used. 'While writing this my very heart flutters at hearing the almost incessant cracking of the whip', he recorded in his diary. One Monday morning he lay in bed and counted a hundred and forty-nine strokes of the whip as one unfortunate was punished. His work and sympathy were 'for the comfort of Christians who were scattered and persecuted, which is the case with our people'.

The general sympathies of the missionaries could hardly have been otherwise in view of their calling. Although they did not organise any anti-slavery movement in the West Indies, there was little doubt as to where their sympathies lay. They were always subject to attack when there was unrest in the area or protests against slavery in England. A newly started Methodist mission in Montego Bay, for instance, died during the Maroon War of 1795. The missionaries of Nevis came near to having their chapel burnt over their heads while the campaign against the slave trade was in progress, although the planters of that island were usually tolerant of their work. Much of the early work of the missions was made difficult by the fact that it coincided in time with the main anti-slavery movements.

In May 1823, a campaign opened in the House of Commons for the emancipation of the slaves. In July of that year the Colonial Secretary sent instructions to the Crown colonies for improving the condition of the slaves. In the Crown colony of Demerara, the Governor received his instructions, and did nothing about publishing them. The slaves knew that something had been done to improve their lot and when the Governor made no move, the idea spread that freedom had been granted and was being withheld. In the trouble that followed, the planters turned on the missionary, John Smith, imprisoned him for seven weeks, then tried and condemned him.

It was charged at his trial that he 'did promote as far as in him lay discontent and dissatisfaction in the minds of the Negro slaves toward their lawful masters', and, 'having knowledge of certain revolt and rebellion, he did not use utmost endeavours to suppress the same'. Slave witnesses were called and were all asked similar questions:

Magistrate. When the prisoner talked to you about finishing half a row on a Sunday did he not tell you it was not right to finish it on a Sunday?

Slave. He did not tell us not to finish it on a Sunday, but, only, that it was not right.

Magistrate. When the prisoner talked to you about the state of the children of Israel did he not tell you that the state of the negro was like to that of the children of Israel?

Slave. No.

Magistrate. Did you hear Mr. Smith tell the negroes that they must not mind a few lashes (for attending church)?

Slave. No, I did not hear him say so; he said if the master gave them work, to do it patiently, and if the master punished them unjustly they must not grieve for it.

The fact that the rebels demanded the right to go to church was interpreted by the planters to mean that Smith was a cause of the rebellion. But his diary showed that his influence had been toward restraint. He recorded that on 25 July, 'Quamina, senior deacon of Success, came to enquire if I had heard the report that the King had sent out orders to the Government to free the slaves. I told him I had not heard it, and that if such a report was in circulation, it must not be believed for it was false. I told him it was likely the Governor had some orders, because the Government at home wished to make some regulations for the benefit of the slaves, but not to make them free. This answer however scarcely satisfied him.'

Quamina was an elderly slave of a steady disposition. Yet he was 'scarcely satisfied' with what Smith had told him. Others were less patient and ready to turn against Smith for his very moderation. A slave described how 'the negroes said that Mr. Smith was making them fools; he would not deny his own colour for the sake of black people'. The planters were nonetheless convinced that Smith had caused the rebellion and sentenced him to be hanged, although they knew that the sentence would be quashed by the authorities in London. Smith, however, died in prison before any reprieve arrived. He was buried in an unmarked grave, a missionary martyr to a cause which even he had not dared to support wholeheartedly.

The Jamaican planters were no less vengeful but, as they had their own representative assembly, they could still cloak some of their persecution of missionaries under the guise of law. Their revised slave code, the result of the Colonial Secretary's appeal of 1823, was passed three years later and contained many attacks on missionary work. Some of these were based on the most fanciful accusations. 'And whereas, under pretence of offerings and contributions, large sums of money have been extorted by designing men professing to be leaders of religion,' began the clause forbidding any fee from slaves for religious instruction. The restrictions on services between sunset and sunrise were re-imposed. Another law made it a case for whipping or the workhouse if slaves were found preaching or teaching without their owners' permission. This incidentally revealed that slaves, presumably 'ticket'-holders, were instructors in some of the churches.

The missionaries had every reason to fear the results of this enactment. It was, however, not approved by the British Government. The Colonial Secretary sent a despatch to the Governor of Jamaica declaring that 'I cannot too distinctly impress upon you that it is the settled purpose of His Majesty's Government to sanction no colonial law which needlessly infringes on the religious liberty of any class of His Majesty's subjects.' This immediately aroused the resentment of the planters, who retorted by re-enacting the rejected law and setting up a committee to enquire into the activities of the missionaries.

Thomas Burchell, Baptist Missionary at Montego Bay, writing home to his missionary society headquarters, described how this 'Sectarian Committee' asked questions about the organisation of the church, what was taught there, how money was collected and used.

He complained that 'in addition to the mortification of being arraigned before such a tribunal . . . my expenses amounted to £35. Mr. Alsopp was called from Lucea, distant one hundred and thirty miles, to answer one single question—"Are you a Baptist missionary ?" Is it not evident that the design of the Assembly was not so much to obtain information as to harass and involve us in unnecessary expense?' The report was, of course, hostile to the missionaries and accused them of preaching sedition and raising money by the basest methods. In England, however, it had no effect. The movement for the total abolition of slavery was growing from strength to strength.

The Jamaican slaves, as in Demerara, got wind of what was happening and the rumour started that 'free paper come'. There were grounds for this belief because slaves on Crown property had been emancipated four months before. Rebellion broke out after Christmas, 1831, and the planters turned at once on the missionaries. The rebellion centred on St. James and Trelawny; missionaries in that area were imprisoned and put on trial. Many of the chapels were destroyed, some of them by savage persistence; it was said that it took fourteen nights of destruction with crowbars to demolish the Methodist chapel in Falmouth. This was a cold, calculated fury and was expressed in more than one way. The *Jamaica Courant*, commenting on the arrest of three Baptist preachers, said, 'shooting is, however, too honourable a death for men whose conduct has occasioned so much bloodshed and the loss of so much property. There are five hanging woods in St. James and Trelawny and we do sincerely hope that the bodies of the Methodist preachers who may be convicted of sedition may diversify the scene.'

The planters who shared such extreme sentiments joined together in an organisation called the Colonial Church Union. Church Union members instigated and led many of the attacks on missionary property; they also influenced the magistrates to use their powers to withdraw licences to preach. But no missionary in Jamaica was condemned to death, as Smith had been, and the Governor of the island eventually banned the Colonial Church Union.

The Jamaican missionaries in fact took the same attitude towards the rebellion as John Smith had done in Demerara. When the slaves were on the verge of revolt, William Knibb at Falmouth spent all his energies in trying to keep his church-members from joining the rebels. 'I learn that some wicked persons have persuaded you that the King of England has made you free,' he addressed them. 'Hear me!, I love your souls, and I would not tell you a lie for the whole world; I assure you that it is false, false as hell can make it! I entreat you not to believe it, but to go about your work as formerly.'

Not all the slaves responded to his words but some of his flock believed him, one remarking, 'If minister had not been so urgent we really would have believed freedom was come.' On two estates, Knibb's church leaders were entrusted with looking after the property while the planters were away on militia duty. But some of the slaves were led to question, 'Minister never say a word about freedom before; why does he come and talk to us about freedom now? The white people must have bribed him to it,' meaning that he must be conspiring with the planters to keep the news from them.

In the end the missionaries could not control events. It will be noticed that both Knibb and Smith were suspected by their flock of really being in league with other white men to withhold freedom from the slaves. This was because the missionaries could not in the hostile atmosphere here openly support the movement in England for the abolition of slavery. Knibb wrote to the Baptist headquarters in London for instructions. 'While you are exerting all your energies at home, ought we to sit here all the day idle?' he asked. He was answered by events, for the effective action to end the legal system of slavery was coming to a head on the other side of the Atlantic.

FURTHER READING

Sources of West Indian History, Religion and Education, pp. 142–3, 146–57, Slavery and its Abolition, pp. 180–4.

Ragatz, *Fall of the Planter Class*, Chapter I, Caribbean Society in the Eighteenth Century, pp. 18–23.

C. B. Firth, *From William III to Waterloo*, Chapter IX.

Hoyos, *Our Heritage*, William Hart Coleridge.

QUESTIONS TO CONSIDER

1. Which religious bodies were active in your territory before the abolition of slavery and what was their work amongst slaves?

2. Why did the planters regard the missionaries in a different way from the clergy of the Anglican or the Catholic Churches?

3. How did the magistrates in Demerara argue their case against John Smith? Do you think that they had any justification?

4. Why were the religious bodies in the West Indies not active in the movement to abolish slavery?

CHAPTER THIRTEEN

The Chance for Charity

SOCIETY FOR EFFECTING THE ABOLITION OF THE SLAVE TRADE

There were members of the House of Commons directly concerned to abolish the slave trade. Their interest in the cause was created by the Society for Effecting the Abolition of the Slave Trade, founded in 1787. The Quakers, who had forbidden members to buy slaves as early as 1755, were the core of the movement, but every denomination, class and occupation was represented among the supporters. The Society set out to carry the arguments against the slave trade into every home in England through the press, through pamphlets, through the Sunday sermon at the local church. Then, having won the support of public opinion, they planned to carry the attack into Parliament.

Before the Society was founded, individual protests against slavery had reached the public. The most striking was the campaign against slavery in England by the Quaker, Granville Sharp, who worked as a clerk in the Ordinance Department. He became interested in the condition of Negroes in England through meeting a Barbadian slave who had been brought to England and abandoned as unfit for work after his master had beaten his head with a pistol. Sharp was appalled to find that slaves brought from the West Indies to serve their owners in Britain were often turned loose when unwanted, or sold openly as 'bond servants'. He determined to get a decision from the law-courts to find if a man could be a slave at all in England. The famous test case of James Somerset, a Jamaican slave abandoned by his master in England, reclaimed years later and put forcibly aboard a ship bound for the West Indies, was tried in 1772 before Lord Mansfield. The judge ruled that, since there was no definite law sanctioning slavery in England, it must be considered illegal. Sales of 'bond servants' in England came to an end, but the slave trade remained a legitimate form of commerce. Only an Act of Parliament could put an end to that.

Branches of the Abolition Society were formed in the big towns to organise local meetings and draw up petitions. A hundred petitions reached Parliament in 1787 and 1788 and five hundred in 1792. The London Corporation, the Universities of Oxford and Cambridge, as well as groups of clergymen, registered their protest in this way. A wider public was reached by the pamphlet writers who used every type of argument. There was Thomas Clarkson's straightforward discussion, *A Summary View of the Slave Trade and the Probable Consequence of its Abolition*, fifteen thousand copies of which were distributed in 1788 alone. There were lurid accounts of atrocities such as *The Trial of Capt. John Kimber for the Murder of Two Female Slaves on Board the Recovery*. One writer argued that 'the CONSUMER of West Indian produce may be considered the *Master Spring* that gives motion to the whole machine of cruelties'. He calculated that if thirty-eight thousand people stopped using West Indian produce, the slave trade would automatically come to an end. On this basis, children were urged not to eat sweets for the sake of the poor Negro. The Bible was scanned for texts that might be interpreted to show that slavery was against the will of God. People all over the country took up the cause with enthusiasm preaching from texts like 'Thou shalt not oppress an hired servant that is poor and needy'.

The poet Cowper wrote *The Negro's Complaint*, which ran:

> Still in thought as free as ever,
>   What are England's rights, I ask,
> Me from my delights to sever,
>   Me to torture, me to task?
> Fleecy locks, and black complexion
>   Cannot forfeit nature's claim;
> Skins may differ, but affection
>   Dwells in white and black the same.

Clarkson commented that it 'gave a plain account of the subject with appropriate feeling'. Thousands of copies were printed on the finest paper. This was intended to appeal to the ladies, and was circulated with the superscription, 'A subject for conversation at the Tea-table'. It was also set to music and became a popular ballad.

When this campaign started, the West Indian lobby was by no means as uncertain of its best interest as it was by 1807. In face of this propaganda they began by organising their own opposition, and used all their influence in Parliament to discredit the anti-slavery cause. They printed pamphlets and distributed them to members of the House and to newspapers. They argued that the slave trade relieved Africa of criminals who would otherwise be put to death, that the Negro was created to serve and that slavery was justified by Scripture. But the West India Society were defending an interest not pursuing a cause, and their campaign was never so intensive as that of their opponents, who printed twice the number of pamphlets.

For their chief spokesman in the House of Commons, the Society obtained the services of William Wilberforce, M.P. for Yorkshire. Shortly before Wilberforce was asked to take up the cause, he had changed his way of life completely. He had been a gay and irresponsible undergraduate at Cambridge and a favourite in the London drawing-rooms, where his wit and fine singing voice were much admired. He had become a Member of Parliament at the age of twenty-one and there, in his own words, 'my own distinction was my darling object'. He was a great friend of the youthful Prime Minister, William Pitt; the two talked politics at length. Then Wilberforce was converted to Evangelical Christianity. He gave up the gay parties, dissociated himself from the intrigue of politics and addressed himself seriously to the business of reform. When asked to take up the fight against the slave trade, he discussed the matter with men like Rev. James Ramsay and read all the information he could find before deciding in favour. The rest of his political life was devoted to the cause of abolishing first the slave trade, then slavery itself.

The West India interest found it embarrassing to have such a well-connected man as Wilberforce opposing them in the House of Commons. But they did their best to discredit his associates. The Rev. James Ramsay was the easiest target. After spending nineteen years in St. Kitts, he had published, in 1784, an *Essay on the Treatment and Conversion of the African slaves in the Sugar Colonies*, in which he had fully described the conditions of slavery. Tales of his depravity during his residence in the West Indies were circulated vigorously until the calumny was said to have affected his health. When he died in 1789, a West Indian planter called Molyneux was reported to have boasted, 'Ramsay is dead—I have killed him'.

It was a bitter fight, even leading to physical violence at times. Clarkson, for instance, was attacked by a Liverpool gang who tried to edge him off the end of a pier when he was collecting evidence against a captain who had murdered a seaman. Most of it was a battle of words and a conflict of ideas, however, and the losing side would be the one whose case was first weakened by new circumstances. The decline of the popularity of West Indian sugar was enough to sow the seeds of doubt about the planters' argument.

ABOLITION OF THE SLAVE TRADE

It was not enough for the Abolition Society to have public support in their campaign and votes in the House of Commons. What they needed was government backing. Pitt supported the cause in the House until the 1797 attempt to pass a Bill which was rejected in the House of Lords. The attitude of that body was well expressed by Lord Abingdon. 'What', he asked, 'does abolition of the slave trade mean more or less in effect than liberty and equality? What more or less than the rights of man?' This was intended as the greatest condemnation, for these were the ideas most feared by the English ruling classes. They had seen the fate of their kind in the French Revolution and trembled for their own security. Any social change was to be avoided; any such change was to be dubbed with the revolutionary slogans; and the abolition of the slave trade was such a change. After this, Pitt's ministers held divided opinions on the matter and he could not risk splitting his government by himself publicly advocating the cause any longer.

Pitt's death in 1806 made way for an active supporter of the bill for the abolition of the slave trade. He was succeeded by his political opponent, Charles James Fox, who was ready to give government backing to the measure. Wilberforce had unsuccessfully presented bills in 1804 and 1805, but a resolution in favour of abolition passed the House of Commons in 1806. This time, with the backing of Fox and the rest of the Government, the bill passed both Houses in 1807.

The slave trade was still earning considerable profits; the *Enterprise* of Liverpool earned £24,430 8s. 11d. on an outstanding voyage in 1804, and profits of £15,000 were not uncommon. The trade, however, was confined to three towns, London, Bristol and Liverpool. The London Corporation represented enough interests other than slave-trading to present their petition for its abolition in 1790. Liverpool was the most important slave-trading town, though even there the proportion of slave ships dropped from one in twelve in 1782 to one in twenty-four in 1807. Liverpool, however, had a new interest in the import of raw cotton from the United States for the mills of new, industrial Manchester, and so had another trade to compensate her merchants for the loss of the slave trade. There was no further resistance to the operation of the new Act.

The last English slave trader, *Kitty's Amelia* left Liverpool on 1 May, 1808. It took another fifty years of diplomatic pressure and a ban enforced by the British navy to bring the whole European slave trade to an end. At the end of the Napoleonic Wars, when all the European nations met to discuss the peace settlement at Vienna, England used her prestige as leader of the victory to make delegates there accept in theory the abolition of the slave trade. Nevertheless, it continued. The French Government eventually took steps in the eighteen-thirties to end their slave trade, but Spain and Portugal continued to develop their colonies with slaves. Above all, the Americans carried slaves for themselves and for the Spanish and Portuguese territories, particularly those rivals of the British West Indian islands, Cuba and Brazil; the Americans continued the trade until the issue of slavery was taken to the point of civil war in the United States in 1861.

PLAN FOR AMELIORATION

After the victory of 1807, members of the Society for the Abolition of the Slave Trade turned to the question of slavery itself. The trade was illegal so that new supplies of slaves could not be taken to the West Indies, but after the mass of slave transportation across the Atlantic in the eighteenth century there was a large creole slave population in the West Indies. The abolitionists therefore soon turned their attention to the conditions of existing slavery.

In addition to Wilberforce and Clarkson, a new generation of abolitionists was emerging. Thomas Fowell Buxton, James Stephen, Canning, Huskisson and Zachary Macaulay were civil servants and politicians who were to play a big part in making improved conditions in the colonies part of the British Government's official policy. In 1823 a new society was organised, this time for the Gradual Abolition of Slavery itself. The plan of the reformers was to campaign for an immediate improvement, or amelioration, of the conditions of slaves to be enforced by law, and to press for the abolition of slavery at an early date. Public opinion was more rapidly recruited this time and, within a year, two hundred and twenty branch societies were scattered over England. Seven hundred and fifty petitions to abolish slavery had reached Parliament. The reforming zeal of the articulate British public was remarkably evident in this cause.

The West Indian interest had realised that theirs was not a popular cause in England and that they would need clever tactics to secure support. They made an astute move over the amelioration proposal. They formed a committee of fifteen, including ten of their Members of Parliament, to work out their own amelioration policy and forward it to the Colonial Secretary, Lord Bathurst. They made their position clear. 'The various parties, who from different motives are hostile to the West India interest,' they realised, 'are at least as powerful and act upon a more extensive system and with greater means of influence on the public mind than the Proprietors and Merchants connected with the colonies. We cannot therefore beat them by influence—we must trust to reason—and the only way of getting that weapon into our hands is by doing ourselves all that is right to be done—and doing it speedily and effectively.'

The suggestions for amelioration therefore came from the London representatives of the planters themselves. Bathurst accepted the suggestions and incorporated them in a circular despatch to the self-governing islands for consideration by their assemblies. In the recently acquired territories of Trinidad, Demerara and St. Lucia, where the Crown had greater powers, the reforms were enforced by Orders in Council. This was the despatch that began John Smith's sad story in Demerara.

The despatch suggested the abolition of flogging for women, a delay of at least one day before a male was flogged for an offence and a record of all punishments of more than three lashes to be kept by plantation officials and to be presented to magistrates at the quarterly sessions. Slave families should not be divided and the selling of slaves as a payment for debts should be prohibited. Adequate religious instruction should be provided for slaves; in the case of the Crown colonies, this should be done at the expense of the Imperial Government if necessary. Finally, slaves should be able to give evidence in court if a religious instructor would vouch for them.

This was not the first time that the Imperial Government had urged the West Indian representative assemblies to legislate for the benefit of the slaves. The Slave Laws urged on the assemblies at the end of the eighteenth century had a similar intention. They had been both resisted and disregarded, even when they became law. The question was whether the planters in the West Indies would now accept the suggestions more readily since they originated from the absentee planters and merchants in London who might be expected to have the same interests as themselves. The London group's intention of regaining the initiative in West India affairs, 'by doing ourselves all that is right to be done', was not shared by their counterparts here. The assemblies in Jamaica, Barbados, Dominica and St. Vincent protested strongly against the suggestions. They consented to enact only a few of the amelioration measures, and such as they adopted made little real difference to the practice of slavery. They certainly did not accept the notion of ever giving a slave a voice in a law-court, and such opportunities as they permitted for religious education were so encompassed by regulations that only the most determined preacher or missionary could make much headway against them.

The case of John Smith demonstrated the strength of feeling that was engendered by these threats to the old system of slavery. The attitude of the planters in the West Indies was publicised by the Abolition Society and aroused much indignation in England. This was further inflamed by the fate of John Smith and by that of another missionary, Shrewsbury, a Wesleyan in Barbados, who was driven from the island after his church and home had been destroyed.

This violent action against missionaries touched the large religious public in England closely. The new evangelical nonconformist churches were still foremost in missionary work and their following remained large and enthusiastic in England. Congregations made regular collections for the furtherance of their churches' work abroad; the task of preaching Christianity to the heathen was regarded as a duty to be supported. People who had not questioned the right of the planters to have slaves, or thought about their treatment, were horrified by the stories of Smith and Shrewsbury. A new light was thrown on the powers of life and death which could still be wielded by the West Indian plantocracy.

In a parliamentary speech Wilberforce called for an investigation of the Smith case. An earnest debate took place in the House of Commons, but the motion was lost; the instinct of one ruling class to defend the authority of their opposite numbers in the colonies proved too strong. But the influence of both the Smith and Shrewsbury cases on public opinion was great; their names became slogans in the fight against slavery. The failure of the amelioration policy was clearly recognised by 1830. To change the situation in the West Indies at all, only the second stage of the abolitionists' policy would have any effect. The battle was now joined for complete abolition of slavery.

CAMPAIGN FOR THE ABOLITION OF SLAVERY

In 1831, the Abolition Society started a new intensive campaign to stir up public opinion. Their task now, however, had more chance of success than it had ever had, for the idea of reform was in the air; it was mainly a matter of seeing that the abolition of slavery was included with the rest. Above all a reform of the British Parliament would bring in new members who would be sympathetic to the cause of the abolition of slavery and ready to make it law.

The main concern was to find a sufficient number of people who were prepared to take their criticism of the West Indian planters and merchants to the point of voting against them in the House of Commons. There were many of them in England, but few were Members of Parliament. Nevertheless, during the years that the anti-slavery movement had been in existence a new group of influential men had emerged. Traditionally the land-owners were the ruling class. The right to vote at all was based on property, which excluded most of the population. Furthermore, there were many pocket or rotten boroughs in which few, or even no, people lived, but which had a Member of Parliament chosen by the owner of that property. Several of the prosperous West Indian planters who returned to England with their profits sought positions of social and political power through buying a seat in the House of Commons from such an owner.

The new influential group were largely manufacturers and businessmen who had become wealthy during the period of industrial invention, with its extension of factories to accommodate the inventions and the congregation of people around the factories to earn their living there. These changes in manufacture and ways of living were striking enough to earn the name of the Industrial Revolution. One of the effects of the Industrial Revolution was to create a group of people with different interests from the great land-owners. The industrialists were prepared to attack the landed interests if this was necessary for them to advance their own. For them the West Indies was a potential market like anywhere else where they did trade. Its importance in that connection was easily measured, and it was obviously a declining market. Given political power the new manufacturing potentates were not likely to preserve the slave societies in the West Indies for any benefit to themselves.

The abolition movement therefore worked against a background of striking change and developing political excitement which could be turned to its own ends. In 1830 George IV, who had stoutly resisted changes in parliamentary elections, died. A new election brought in a majority of members prepared for change, and a leader in Lord Grey, who had long worked for it. After a few political crises and

155

threats, the first Reform Act was passed, and its measures immediately affected the issue of abolition of slavery. Fifty-five of the old towns that had provided seats for whoever could buy them lost representation; thirty more lost one of their members. The vacant seats were transferred to the new industrial towns, Manchester, Birmingham, Leeds and Sheffield, and to the counties, to represent the small farmer. At the same time the vote was given to all townsmen paying £10 a year rent on a short lease. Altogether one in twenty-four of the population now had a vote.

The new voters included the factory owner and the respectable tradesmen who served his family. These were the people who had signed petitions for the removal of the slave trade, had discussed after the Sunday sermon the fates of Smith and Shrewsbury, and who were also looking round for the best markets for their manufactured goods. It was on these people that the Abolition Society urged its cause throughout the months of agitation that attended the Reform Bill.

Enthusiastic young members of the Society formed what they called the Agency Committee which divided the country into districts, and employed six paid lecturers and a panel of honorary lecturers to work the districts. The speeches took an uncompromising line. 'To uphold slavery is a crime before God,' the speaker would declare, 'and the condition thereof must be immediately abolished.' During the 1832 election, the Agency Committee tried to make the candidates pledge themselves publicly to support abolition; many of them, sensing the feelings of their audience, did so.

The work of the Committee was helped by the arrival of William Knibb and Thomas Burchell, the two Baptist missionaries from Jamaica, with first-hand accounts of the slave rising and the planter reprisals there. The same news reached the Colonial Office in despatches from the Governor of Jamaica. The government was learning from official sources what Knibb and Burchell were telling the public, that the result of trying to maintain slavery would be racial war. The Christmas Rebellion had been subdued by the following February, but the slaves were now set to win their freedom if it was not granted them.

With the slaves under control again, the Governor of Jamaica and the Colonial Office in London found themselves faced with the problem of how to control the planters. There had been much talk among the whites of secession from the British Government to join the United States, where no anti-slavery movement would yet threaten their interests. There had even been a conference in Barbados in 1831 to discuss the idea. The Imperial Government disliked this development but could do nothing about it. Furthermore, in Jamaica, the vicious activities of the Colonial Church Union against the nonconformist missionaries continued long after the real danger of the rebellion had passed. Sixteen churches were destroyed in all. Knibb and Burchell had been brought to trial on trumped-up charges, as was Edward Jordon, the free coloured editor of the *Watchman and Jamaica Free Press*, who was presumably charged as a warning to his group not to interfere with the existing state of society.

So far as the Imperial Government was concerned, the Union was disturbing the uneasy balance of Jamaican society and challenging the political power of Britain. The Governor, Lord Mulgrave, forced public officials who were prominent in the Union to resign their posts, and in January 1833 declared the whole organisation illegal. It was a reflection on the real weakness of the planter class that the movement immediately collapsed.

By 1833 the planters were politically stranded; they had rejected the advice of the group of absentee planters and merchants in London; they offered no marketing prospects to the newly represented interests in the House of Commons; they sold expensive sugar compared with Mauritius, Cuba, Brazil and India, and they had challenged the authority of the Imperial Government. Throughout these developments the abolitionists were urging action.

The reform government was ready to take action. Some members were as convinced of the need to end slavery as they were of the need to stop children working in English factories; others considered ties with the West Indies no longer profitable and many could see that the amelioration policy had been destroyed by the attitude of the planters. There could be no compromise with slavery. Buxton introduced the bill early in the new session and by August 1833, the Emancipation Act was passed. Slavery was to be abolished from 1 August 1834, and children under the age of six at that date were to be free. There were three main proposals to meet the situation as the Imperial Government saw it. In the first place the planters were to receive £20,000,000 in compensation for the loss of their unpaid labour. To create a period of transition before full freedom was granted to the slaves, an apprenticeship scheme was adopted. By this the ex-slaves could not leave the estates until the period was over, but they were now to receive wages for work done in excess of forty hours a week. ·The apprenticeship period was to last six years for field labourers and four for domestic workers. The third provision was a sum of money granted by the Imperial Government both for the employment of special magistrates to deal with disputes arising on the estates and for Negro education.

The abolitionists had won their cause for all British colonies. The slaves were freed by a movement in England that finally found an opportunity for the successful outcome of a decade of campaigning. Freedom, however, had to be worked out in the West Indies. Here the vast majority of the population, who had been born into slavery, would want to use their freedom for their own independent interests; these interests were expected to be entirely different from those of the influential minority whose main concern was to preserve as much as possible of a way of life which gave them personal wealth and privilege in the West Indies.

FURTHER READING

Sources of West Indian History, Religion and Education, p. 161, Slavery and its Abolition, pp. 178–91, Government and Politics, pp. 102–4.

Parry and Sherlock, *A Short History of the West Indies*, Chapter XII, Hoyos, *Our Common Heritage*, John Beckles.

QUESTIONS TO CONSIDER

1. It is not easy to say exactly why the Act for the Abolition of the Slave Trade was passed in 1807 after many earlier attempts. What reasons do you find most convincing?

2. What circumstances favoured the work of the leaders of the Abolition movement?

3. How did the attitude of the West Indian planters in London differ from that of the planters in the West Indies? Can you account for the difference?

4. What problems do you anticipate for the apprenticeship scheme introduced by the Act of Emancipation?

CHAPTER FOURTEEN

West Indian Society on the Eve of Emancipation

THE SOCIAL GROUPS

While striking changes were taking place in the fortunes of sugar-planters and in the attitude of the British Government to their slave colonies, certain changes were taking place in West Indian societies even before the emancipation of the slaves. The slave societies were necessarily rigid since the mass of the population were confined to being slaves. But there were three main groups, and individuals shifted from one to another occasionally even though the occupations followed by the groups were limited by the accepted rules of society, by economic opportunities, and sometimes by the laws of imperial governments or colonial legislatures.

The whites were mainly engaged in planting, as owners of big estates or as smaller-scale growers of sugar or other export crops. Others were in various professions, as doctors, lawyers, clergymen, missionaries and schoolteachers; in trade and commerce, as factors or as merchants in their own right; in the military or naval forces; in the performance of skilled trades, especially on the estates; in supervisory work as attorneys, overseers and book-keepers. A few were travelling salesmen, conjurors, or public performers, appearing wherever they thought there was money to be had for what they offered.

The free coloured were an intermediate class in the society. There were also the free black people, usually slaves who had been given their freedom by their owners in return for some exceptional service, or sometimes, for reasons the opposite of gratitude, when an old or disabled slave was ejected to save the cost of his food, clothing or care in his sickness. On rare occasions, a slave could use money accumulated by sale of his ground provisions in the market to buy his freedom, but only with his master's permission.

The free black and coloured people, living in a society which allowed personal prestige to the white and wealthy, were seldom fair-skinned enough or sufficiently wealthy to be accepted without reserve, and it is clear that the white population feared their numerical increase or rise to power. Consequently, during the eighteenth century, all the assemblies in the British colonies excluded them from public office and the right to vote. There were also laws limiting their rights in law-courts and forbidding them to serve on juries. Their right to inheritance was sometimes restricted, and there were petty laws in some islands forbidding coloured people to own ships or vehicles or to send their children to public schools.

In 1713, an act of the Jamaica Assembly, annually repeated until 1826, excluded all free black and coloured people from employment on the plantations. The coloured children of estate owners, if acknowledged by their fathers, were thus compelled to choose between slave status on the estate, or freedom with less personal security in the towns or rural villages. The gradual result was the rise of a free black and coloured population in the towns and in agricultural communities on the outskirts of the big estates.

We have already seen that the free coloured in the French islands had been granted full rights of freedom which were later withdrawn. The effects of this were a smouldering resentment which eventually caught fire. It took a revolution to restore these coloured people to their position as fully free.

Land-owning by free coloureds was less encouraged by the assemblies of the English islands. By 1762 the free black and coloured people of Jamaica owned between them property to the value of £250,000 but only four of them were plantation owners. Much of this property had come to them as bequests and allowances from their white relatives. The assembly in 1761 limited the value of any bequest from a white to a coloured person to £1,400, and forbade free coloured people to purchase land exceeding that value. The rural free black and coloured people were thus limited to the growing of provisions or to small enterprises in crops for export. Many preferred employment in the towns, chiefly as assistants to white craftsmen who lacked the money to buy slave labour.

As they were barred from easy entrance into large-scale agriculture, those who had money sought other ways of using it. Some bought houses to be run as inns or lodging-places; others bought slaves and lived on the proceeds of hiring them out; others bought the tools of trades they had learnt and set up as independent craftsmen, and others bought goods from visiting sea-captains, or imported them from Britain and opened merchant establishments. It was in this last enterprise that the free black and coloured people found their greatest financial success. Despite the laws and the social attitudes which obstructed them, they had managed as a class by the end of the eighteenth century to improve their wealth and economic importance considerably. Moreover, during the years of war between 1790 and 1815, higher prices for goods in the markets and increased local trading advanced their prosperity. The money saved during the war years enabled them to buy land during the post-war depression when many of the large estates were in difficulty and their owners willing to sell them at low prices. By the time of emancipation, therefore, there were considerable land-owners among the free coloured.

GROWTH OF POPULATION

Before emancipation there was also some change in the planters' attitude to their slaves. As long as the planter had found it cheaper to buy slaves than to breed them, they had been treated as animal stock, though it was always wise to keep them healthy because they represented a large capital investment. After the ending of the slave trade, however, it had become necessary for the planters to encourage their slaves to have children in order to ensure the future labour supply. Mothers of large families were rewarded by promotion to lighter work, and the general treatment meted out to the slaves tended to improve. It is noteworthy that on the Codrington Estates, in the middle of the eighteenth century, a deliberate experiment in slave-breeding was conducted as a possible economy in ensuring healthy workers; the island of Barbuda was used for the purpose.

It is impossible to give reliable figures of the growth of West Indan population before the present century, and before emancipation the only figures available were rough estimates made by the local clergy or magistrates. Still, there are certain facts from which we can guess the general trends. Until 1808 the main source of increased population was the importation of slaves. Among the creoles, or West Indian born, whether free or slave, only the free black and coloured population showed any steady increase. We have no records of births and deaths or of immigration or emigration, and these are the figures we need to calculate changes in population. But we do know something of the conditions which would have hampered population growth by natural increase in the West Indies. This is only achieved when there are more births than deaths occuring in a community, and this was not the case in the eighteenth century.

Before medical science had developed far and before necessary standards of public and private hygiene were understood, the death-rate was appallingly high everywhere. There is always too a high death-rate amongst infants in a poor community; this is only now being overcome in the West Indies. Moreover, there were the special hazards of living in a tropical climate. Malaria and yellow fever were prevalent and their cause was unknown; swamps and dank forests in many territories added to the ill health of those living there. The natural increase of slave population was also handicapped by the un-happy insecurity of slave society and by the conditions of estate life. Expectant mothers were not always treated favourably or required to do lighter labour. Even more important was the fact that, until the planters became increasingly concerned about the breeding of slaves, the slaves imported always consisted of more men than women.

Generalisation about the growth of the white population is more difficult. It is clear that immigration was very important. The first wave of white immigrants went, in the first half of the seventeenth century, to Barbados. From there, the Leeward Islands, the American mainland, and nearly every colony in the British West Indies received immigrants. The second wave of settlers went, in the second half of the seventeenth century, to Jamaica. There was an important difference between these large immigrations to Barbados and Jamaica, which included whole families, and the smaller migrations to the other colonies. In these two islands the presence of relatively large numbers of women allowed families to increase naturally, whereas in the Leeward Islands, where white women were fewer, natural increase of white families was handicapped. It was in the Leewards, therefore, that any emigration would be most likely to affect the total number of whites noticeably. The growth of absenteeism, for instance, affected the size of the white populations in the Leewards far more than in Barbados and Jamaica.

In general, for the whole population, because of large slave imports, the long-term trend was one of a steady population growth. But, because the whites were far outnumbered by the black and coloured populations and because the white rate of natural increase tended to be lower, they became an ever-diminishing percentage of the total British West Indian population.

RECOGNITION OF THE FREE COLOURED

The whites of the British West Indian colonies had not forgotten the combination of the slaves and free coloured people which had upset the old regime in Haiti. It seemed, therefore, to certain of the whites that it might be good policy to win the alliance of at least some of the free black and coloured people in case the restlesness of the slaves, excited by rumours of emancipation, should break out into more open revolt.

There were distinctions of colour among the general class of free black and coloured people ranging from the Mustifino, who was 'fifteen-sixteenths white', through the Mustee, Quadroon and Mulatto to the Sambo, who was only 'one-fourth white'. These distinctions led to a general striving after 'whiteness' for social, political and economic reasons and tended to prevent the free coloured from combining amongst themselves. But their increase in prosperity and the fact that some of the whites were willing to conciliate them, led to a gradual withdrawal of the laws against them. The move started in Grenada in 1823 and, in 1828, by order of the British Government, disabilities were removed from the free coloured in the Crown colonies.

In Jamaica they took a hand in their own release from subjection by starting their newspaper, *The Watchman* in 1829, with Edward Jordon as proprietor. As we have already seen, Jordon was brought to trial later for remarks in the paper at the time of the Christmas rebellion in 1831. He had already shown his sympathies in the previous year in replying to a white correspondent in another newspaper who had said 'the whites should place the browns gradually on a footing with ourselves, to create a defensive alliance which may prove a security to us in the hour of need'. Jordon replied that this was too late because the browns and blacks were no longer divided; the 'divide and rule' policy of the whites had already brought them together.

In 1830, all legal discrimination on grounds of colour was abolished in Jamaica, and in Barbados, Dominica and Tobago in the following year. Elsewhere there was only a repeal of parts of the restrictive laws at first, but, during the eighteen-thirties, the free black and coloured populations throughout the British West Indies won their legal equality with the whites. This victory was due to circumstances as well as to the efforts of the free coloureds to rid themselves of the restrictions put on them by the eighteenth-century plantocracy; the fact that the whites were now afraid of the coloureds inciting the slaves to revolt changed their attitude. Since their own members were becoming fewer in proportion to the rest of the population, some of them could now envisage the point when coloureds might become public officials and even legislators.

The long post-war depression in the West Indies was aggravated for the planters in the early eighteen-thirties by the fear that emancipation was coming. Many owners preferred to give up at this point. Property was going cheap, but not everybody could afford to buy. The people who were most likely to have the money were those who received fixed salaries or allowances, and those who had saved in the previous days of high wages and commercial prosperity. This was once again the coloured group and they considerably added to their landholding in the years immediately before emancipation.

The progress of the free coloured in agriculture was described by a Presbyterian visitor to the West Indies in 1830. He reported that 'the coloured inhabitants, although borne down and disdained, are by no means so poor, helpless, and uninfluential as is generally supposed. In Jamaica alone they are in possession of wealth which on a moderate computation has been estimated at not less than three million sterling. All the pimento plantations, with the exception of one only, are in their hands, and they are the owners of several coffee estates, besides having the property of numerous houses in the various towns of the island.' The price for sugar was unattractive and, in any case, they often preferred to produce other crops requiring less capital and labour. In the eighteen-thirties the prices of slaves were low, but that was because nobody wanted to buy slaves when it was becoming clear that they might soon be given their freedom.

SLAVE PROPERTY

The slaves, too, had their personal possessions. The slave's property, however, was nearly always of small value, and since he might suddenly be sold or transferred to another property, or even to another colony, he preferred to hold cash, which he could easily take with him, rather than goods. The amount of personal property which a slave might acquire depended on the administration of the estate to which he belonged, as well as on his own industry and desire to accumulate wealth. On estates where slaves were allowed sufficient

SLAVE PROPERTY

garden-land for their own use, and time to work it, they could produce profitable surpluses of food crops to sell in the local markets.
Some slaves with their owner's agreement even reared poultry and
animals of their own.

It is understandable that masters should encourage slaves to grow
foodstuffs in their spare time. Such produce could reduce the money
that the master had to spend on food for his slaves. It was also no
doubt regarded as a way of keeping them occupied and more con-
tented in any period when estate labour did not demand their full
attention. Letting the slave have a little land to work was much safer
for the planter than letting him idle and gossip over the hardness of
his life.

The motives which particularly led slaves to try to acquire money
were: the possibility, though a very faint one after 1807, of purchasing
their freedom; the obvious advantage of being able to buy small
items for themselves in the market, such as finery for Christmas
time; the desire of some of them to contribute to missionary church
funds; and possibly the wish to leave something for their children.

The town slave performed domestic duties or was hired out by his
master for occasional work. In the latter case the master often allowed
him a percentage of his earnings for his keep. This type of employment usually brought certain special liberties. The slave was often responsible for finding his own food and lodgings, and sometimes he
even sought his own employment, subject to his master's approval.
In such cases, the chances of unobserved accumulation of property
were greater; the town slave was readier to hold on to goods than
was the estate slave. The possibility that he might be sold was hardly
less, but as a town slave he was more likely to be sold to another
master in the town than to an estate owner. After 1807, however,
slave-owners became reluctant to sell their slaves even if they did not
have enough work to keep them all employed. It was then much
more profitable to hire out the slaves to those who needed additional
labour. Slaves thus hired out were known as jobbing slaves and their
owners demanded high daily rates for their services.

LIMITED CHANGES OF OCCUPATION

Neither in town nor country was it easy for the individual to change
the nature of his occupation. The whites in a slave society would
perform none of the tasks performed by slaves. The free black and

165

coloured people were no less opposed to working beside slaves and in any case, the laws of the island assemblies imposed restrictions on their employment. These conditions were of great importance. As the number of free black and coloured people increased so that it became difficult for many of them to find profitable employment in the limited spheres open to them, they invaded those occupations in the public service, in the professions, in commerce and in agriculture which had originally been the exclusive preserve of the whites. This was made easier by the declining numbers of the white population, which meant that there were more 'white jobs' than there were whites to fill them.

But one great difficulty was that in addition to restrictions in occupations open to different classes, there were conditions which prevented the easy movement of labour from one place to another in search of employment. As far as the free black and coloured people were concerned, unless they carried indisputable certificates of their freedom, they were likely to be arrested as runaway slaves. After the abolition of the slave trade and as slaves became scarcer, this danger to the free people was increased. Between 1792 and 1814 nearly every colonial legislature passed laws imposing heavy fines or charges on future manumissions of slaves, and ordering the free black and coloured people to carry proof of their freedom. In 1815 the British Slave Register Act 'to prevent unlawful importation of slaves, and the holding of Free Persons in Slavery, in the British Colonies' was partly intended to protect the freedom of coloured people.

There was nevertheless a certain limited shift between town and country occupations. The increase in the number of jobbing slaves for hire has already been remarked upon. The towns were also becoming centres of skilled trades and crafts. At first the planters had maintained most of the skilled labour they needed on their estates. They had their own millwrights, coopers, coppersmiths, blacksmiths, carpenters, masons, wheelwrights, and so on; but, as it became increasingly expensive to maintain a large labour force, it was cheaper for them to keep the barest minimum of skilled workers on the estate, and instead to employ outsiders when necessary. The practice of skills was therefore slowly, and of course only partly, transferred to the towns.

It was the smaller planters who contributed most to the increase of commercial interests in the towns. The big planters generally continued to send their estate produce direct to their agents in Britain, but, wherever small planters were numerous, the commercial life grew despite the lack of business from big planters. Not only did it grow in volume, but, because the small planters produced a variety of crops, it extended the experience of the local merchants and factors from the marketing of sugar to dealings in a variety of produce. The smallholders too were interested in the labour to be hired in towns. They were relatively poor men who had never been able to afford the full-time services of a large number of skilled workers. It suited them particularly to hire such workers when their services were needed.

On the other hand there was a certain movement away from the towns as well. They were always the professional centres where most lawyers, doctors, clergy and schoolteachers could be found. This changed little in the case of the lawyers, but the requirement for planters to provide medical attention for their slaves and the increasing attention to religious education and missionary work meant that some of the others tended to move nearer the estates, Moreover, with the growth of absenteeism and the loss of prosperity, social life in the towns was not as attractive as it had been in the heyday of the plantocracy.

There were changes, but their effect must not be exaggerated. Overwhelmingly the old order continued on the estates. In some areas there was plentiful labour for the work that needed doing; in others labour was very scarce. This was true in individual colonies. Still more was it true over the British West Indies as a whole. After emancipation, ex-slaves would be free to dispose of their labour as they pleased and West Indian planters and governments alike were anxious lest the estates were in consequence left without enough workers to cultivate and harvest the crops.

FURTHER READING

Sources of West Indian History, People of the Caribbean, pp. 16–22, Government and Politics, pp. 107–9.
Roberts, *Six Great Jamaicans*, Edward Jordon.

QUESTIONS TO CONSIDER

1. What were the main distinctions between the social groups in the West Indies just before emancipation?
2. In what ways had the free coloured improved their position in the same period?

3. What importance in West Indian history do you give to the free coloured as a group?

4. What changes in the position of slaves described in this chapter do you consider would prepare them for a different life when they were emancipated?

PART III

ESTABLISHING FREEDOM

PART III

ESTABLISHING FREEDOM

CHAPTER FIFTEEN

The Organisation of Freedom

THE PEOPLE CONCERNED

At midnight on 31 July, 1834, nearly three-quarters of a million men, women and children in the British West Indies ceased to be slaves. The Act of Emancipation passed by the British Government made them apprentices to their old masters, and only able to earn wages or choose their own occupations after they had given about forty hours of unpaid labour each week. This was a very limited freedom which postponed the answer to the vital question whether the ex-slaves would continue to work for their masters once they had full choice in the matter. Nonetheless, there were plenty of gloomy forebodings about the effects of even this limited freedom. It was said that the newly emancipated population might riot as the Jamaican slaves had done in 1831. More troublesome in the long run was the fear that they might refuse to work.

In the event, it was reported with pride by many observers that 1 August, a Friday, saw large congregations joining in services of thanksgiving in chapels and churches. The weekend passed quietly, and the ex-slaves returned to work as apprentices on the following Monday. In Antigua, where immediate freedom was granted to the slaves, two-thirds of them returned to the estates as free labourers within two months of their emancipation, and the actual production of sugar increased despite the reduced number of workers. Here, however, there was not much free land for the ex-slaves to procure for themselves, so they had little alternative to working for their living on the estates; the results of freedom in Antigua could hardly be taken as a guide to what might happen elsewhere.

The British and West Indian governments were anxious to maintain production of sugar on the estates in the West Indies, but, since they had different points of view in the matter, they went about it in different ways. The Act of Emancipation committed the Imperial Government to provide and pay for additional magistrates whose main duty was to deal with complaints from both masters and apprentices on the estates. Furthermore, the Imperial Government provided funds to promote 'the religious and moral education of the Negro population to be emancipated'. Both these measures were intended to keep the people where they were, and satisfied with their position.

In fact, once the British Government had passed the Act and organised the payment of £20,000,000 in compensation to slave-owners, they left the details of emancipation to the local government in each colony. Laws passed after emancipation therefore differed in the West Indian territories, but they were all calculated to discourage any movement of workers away from the estates. There were harsh measures against vagrancy, taxes to discourage small scale landholding, and high rates for licences to traders and dealers; these attacked the main alternatives to work on the estates. There were also efforts to introduce contracts which would hold the labourer on the estates for long periods.

West Indian laws which promised to be unduly oppressive for the mass of the people could be, and often were, disallowed by the British Government; they consistently rejected the suggestions for contracts to bind workers to particular estates, for instance. The Colonial Office was manned by a group of civil servants who were anxious that the ex-slaves should in fact gain benefits from their freedom; these officials constantly urged the West Indian Governments to pay attention to their needs, such as education, hospitals and protection against lawlessness and hazards like fire. On the slave estate, only the master had been responsible for the condition of his slave and it had paid him not to let this fall below a reasonable working standard. These responsibilities no longer held in the new order, and the planters could decline to accept them if they wished. If the ex-slaves were to have any social services at all, what had been provided before at the master's expense should now be provided publicly at the government's expense. Governors and Colonial Office officials tried to persuade the assemblies to provide such services.

The most notable official reformer was James Stephen, son of the James Stephen senior who had been active in the Society for the Abolition of Slavery. He was for many years the legal adviser to the Colonial Office, and gave his opinion on the laws sent in by the colonial assemblies for confirmation. The Bill for the Emancipation of Slaves was drafted by him, so that he was already intimately concerned with the progress of emancipation when in 1835 he became the chief civil servant at the Colonial Office. He held this position for eleven years, while the problems of the change were being faced. As a reformer, Stephen wanted the ex-slaves to improve themselves in their new status, and he felt a constant need to protect them against hard laws made by men who were their rulers and who also wanted to remain their employers. He expressed this point of view when commenting on one law which he thought should be disallowed. 'The desire to extinguish the freedom of those on whose labour the profit of Capital depends,' he wrote, 'is a passion always at work, and almost always working by subtleties, and petty encroachments like those with which this Law seems to me to abound.' Such a sympathetic attitude could have greatly benefited the West Indian population at large, but it existed on the other side of the Atlantic and could only reach the West Indies through the activities of the governors here. They in their turn, even in the Crown colonies, had to face the comment and criticsm of their legislatures, which were often quite enough to kill any suggestions unwelcome to the sugar interest.

The missionary bodies and, to a lesser extent, the clergy of the Anglican and Catholic Churches were also active reformers. These were people on the spot, who can usually be more effective than a distant authority. Some denominations challenged the planting interest more than others. The most uncompromising were the Baptists, who worked mainly in Jamaica. They adopted wholeheartedly the cause of the betterment of the Negro, and some Baptist missionaries very soon came to think that such betterment could come only by escape from the estate labour which was so similar to slavery. The Methodist Missionary Society made it a policy not to interfere in public affairs, but in their day-to-day work, although they did not directly challenge the authorities, their missionaries could not avoid giving practical advice which might have the same effect. The Moravians, where they gained a foothold, mainly in Antigua and Jamaica, frequently worked on an estate with a sympathetic owner who allowed them to teach and preach amongst his hired labourers.

The Catholic Church was active in those islands which had previously been French or Spanish, St. Lucia, Grenada and Trinidad. Like the other religious bodies, the Catholic Church embarked upon a more systematic policy of conversion after emancipation, but they had less opportunity for extensive work in education, for instance, because the British Government was reluctant to give funds to Catholics for the purpose. In Catholic islands, the Established Anglican

Church was at first financed with public money far more generously than the church of the majority of the people.

It is harder to generalise about the role of the Anglican clergy immediately after emancipation. Many of them were land-owners themselves and so shared the interests and attitudes of other planters, even to the extent of opposing the emancipation of slaves in several cases. On the other hand, individual clergy, notably Dr. Rawle in Barbados, worked untiringly for the betterment and education of the ex-slaves in the island.

These were the groups which, each in its way, had to adapt themselves to whatever problems were created by the abolition of slavery. In addition, the paid Stipendiary or Special Magistrates, provided for in the Act of Emancipation, were a group deliberately formed by the Imperial Government to be 'the architects of freedom'. While preserving 'the public tranquility', they were to assist in the transformation of masters and slaves into employers and hired labourers. How far were they able to effect such a social revolution?

THE ARCHITECTS OF FREEDOM

The abolition of slavery meant the abolition of slave laws and of internal estate discipline. It was the effect of this that was so much feared at first; it seemed to the planters and to some of the English civil servants that outbreaks of disorder, crime and idleness were bound to follow. The Stipendiary Magistrates were therefore to establish themselves first as guardians of public order, but they were to ensure also that the apprentices in fact obtained their legal rights.

The success of this naturally depended on who the Special Magistrates were to be and how far they would be accepted by both the planters and the ex-slaves in the colonies. The permanent unpaid magistrates, or Justices of the Peace, represented the planter interests and were not by their experience likely to give a Negro estate labourer a sympathetic hearing in court. Much of the appointment of the Special Magistrates was done in England, from the large group of retired army and naval officers there. Comparatively few Special Magistrates were appointed on the spot, although in islands, such as Trinidad and St. Lucia, where a French *patois* was spoken, more were chosen by the governors in the territories. Perhaps the most notable West Indian appointed was the Jamaican, Richard Hill, who, despite attractive offers of promotion elsewhere, remained head of the Special Magistrates in Jamaica until his death in 1872. Hill had been associated with Jordon's movement to abolish the disabilities against coloured Jamaicans and so was clearly no ally of the white planters.

The Special Magistrates were to be 'men uninfluenced by the local assemblies, free from local passions', as the Secretary of State put it. The policy of having disinterested appointments, however, broke down in the face of the numbers required. The British Government had underestimated the situation in every possible way. They were slow to make the first appointments, and governors of some islands had to put in stopgaps in the crucial first months of apprenticeship. The following figures show what a poor beginning was made.

SPECIAL MAGISTRATES

	Number originally allotted.	Present on August 1, 1834.	Finally allotted.
Jamaica	33	28	63
British Guiana . . .	13	5	15
Trinidad	6	2	11
Bahamas	3	0	6
Barbados . . .	6	6	8
St. Kitts and Anguilla . .	4	2	5
Tobago	2	0	4
Grenada and Cariacou . .	3	1	5
St. Vincent and the Grenadines .	3	3	3
Nevis	1	0	2
Montserrat	1	0	2
Dominica	3	1	5
Virgin Islands	1	0	1
British Honduras . . .	1	1	2
	80	49	132

The Special Magistrates received, from governors on the one hand, the highest praise for their work, and, on the other, much criticism from some of the planters. There is little doubt that the majority applied themselves to their multiple task with diligence, phenomenal physical energy and a high degree of impartiality. It is no exaggeration to say that they often did so at the risk of their lives. They were never numerous enough, and the financial reward was miserably inadequate. They were, however, a new group in the West Indies, and their ideas on the organisation of the people were not influenced by recollections of slavery.

The definition of their task was based on the idea that estate labour would remain the principal form of employment. The Magistrates were literally on call to any estate manager or worker who appealed to them. They were constantly in the saddle, summoned to scattered estates. A Magistrate could be called from the peace of his home for anything from a 'chopping' case to an allegation that a man was late for his work or had an insolent manner. Summary justice was applied in such cases, and there is little doubt that the use of the whip continued during apprenticeship much as it had done under slavery. The apprentices, for their part, increasingly called in the Magistrates to settle questions of wages for additional labour and to listen to charges of victimisation. The exact duties of the Special Magistrates, beyond those outlined by the Act of Emancipation itself, were defined by different West Indian Governments. Many acts concerning discipline and punishment were disallowed by the British Government. Laws forbidding the use of the whip on women and the undue use of the treadmill, which were introduced during this period, indicate the nature of the rough justice that was used. Whipping was abolished as a punishment by the Magistrates in most places only when full freedom was granted.

The Special Magistrates might also have been the 'architects of freedom', as the Colonial Office hoped; but, for two reasons, only the exceptional were. The first thing that stood in their way was the fact that apprenticeship was one system and freedom another. There was no gradual relaxation of the hard rules of apprenticeship to prepare the ex-slaves for their coming freedom. This meant that, throughout the earlier period, the Special Magistrates had to operate a system of rough justice that had really been worked out for emergencies in the months immediately after emancipation, when trouble was expected. The fact that trouble did not come did not lead either the British or the West Indian Governments to suggest a less rigid system. It is little wonder that apprenticeship was unpopular and the Special Magistrates in an awkward position. Overburdened with the demands of petty estate discipline, they had little time to work out schemes for social improvement.

In any case, the second difficulty would have been insuperable. As was the custom of the time, the plan was done on the cheap. For £400 a year a man was asked to settle in a region where the climate and tropical diseases had already killed many missionaries living a similar way of life here. The fact that the military establishment was now expected to be renewed every two years for just this reason should also have been a warning to the authorities. Furthermore, no special allowance was made for the stable of horses which were essential for the Magistrate's work, and for lodgings when he was caught far from home at nightfall. Since the system was regarded as temporary, there was no provision for leave or for pensions. It was almost as if the authorities thought that survival was so uncertain that they need not provide for the future. The death-rate and retirement on account of illness were both very high indeed.

These conditions hardly helped the Special Magistrates to do what the British Government hoped of them, and it is quite remarkable that they achieved as much as they did. Their presence did prevent punishment continuing as the private concern of plantations, as it had been under slavery. The outsider had to be called in instead. It might be thought that, for the unfortunate apprentices, lashes received at the order of the Special Magistrate were no more welcome than the lashes of the slave overseer. There is no doubt that there was variety in the treatment of apprentices in the different circuits of Special Magistrates, as there had been between the plantations during slavery. Individuals still decided what happened; but a paid Special Magistrate who had to report his activities could be dismissed for his shortcomings, and some of them were.

The fact that the apprentices recognised the system as an improvement was shown by their own increasing use of Magistrates as they saw the benefit of submitting their own difficulties over wages, ejections and other cases of victimisation to an impartial authority. The most attractive course for the apprentice was obviously that of manumission, the buying of freedom. Each application had to be assessed by a panel, which varied from territory to territory but which usually included a Special Magistrate. The number of apprentices who applied to the panels to ascertain the price of their freedom was certainly far higher than the number who in fact bought it.

One of the Magistrates' most useful activities, but one which must have been a great trial to them at the time, was a report on the general state of their area which they were required to submit to the governor, in some territories as often as once a month. These documents, frequently written at night after weary hours of rough riding, gave a regular account of the practical working of the new system, of the estate owners' grim struggle to retain their workers, of vindictiveness amongst planters who ejected workers from their homes on estates in some cases, and generosity in others. We also learn from the reports of the reluctance of some apprentices to work on the estates, the beginnings of wandering, the attractions of independence from hired labour, the problems of the sick, the very old and the very young, who were no longer necessarily provided for on the estates. These reports were of enormous value to the Colonial Office and to governors who wanted an overall picture of the detailed working of apprenticeship. In most cases they show a ready sympathy for the difficulties of the apprentices and make urgent suggestions for their education, medical care and fair treatment generally. It must have been some compensation for the Special Magistrates to realise how much they were quoted by the authorities. The debates which led to the total abolition of the apprenticeship system, two years before it had been intended for the field labourers, were frequently marked by quotations from Special Magistrates' reports.

Governor Sligo of Jamaica was perhaps their greatest supporter. His testimonial to them is well known. 'What was in the physical power of man to do, they did,' he wrote, 'and it is a matter of the greatest wonder that so much zeal, so much energy and such an in-defatigable spirit of humanity as pervaded the vast majority of that body, should have been displayed by them. In such a climate as Jamaica . . . these gentlemen, with a courage and perseverance un-equalled by any on record, rode about the island defying the sun and the rain and disease. The mortality among them was in consequence quite lamentable but the slightest indifference or unwillingness to continue their exertions has never been in a single instance exhibited.' Sligo no doubt exaggerated and oversimplified. But it seems fair to say that these mostly elderly, half-pay army officers, retired pro-fessional people, with some West Indians among them, did serve, especially in Jamaica, in checking any serious disorder and perhaps some of the bitterness between the different groups of West Indian society after emancipation. What they were unable to do was to se-cure much improvement for the people's conditions of living or to keep them attracted to estate labour.

THE NEGRO EDUCATION GRANT

The British Government may not have been clear on the role to be played by the Special Magistrates as reformers. They were, however, entirely clear that education should be supported to improve and convert the ex-slaves. In 1833 the British Government made a grant of £30,000 for English elementary education; two years later, they paid the same sum for the education of ex-slaves in the colonies. It was not an ambitious scheme so much as a way of teaching people the

Christian religion so that they should wish to accept the position in life in which they found themselves. This was the intention; it did not always have that effect.

The British Government had to find an agency to start the education. They chose first to use the missionaries who had already done what they could for education under slavery. The money was allotted to the religious bodies for the provision of new schools. This led to a vast increase of schools immediately after emancipation, and they were at first well supported by the apprentices, who thought that if their children could read they would be able to rise in life beyond the hated position of field labourers.

Like so many matters after emancipation, this was an apparent success until the difficulties appeared. The missionaries found the running expenses of their schools a great burden and had to check their expansion. The whole arrangement was uneven in its results. Obviously where the missionaries liked to go, there were most schools. While the families were on the estates it was easier to provide a school which a reasonable number of children could reach, but any movement away from the estates made this almost impossible. Jamaica, which had the biggest variety of missionary societies, did well in the beginning. In the islands where the Catholic Church was strongest, there was a very poor start because the British Government was prejudiced against Catholics, and the Catholics were not happy to take government money. In Trinidad, St. Lucia and Grenada, therefore, little was done immediately about school education.

In areas where the Established Church prevailed, money from Church funds could be added to the Negro Education Grant to start schools in connection with the vestries. Barbados was in a particularly good position to develop a school system in this way, but in practice, although there were fewer denominations to split the resources for education, daunting difficulties were encountered there as elsewhere. Everywhere there was an acute shortage of teachers, and those who could be found had very little idea of how to give any effective schooling.

A praiseworthy but wholly inadequate attempt to train West Indian teachers was made by the Mico Trustees. They held the funds left by Lady Mico, who had, in 1670, bequeathed her estate of £1,000 to her nephew, Samuel, on condition that he married one of his six cousins. If he declined, as he did, the money was to go to the ransom of any poor Christian seamen captured by the Barbary pirates of

North Africa. But the Barbary pirates had by then been brought under control, so that Lady Mico's second provision had proved fruitless too. The money was invested and left to accumulate; by the time of emancipation the sum had grown to £120,000. The abolitionist Thomas Fowell Buxton applied for it to be used for the education of ex-slaves on the grounds that this was close to the intention of Lady Mico; his application was allowed by the Court of Chancery, which deals with such matters in England.

This timely grant of money was used for the two most crying needs for education in the West Indies. Three Mico Training colleges were started in 1835 and 1836 in Jamaica, Trinidad and Demerara, to train teachers for the new schools of all denominations. Secondly, Christian schools, not however attached to any particular denomination, were set up to supplement the Anglican and missionary schools. The Mico Schools were the only schools provided in Catholic St. Lucia and they accounted for the majority in Trinidad too.

Altogether this was a vigorous start on a great plan for education and conversion. There is no doubt that all concerned were ambitious for a full and complete scheme of education for the whole population. As one missionary wrote, he looked to the day when 'the sable emancipated infants we are now receiving into our schools shall respectably and successfully occupy their stations in the pulpit, on the bench and at the bar'. Plans included secondary schools and colleges; there was no lack of ambition. It is easy now to see how far well-intentioned missionaries and reformers were short of the mark, but they did get schools started immediately after emancipation in such a way that they have existed, despite great setbacks to education, ever since. Above all, if conversion can be assessed by church membership, religious education in all branches was a great success, for all denominations claimed much multiplication in the numbers of their congregations. The problem after this was to find an equally compelling argument for general education, to follow the religious one. Other events and circumstances made it difficult.

FURTHER READING

Sources of West Indian History, Slavery and its Abolition, pp. 191–2, Emancipation and Apprenticeship, pp. 193–7, 202–3, 206–8, Social Conditions since Emancipation, pp. 216–22.

Black, *History of Jamaica*, Chapter XIV, The End of Slavery, pp. 159–67.

Hoyos, *Our Common Heritage*, Richard Rawle.
Ottley, *History of Tobago*, Chapter XVI.

QUESTIONS TO CONSIDER

1. Which of the measures taken by the British Government to assist the ex-slaves would you consider to be the most helpful to them?

2. What part do you think that the Special Magistrates played in preparing the apprentices for full freedom?

3. What problems do you anticipate for the development of education after the end of the Negro Education Grant in 1845?

4. Which of the groups mentioned in this chapter do you think most deserves the title 'architects of freedom'?

CHAPTER SIXTEEN

The Problem of Labour

APPRENTICED LABOUR

Apprenticeship served to postpone the final answer to the question which worried the planters most. Would the ex-slaves continue to work for them when they had a choice in the matter? As we have seen, the planters had been in difficulties before the emancipation of their slaves, and these difficulties remained with them afterwards. Apart from the natural hazards of poor crops, hurricanes and floods, many estates were encumbered by debt and regular commitments from earlier and more prosperous days. Some planters sold their estates, or surrendered them to their creditors, and abandoned both sugar and the West Indies. Others found that, with the compensation money from the British Government, they could clear their standing debts and start again unencumbered.

The compensation payments in each territory were different. This was because they were based on the average prices offered for slaves in each territory during the eight years before emancipation. Thus, in Trinidad and British Guiana, the compensation payments were generally higher than they were, for instance, in Barbados, or even in Jamaica. This agrees with what we already know of these territories. Slaves were scarcer and dearer in newly acquired and newly developing territories than in longer settled and more developed ones. In these newer territories the labour even of the old and infirm was valuable, as the table for the rates of compensation shows.

There were many difficulties in the scheme of apprenticeship. Its greatest weakness was simply that it was neither one thing nor the other, neither full slavery nor full freedom. During the hours of enforced labour the planters, though controlled by the activities of the Stipendiary Magistrates, were still unquestionably in the dominant position. But in the hours when the apprentice was entitled to demand a wage for his labour, it was he who held the stronger bargaining position, especially in crop-season when his additional labour was absolutely necessary to the planter. It was then that he could refuse

SLAVE POPULATION AND COMPENSATION PAID

Colony	Field Slaves	Average Compensation £ stg.	Non-field Slaves	Average Compensation £ stg.	Children under 6 years	Average Compensation £ stg.	Aged and Infirm	Average Compensation £ stg.	Total Slaves
ANTIGUA	20,380	18	2,985	15	4,325	2	1,445	0	29,135
BARBADOS	52,200	25	14,445	23	14,730	4	1,780	2	83,155
BRITISH GUIANA	63,280	61	6,300	54	9,900	19	3,350	11	82,830
DOMINICA	10,465	23	1,200	21	2,115	5	400	2	14,180
GRENADA	16,940	30	2,070	27	3,320	10	1,310	9	23,640
JAMAICA	218,455	23	36,835	24	39,015	6	16,765	5	311,070
MONTSERRAT	4,510	21	515	10	1,145	3	230	0	6,400
NEVIS	5,300	21	1,925	19	1,260	4	330	0	8,815
ST. KITTS	12,600	20	3,065	20	3,200	6	915	2	19,780
ST. LUCIA	8,725	31	1,600	30	1,960	8	1,000	8	13,285
ST. VINCENT	15,310	31	2,800	30	2,965	11	1,190	3	22,265
TOBAGO	8,265	27	810	30	1,480	5	1,030	0	11,585
TRINIDAD	13,775	55	3,765	56	2,245	22	875	12	20,660
VIRGIN ISLANDS	3,415	16	900	14	730	3	70	0	5,115
TOTALS	453,620	31	79,215	29	88,390	9	30,690	4	651,915

to work unless he was given the wage he asked for. The extent to which the apprentices took advantage of this position is revealed by the fact that wages before full emancipation were often double what they came to be afterwards. It was difficult for masters and apprentices to adjust their attitudes and their behaviour to this new and delicate situation. Each side sought to test the strength of the other, and the innumerable instances of argument and dispute over wages and hours of work offered are catalogued in the reports of the Stipendiary Magistrates who had to settle them.

THE END OF APPRENTICESHIP

The calculation which had made the planters of Antigua decide against any period of apprenticeship came to impress other West Indian planters as they put the system into practice. The reason had not been entirely unselfish or humanitarian, as was revealed at a meeting of influential planters held in St. John's just before emancipation. They intended to frame a memorial to Parliament protesting against the abolition of slavery. To the amazement of many who were there, several prominent planters spoke in favour of freedom. 'Gentlemen,' one proclaimed, 'my previous sentiments on this subject are well known to you all: be not surprised to learn that they have undergone an entire change. I have not altered my views without mature deliberation. For several days past, I have been making calculations with regard to the probable results of emancipation, and I have ascertained beyond a doubt that I can cultivate my estate at least one-third cheaper by free labour, than by slave labour.' Another gentleman then said that he had long been opposed to slavery but had not dared to say so in public; and a third agreed. The planters in Antigua had made a decision which turned out to be a remarkably accurate calculation of the profits of dispensing with apprenticeship.

This was not too remarkable a change of opinion in a small island, well populated, and with little apparent opportunity for free people to make a living in any other way than by estate labour. The slave-owner had usually maintained more slaves than he could profitably use in the dull season. If he was sensible he had clothed, fed and housed them well enough to keep them fit for labour. He had been responsible for the maintenance of infants and old people whose labour was of little value to him. He had provided some medical attendance and, perhaps, some religious instruction. The employer of free labourers would be clear of all such expensive responsibilities. He would pay the lowest wage which would attract the number of labourers he required, in and out of crop, and the wage-earner him· self would be responsible for the physical and spiritual welfare of his family. In Antigua, as the knowledgeable planter had calculated, the necessary wage-rate would not be high and a great reduction of cost would be achieved.

Similar conclusions had been reached in other territories by 1838, when the non-field apprentices were due to receive full freedom. The island assemblies in turn decided to abolish the whole system. In the spring of 1838, Montserrat, Nevis, the Virgin Islands and St. Kitts, in that order, took the initiative; Barbados, St. Vincent, Grenada, Jamaica. Tobago, the Bahamas and British Guiana followed suit during the summer months. In the more densely populated islands, no party found any further use for the system of apprenticeship; in the more sparsely populated areas, it became impossible to maintain apprenticeship when the others gave it up.

The Imperial Government was also aware that the scheme was not succeeding as the transition period of training for freedom which they had envisaged. There might also be difficulties if the domestic apprentices became free and the land labourers were kept apprenticed. Also, the Anti-Slavery Society had returned to the methods and persuasions of pre-emancipation days, holding meetings and circulating pamphlets. 'The interest of the Negro,' declared the indefatigable reformer Lord Brougham, 'is to be looked at, and only the interest of the Negro.' The humanitarians were convinced that the ex-slave had not yet tasted the sweets of freedom and that it was now certainly time that he should.

The second momentous 1 August passed as peacefully as the earlier one had. Men became free of the legal restrictions of apprenticeship, and all labour henceforth was to be paid labour. 'The interest of the Negro' would now be shown wherever there was a chance for him to change his way of life from the old conditions of estate labour.

'ME NO CARE TO HIRE MESELF OUT AGAIN'

Freedom of choice had at last come; the abiding question of whether or not labourers would remain on the sugar estates was to be answered. The answer was largely decided by the alternatives available; but it was clear what most ex-slaves wanted to do, if they had any real choice. Where there was opportunity of a living off the estates, they departed in large numbers. Where they had little option, they continued as hired labourers for the planters.

Since these were agricultural territories, the decision mainly turned, as the planters knew it would, on the question of available land. As one Jamaican put it, 'if the lands in the interior get into the possession of the Negro, goodbye to lowland cultivation and to any cultivation'. If there was idle land or if estate owners were prepared to sell or rent land, it was eagerly sought after by the ex-slaves.

To get a picture of the different ways the ex-slaves used their freedom, it is necessary to consider the alternatives open to them. First, there was small-scale independent agriculture. In certain colonies, such as Trinidad, British Guiana and Jamaica, there was land lying idle. In Jamaica, most of this idle land belonged to estate-owners whose estates had failed. In every colony there was at least some idle land of this sort. However much planters as a group might say that they wanted to deprive ex-slaves of the opportunity to acquire land, there were always individual landowners who were ready to sell property. Some of them wished to sell entire estates, others wanted to dispose of a number of acres.

These idle estate lands were easily sold, to individuals who wanted to farm, to groups of people who intended to work the land together, to missionary bodies like the Baptists, Wesleyans and Moravians, who generally sub-divided it into small lots for re-sale to their members on reasonable terms; and to land speculators who were busy making profits by buying up properties, sub-dividing and re-selling. Land prices throughout the British Caribbean ranged from about £4 to £10 per acre, depending on the territory and the quality of the land. These prices were not beyond the pockets of those ex-slaves who had saved during slavery and who had been working for good hourly wages during the apprenticeship period.

Any ex-slave who acquired his own land would obviously use his family's help to cultivate it and to market the produce. An ex-slave who bought more acres than he and his family could work would probably employ a few labourers himself. The Jamaica planter quoted above had something to say about this too. 'Very many of the apprentices are purchasing their apprenticeship and buying 5, 10, 50 and even 100 acres,' he reported, 'I myself sold a Head Constable 100 acres of outlying land at £4 10s. and another 100 acres is now offered for by three or four people at £5 per acre. The man who can buy such a quantity looks forward to the cultivation of his property by the labour of others.'

In Trinidad and British Guiana, apart from land which was being sold by estate owners, there was also much idle land which belonged to the government. This was Crown land, and although it was not offered for sale in the same way as unproductive estate land, the existence of cultivable Crown land gave an opportunity to 'squatters', who moved in without permission and began to cultivate without buying or renting.

A description of conditions in Berbice in British Guiana gives a picture of the rapid changes which could occur in places where idle land was plentiful and cheap. It ran, 'the population of the district or county of Berbice is about twenty thousand persons, of whom fifteen thousand belonged to the class made free on the 1st of August, 1838. At this period, not one possessed an inch of land. About the middle of 1842, after a lapse of four years, twelve hundred and twenty-three families, comprising four thousand six hundred and forty-six individuals—that is to say, the greater part of the freed population—were proprietors in the different localities of seven thousand acres . . . which had cost them more than one hundred thousand dollars . . . and on which they had erected at their expense eleven hundred and eighty-four cottages. As for the land, it was in cultivation and abundantly produced plantain, maize, Indian corn, yam, fruits, and a quantity of other provisions, which secured the proprietors a perfect independence.'

The emancipation of slaves had other effects which offered other employment. Trade increased because the ex-slaves now had to buy their own food, clothing and essential equipment, and they were no longer satisfied with the bare necessities of life. Also they produced more for sale and export themselves, particularly of minor crops such as honey, beeswax, cassava, ginger and arrowroot. All this meant openings for retail traders, tally clerks, porters, boatmen, stevedores, carters, packers and so forth.

The small-scale retail traders, the 'hucksters' of Antigua and the 'higglers' of Jamaica, were the most rapidly expanding group. They required little ready cash. Goods, such as bags of flour or barrels of fish, could be bought on credit in small numbers from importing merchants at wholesale prices. Small profits from sales could be used to build up the business gradually. Another way of getting goods to sell at retail, which is equally common today, was for the retailer to attend a merchant's sale of surplus perishable stocks, buy up as much as he could afford and re-sell speedily.

Small-scale agriculture and retail trading were the most popular employments for those who left the estates. There were other losses to the estates too. During slavery the planters had used women and children as field-workers, and had been able to put even the aged and infirm to light labour. After emancipation, many women devoted their time to housekeeping and family raising. They would help their menfolk to cultivate their own land and to market the produce, but they might never give their labour to any outside employer.

Many ex-slaves had high ambitions for their children. Manual labour, the mark of servitude, was not to be for them. The demand was for education so that the children might learn to read and write and use the power of knowledge to raise themselves economically and socially. After emancipation, few children were allowed by their parents to give labour to outside employers, least of all to estate owners. Most parents were in fact disappointed in these ambitions, but the immediate result was that child labour on the estates became rare.

THE PLANTER'S DILEMMA

It is now clear that after emancipation, the British West Indian sugar territories tended to fall into one of three categories. Firstly, there were those in which idle cultivable land was scarce, labour was relatively cheap, and the production of sugar continued as before. Then there were those in which idle cultivable land was available to the ex-slaves, labour was relatively dear and production of sugar was maintained by importing large numbers of indentured workers. In most territories there were special circumstances to be taken into consideration which made the alternatives less simple.

The table on pages 190–91 shows the position in certain key periods beginning with the average output annually during the five years before the abolition of slavery. Between 1834 and 1842 there was the apprenticeship scheme, followed by a period of labour unrest during the adjustment to full freedom. A fall in the output of all the territories was to be expected during these years. After 1842, we can expect, firstly, a return to former output in those territories where local labour was sufficient; secondly, a rather slower return to former output where local labour was scarce and, thirdly, a decline where planters were either unable to solve their labour problem or were faced with other insurmountable difficulties. The territories have been listed in these categories. Antigua and St. Kitts, Barbados, Trinidad and British Guiana fall into either the first or second groups, so that the reasons for the state of sugar in these territories can be readily arrived at. For others there were special reasons for what happened.

In the Windward Islands in particular, planters found it difficult to improve cultivation in such mountainous and rainy areas; and there, estates had suffered great damage during the wars with the French. Labourers tended to migrate from these islands, particularly from Grenada, to Trinidad and British Guiana where wages were higher.

In the small and relatively crowded colonies, the employers were in a position to gain the upper hand. In 1842 in Barbados, for instance, the labourers were complaining that the work was being rationed out and there was not enough for everyone to do. In Trinidad, on the other hand, the labourers were said to control the price and to have 'the power of fixing the terms of all contracts of service and rates of wages'. In short, the position varied throughout the West Indies.

WAGES IN THE EIGHTEEN-FORTIES

ANTIGUA	Ninepence (with cottage, grounds and medical attendance).
MONTSERRAT	Fourpence (with cottage and grounds).
NEVIS	No money wage. Labourers got a small share of the estate produce.
ST. KITTS	One shilling.
BARBADOS	Ninepence (with cottage and grounds).
DOMINICA	Ninepence (with cottage and grounds).
GRENADA	Eightpence (with cottage and grounds).
ST. VINCENT	Eightpence (with cottage and very small grounds).
ST. LUCIA	One shilling and sixpence (with cottage and grounds).
TRINIDAD	Two shillings.
BRITISH GUIANA	Two shillings.
JAMAICA	One shilling and eightpence (with cottage and grounds).

Some planters were daunted by the labour problem and went out of business. Others decided that they would try methods that they had not bothered to introduce when they could depend on a slave labour supply for manual work. The plough and the harrow were the two most important labour-saving devices introduced after emancipation. They were used first in Trinidad, Jamaica and British Guiana. In Barbados and the Leeward Islands, where labour was plentiful, planters were much slower to introduce these agricultural implements. There was also a growing interest in such subjects as soil chemistry and the use of fertilisers. There were numerous discussions of the best varieties of cane, the best methods of planting and manuring and the advantages of ratooning the canes. Chemists

¼ MN UNITS	1829-34			1836-38			1839-41			1842-44			1845-47		
Antigua [1]															
St. Kitts [1]															
Barbados [1]															
British Guiana [2]															
Trinidad [2]															
Jamaica [3]															
Nevis [3]															

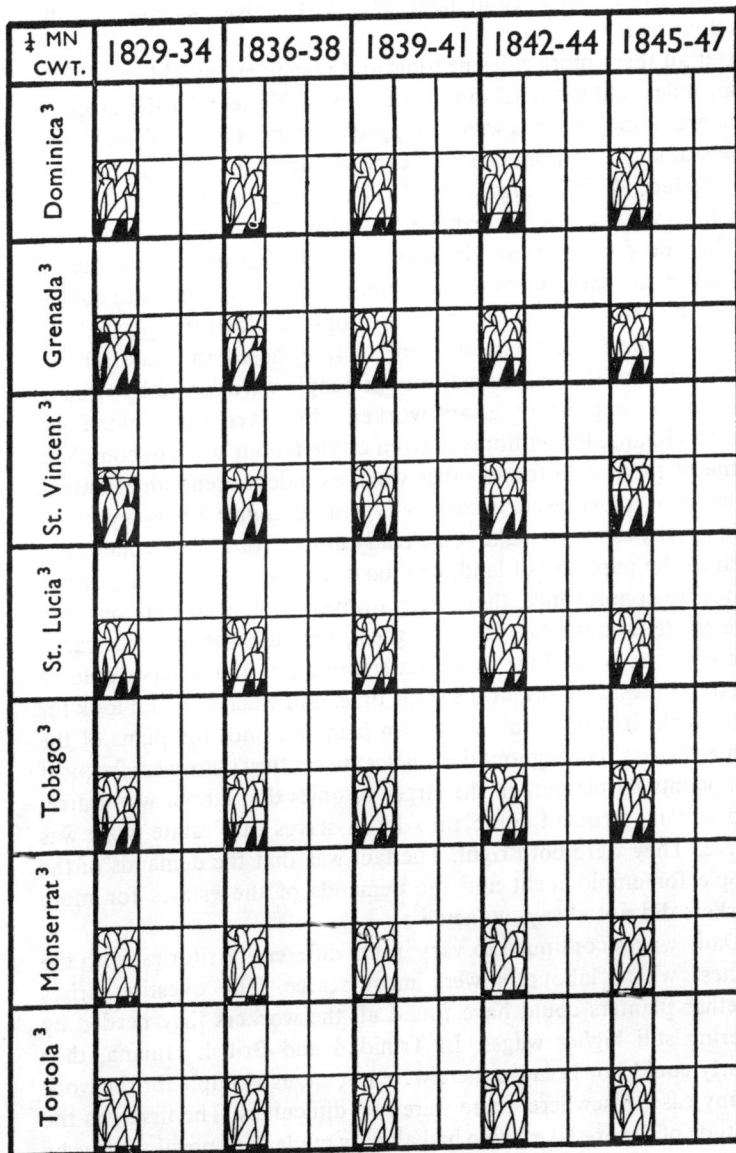

Fig. 10. Average Annual Sugar Output

Lack of land and cheap labour available. [1] Cultivable land available, therefore lack of labour. [2] A mixed situation.

and sugar refiners in Britain wrote about the manufacturing process and the use of better equipment, such as the steam-engine and the vacuum-pan.

But all these more efficient tools and machinery would be of little avail unless sufficient labourers were available to take the crop. In Demerara, the factories were equipped to manufacture 100,000 hogsheads of sugar, but only enough cane was brought in from the fields to produce 40,000 hogsheads. In Demerara, it was labour, not machinery, that was needed. Better cultivating and manufacturing might indeed improve and increase the crop, but only if when crop-season came, there were enough labourers with machetes to cut the improved canes and take them to the improved factories.

The ex-slaves were not all completely opposed to estate labour. In the smaller islands, the majority of people were forced by circumstances to continue as estate workers. But even in Trinidad and British Guiana, the withdrawal from estate labour was not complete. Some of those who found other work as independent small settlers or as retail traders were occasionally willing to give a few days work on a nearby estate to make some ready money for an immediate need such as the purchase of land, or a boat, or a small stock of saleable goods. In consequence, there were always people who were ready to give estate labour when it suited them, but this was not necessarily at crop-time. Not all the small settlers, retailers and others would be looking for estate work at the same time, and when they did look for such work, it was to suit their own plans and not the plans of the estate owners. Throughout the nineteenth century there were frequent complaints by planters in the larger colonies that labour was scarce, and equally frequent complaints by ex-slaves that estate work was scarce. They were both right. The fact was that the demands of the people for employment and the demands of the estates for more workers did not always coincide.

Daily wages continued to vary in the different territories, with the highest where labourers were most scarce. The question arises whether planters could have found all the workers they needed by offering still higher wages. In Trinidad and British Guiana, they clearly could not because there were not enough people for the work in any case. Elsewhere, there were two difficulties. The first was the attitude of the ex-slaves, who had already made their position clear by seeking an independent livelihood; some of them would not have worked on the estates whatever wages were offered, because they wanted to break away completely from the work they had been forced to do during slavery. The second, which was the deciding point for the planter, was the price that he could get for his sugar. This set a limit to the wages he was willing to pay. If rising wages were going to eliminate his chance of profits, planting as a business ceased to have a point.

AN ISSUE AND A DECISION

The year 1846 was a critical one for the planters. Before that, they faced rising wages at home but received sufficient prices in Britain. Until then, the British West Indian sugar industry still had one great advantage over foreign competitors; the same advantage was offered to the other British sugar-producing colonies, Mauritius and India, in 1825 and 1836 respectively. The sugar from all of them was admitted to Britain at low rates of import duty, but higher rates of import duty were levied on all foreign sugar, thus making it more expensive and eliminating competitors of the West Indian product.

The blow came in the eighteen-forties, when the British Government changed its attitude towards trade with its colonies. Quite simply the cheapest goods could often now be found in foreign markets. For instance, Cuba was forging ahead as a sugar producer, and was certainly manufacturing a cheaper product than were the other West Indian areas in the nineteenth century. Free trade, by which British buyers would import their food from the places where it was most cheaply produced, was now attractive to the British Government. The population of England was increasing rapidly and the new industrial occupations had brought people together in large new towns. During the eighteen-forties, there was much hardship for many people in England and this kept the British Government occupied with problems at home. Feeding the population was certainly a problem; cheap food was essential. When a mercantile system was imposed by the European countries on their colonists nearly two centuries earlier, the interest of the home country came first; so it did again when in 1849, with the repeal of the Navigation Acts, England abolished protection in favour of free trade.

By the Sugar Duties Act of 1846 the preferential duties for sugar from British colonies were to be gradually withdrawn. It was intended that the duties on sugar imported into England from all sources should be gradually equalised over the next four years. Vigorous protests from the West Indian assemblies and the West India Committee in London resulted only in a postponement of the full working of the Act for a further two years. By 1852, therefore, British sugar planters no longer had a protected market in Britain. They had lost the security of sale which had helped earlier planters to make their West India fortunes.

In such a situation, the bargaining for wages which had taken place with local workers in the twelve years after emancipation would not help a planter to survive in a now critically competitive business. If local labourers would not work for the wages which the planters could afford, another, cheaper, source of workers must be sought. In these circumstances the large-scale importation of workers was bound to start again in the West Indies if the sugar estates were to be maintained at all.

FURTHER READING

Sources of West Indian History, Economic Life, pp. 68–9, Emancipation and Apprenticeship, pp. 198–206, 208–15.

Hall, *Letters from Monville*.

QUESTIONS TO CONSIDER

1. How were the newly freed workers able to find a living away from the estates?

2. What evidence have you that 'the ex-slaves were completely opposed to estate labour'?

3. Which territories had the most difficult labour problems and why?

4. What results can you anticipate for the West Indies from the introduction of free trade in Britain?

CHAPTER SEVENTEEN

Immigrant Workers

FINDING THE SUPPLY

Three places in the West Indies were particularly concerned with importing people from abroad to work on plantations. One was Jamaica, where the planters lost their labourers from the estates soon after emancipation for the reasons which were given in the last chapter. The others, as you would now know, were Trinidad and British Guiana, which did not have enough labourers in the first place and where there was plenty of vacant land to attract those already there away from the sugar estates.

In Trinidad, the Governor had suggested the importation of Chinese labourers as early as 1806. One reason why the Trinidadian Government chose Chinese workers was because they did not wish to increase their Negro population. For the same reason Trinidadian planters brought Frenchmen from Le Havre, Jamaica looked to England, Ireland and other parts of Europe for its first immigrants after emancipation and St. Kitts imported two hundred English workers in 1845. Small numbers of English, French and German workers were also brought to St. Lucia and British Guiana between 1836 and 1851.

The desire to increase the white population was shared by the Spanish Government in Cuba, where in the eighteen-forties there were 498,000 slaves in a population of 600,000. They wished to keep their promise to the British Government to stamp out the illicit slave trade. Some Cubans also wished to abolish slavery and others thought that more white settlers might help them to win independence from Spain. After slave risings in 1843 the slave-owners themselves welcomed the idea of white immigration. But, although a few Catalans and Canary Islanders came to Cuba, they were not enough for the expanding sugar industry.

In the event, the Chinese and European workers who came to the British islands did not satisfy the planters, because they did not take to estate labour. The Europeans died in large numbers soon after arrrival; those who survived left the plantations for other occupations. The Chinese preferred trade and business to field labour and, as soon as they could earn enough to make a humble start, they abandoned the estates.

When China and Europe failed to provide them with capable plantation labourers, the planters of Trinidad and British Guiana immediately after emancipation found that they could for a time draw upon a much closer source of supply. The higher wages they paid because they were short of workers attracted ex-slaves from Barbados, St. Vincent, Grenada and even the Leewards. In eighteen months from January 1839, about 1,160 West Indian workers arrived in Trinidad from other islands. At first they paid their own passages, but soon the planters advanced them the sum, and also paid a bounty to the ship's captains who brought them.

But these West Indian immigrants had no intention of being full-time estate workers. In fact, before long many of them migrated only for the crop-season. Those who left home permanently moved from the estates to towns, or bought land or squatted on Crown lands. Furthermore, as the estate labourers became fewer in number, those who remained demanded higher wages than before, wages which the planters said they could not afford to pay if they were to continue to make a profit from their sugar plantations. Not only did the planters in Jamaica, Trinidad and British Guiana need more labour than was already available to them, but also they wanted labourers who would work for lower wages than those already living there, and who would remain on the estates to work whenever the planters wanted their labour.

This hardship for the planters attracted the sympathetic notice of the British Parliament and they suggested a remedy. 'One obvious and most desirable mode of endeavouring to compensate for this diminished supply of labour,' ran a report on the subject in 1842, 'is to promote the immigration of a fresh labouring population to such an extent as to create competition for employment.' Where could such people be found? The West Indian planters were prepared to look everywhere. They tried North America with little success. Fewer than a thousand came from North America in 1839 and 1840, the years of the most widespread recruitment there. They continued to use Barbados despite the resentment of the Barbadian planters. From Madeira came a small but regular flow of people until 1882. But most of all they looked to Africa, China and India.

The Madeirans started to come regularly in 1840. Between 1841 and 1848 they were attracted particularly to British Guiana; the wages there were 3s. to 4s. per day as against 4d. to 6d. per day in Madeira. But so many died that the British Guianese Government stopped paying passages from Madeira in the middle of 1842. The higher wages in British Guiana still attracted Madeirans, but now their own government wished to keep them at home. Would-be emigrants were forbidden to leave without a passport, for which they were charged an extravagant price. The numbers of Madeirans bound for British Guiana fell from 4,297 in 1841 to 140 in 1844. But a famine in Madeira in 1846 again sent up the numbers to 5,975 in 1846, and 3,761 in 1847. Madeirans were not, however, very satisfactory to the planters as, like the Chinese, they preferred to leave the fields for commercial pursuits as soon as they could find an opportunity.

In 1841 a committee of planters in Trinidad particularly recommended Africa as an area from which to recruit workers. But attempts to get Africans resident in Sierra Leone and the Kru Coast to migrate to the West Indies were not successful. The Africans there were reluctant to come. There were no local catastrophes to make them leave; and both missionaries and merchants on the West Coast of Africa, for their different reasons, discouraged them from leaving. So the Africans who came to the West Indies were mostly those rescued from captured slavers bound for countries which had not yet abolished slavery. This was the result of the campaign of the British Navy against the Atlantic slave trade after 1833. The years 1848 and 1849, when Brazil imported a greatly increased number of slaves, proved the peak years for captured Africans for the West Indies. By the end of the eighteen-sixties, a total of 36,160 Free Africans had been brought to the West Indies.

AFRICANS BROUGHT TO THE WEST INDIES AFTER 1838

British Guiana	.	.	.	13,970
Jamaica	.	.	.	10,000
Trinidad	.	.	.	8,390
Grenada	.	.	.	1,540
St. Vincent	.	.	.	1,040
St. Lucia	.	.	.	730
St. Kitts	.	.	.	460

No attempts had been made to bring Chinese to the British West Indies after Trinidad's experience with those they had imported in 1806 until, in 1844, British Guiana tried to recruit, not from China itself, but from the Chinese populations in Malacca, Singapore and

Penang. The Chinese there, however, had jobs and did not wish to leave.

The period of sustained Chinese immigration to the British West Indies was between 1859 and 1866, during which time just over 1,000 went to Trinidad and 12,000 to British Guiana. The Chinese who came before 1860 had been recruited neither in the towns nor in the villages. They had been bought from the 'barracoons' at Macao. A visitor described some of the best ones. 'These depots were all that could be desired as regarded space, order and cleanliness,' he reported, 'but the lofty walls and cluster of guards in every direction told but too truly that the buildings were but well conducted gaols and the inmates but hopeless prisoners.' In fact the Chinese emigrants were seldom volunteers. One consequence of this form of recruitment was that no women came to the West Indies from China in those early years.

In 1860 British Guiana appointed an agent and he attempted with fair success to promote 'family emigration' recruited from the southern sea-coast provinces of Fu-Kien and Kuang-tung. From 1864 Trinidad shared the cost of the agency in China, but neither colony benefited very much from Chinese immigration after 1866. The reason was that the Chinese Government had drawn up rules to regulate the engagement of Chinese emigrants by French and British subjects which did not satisfy the French and British Governments, even after long discussions. The Chinese Government were in fact opposed to emigration and they only accepted the task of regulating, rather than prohibiting, it because they had been defeated in war by the European nations. By contrast, the closer relations between the French and British Governments and the Indian Government allowed easier agreement between them on regulations. There were also other reasons why the traffic from China to the West Indies did not flourish. The Chinese themselves, unless kidnapped and sold, chose to go to California or South-East Asia, which were nearer home. Furthermore, ships made higher profits carrying cargo than they did carrying people to the West Indies. Consequently, when the West Indian agents attempted to recruit honestly and to charter suitable ships for the voyage, it was a costly business. In the eighteen-fifties it cost £25 to send an immigrant from China to the West Indies, but only £15 to send one from India. India became the main source of immigrant workers for the West Indies by the second half of the nineteenth century.

Workers had to be induced to come to the West Indies from other parts of the world. Normally people do not leave their homes to go abroad unless their life has been very difficult, or unless the place they are going to can be made to seem very attractive. It was a combination of both these factors which persuaded Indians to come to the West Indies. There are always individuals who will join a general movement abroad for personal reasons, such as family troubles or to escape their creditors. But hard times and famine were also widespread in India in the nineteenth century on account of frequent drought and a rapidly rising birth-rate. Recruiters found thousands of Indians in the villages and in the swarming, over-populated towns of Calcutta, Madras and Bombay, who could readily be persuaded that the West Indies by contrast was a land of promise.

CONTROLLING IMMIGRATION

But before the recruiters could set to work, there were obstacles to remove. In 1838, the Indian Government prohibited Indian emigration to Mauritius and the West Indies. In 1839, the Secretary of State had refused to let British Guiana recruit labour on the West Coast of Africa. In 1839, Great Britain had declared war on China. Moreover, there were those who feared that, in the movement of large numbers of people over the great distances involved in a crossing from Africa, China or India, there would be in effect a return to the conditions of the slave trade. Furthermore, to leave these people in the hands of the old employers without supervision would be practically to revive slavery. In such an event their long years of work in securing the abolition of the trade and the emancipation of slaves would have been in vain.

These views were held most strongly by members of the Anti-Slavery Society in England, and by some of the nonconformist missionaries in the West Indies and in India. Petitions to the House of Commons were organised 'against consigning coolies to such murderous bondage', and the protest was supported and helped by certain members of the House. But arguing strongly on the other side were the West Indian interest in London and the planters in the West Indies. They still had helpers in Parliament too.

With one group denouncing large-scale emigration to the West Indies and the other urging it as the only possible way to ensure that sugar estates would survive, the Imperial Government had to decide whether to allow immigration or not. If they did, they also had to consider whether it was to be treated as a private matter between planters and their imported labourers, or whether it should be a matter primarily between governments, in order to ensure official supervision of the recruitment, the journeys and the conditions under which the emigrant laboured. In 1841 the Secretary of State made it easier to recruit in Sierra Leone; in 1843 he approved emigration from China and, in 1844, he removed the prohibition on Indians coming here. So the Imperial Government had decided not only to support immigration of workers to the West Indies, but also to control it.

In coming to this decision they considered the previous experience of emigration conducted as a private matter in British Guiana, India and Mauritius. During the short time that it had been in operation the frauds committed by recruiters, the inadequate provision made for the long voyages, and the deaths caused by the neglect of some of the immigrants once they had arrived in British Guiana, had given the Anti-Slavery Society and its allies enough reason to agitate very strongly against the private system. After it was suspended in 1838, commissioners both in India and British Guiana were appointed to examine what had gone on. Those who had then protested so strongly hoped that large-scale emigration from Africa, China and India to the West Indies would never again be permitted.

But the Imperial Government was faced with another issue in the eighteen-forties which affected their decision profoundly. The equalisation of the sugar duties as part of the new free trade policy in England was a heavy blow to the West Indian sugar planters and their protest was as loud as their predicament was real. Although the British Government remained adamant over its free trade policy, they helped the West Indian planters in their new crisis. They would not grant preferential import duties for West Indian sugar; but, in 1848, they made loans of money to Jamaica, British Guiana, Trinidad and Barbados, and much of it was used, particularly in Trinidad and British Guiana, to support more immigration of workers. So, by 1848, not only had it been decided to permit large-scale emigration to the West Indies, but now money was provided for the purpose, only on condition, however, that it was supervised by the West Indian, the Imperial and Indian Governments. Official immigration from Asia was now established, and the largest number came from poverty-stricken districts of India, from Behar, the United Provinces of Agra and Oudh and, to a lesser extent, from Madras.

It may be wondered why the Imperial Government should concern itself so actively with ambitious schemes to carry workers halfway round the world to maintain a sugar industry from which they had just withdrawn protection in their market. It was not the maintenance of sugar that was their first concern; rather it was the maintenance of the social organisation of the colonies, with a good proportion of Europeans of influence. This was considered in the best interest of the whole community. A letter from Lord Harris, Governor of Trinidad from 1846, illustrates the point. 'I fully and cordially agree with you,' he wrote to the Secretary of State, 'in the opinion that the highest interest of the negroes requires that the cultivation of sugar should not be abandoned, and that the proprietors of European race should be enabled to maintain their present place in the society of the colony, which can only be done by giving them greater command of labour.'

It was not only the British planters who looked for cheap estate labour outside the West Indies. They had been the first to do so only because their slave trade had ended in 1807, and their slaves were emancipated in 1838. For the French islands, the trade did not end until 1830, and American ships supplied Cuba with slaves until 1862. The French freed their slaves in 1848, the Dutch in 1863 and the Spaniards in 1885. But even before their emancipated slaves had the opportunity to show the same reluctance for plantation labour as had happened in the English islands, the planters in the French and Spanish islands and in Dutch Guiana were seeking labour from other sources. The French began by the forcible recruitment, from 1830 to 1860, of Africans from the Congo, who were freed on landing in Martinique and Guadeloupe. Immediately their slaves were freed in 1848 they began recruiting from the French colonies in India, and in 1860, British India was opened to them. Before emancipation in the Dutch West Indies, planters in Surinam had recruited from Java and in 1870 they too were allowed to use India.

Spain had abolished the slave trade in 1820, but Cuba and Puerto Rico were supplied with slaves by others, mostly French and Americans. The Cubans also made use of the slaves captured from the slave-ships and landed at Havana. They were now supposed to be free men, but they were hired out in gangs to Cuban planters for seven-year terms, during which the planters treated them worse than slaves. To stop the practice, no more captured slaves were landed at Havana after 1835. After 1840, the British Navy made it more difficult to get slaves through to Cuba, Puerto Rico and Brazil. But the demand in Europe for cheap sugar was growing greater, and, after the introduction of free trade in sugar in Britain in 1846 gave them a new market, these colonies wanted labour to expand their production. This was why the Cubans now looked to China for labourers. Between 1852 and 1874 they imported some 125,000. At first they were shipped from Amoy and Canton, through the agency of two British firms; but when those sources were stopped, they used the barracoons of Macao.

The methods of recruitment were kidnapping on a large scale and the buying of prisoners taken in the civil wars in South China. The traffic was not regulated in China, and the emigrants had no protection in Cuba. The labourers were made to sign in China a contract to labour for eight years and they were to receive four pesos a month, plus food, shelter and two changes of clothes a year; but in fact when they landed at Havana they were sold into slavery. At length the Chinese Government sent commissioners to investigate what was happening in Cuba. They found 'almost every Chinese met by us was or had been undergoing suffering. The fractured and maimed limbs, blindness, the heads full of sores, the skin and flesh lacerated—proofs of cruelty patent to the eyes of all.'

In the French colonies too, though conditions were not as bad as in Cuba, the emigrants were not properly cared for and their mortality was high. So the British Government closed India to French Guiana in 1876, and to Martinique and Guadeloupe in 1886. Only in the Dutch colony of Surinam did Indian immigration continue until it was ended for all colonies in 1917.

INDIAN EMIGRANTS

In India, the British West Indians set up emigration officers to be in charge of recruiting. At first, the same men served the Governments of Jamaica, Trinidad and British Guiana, but as the demand increased, and as recruiting also became more difficult, the separate governments appointed their own agents. In fact, until 1848, recruits could be found fairly readily in the bazaars of Madras and Calcutta. These were not skilled in agriculture, any more than many of the Chinese, Madeirans and Africans were. They were untrained for their jobs on the estates, and there was much complaint here about the quality of the Indian immigrants.

Under the agents were the sub-agents in charge of areas in the country, and under them were the actual recruiters who went among the people to persuade them to emigrate. From the beginning of emigration in 1838 to the end in 1917, these recruiters always had a bad name. They were unpopular in the villages and countryside, and were sometimes attacked and beaten. Some of this unpopularity was caused by those recruiters who practised fraud to get simple people to emigrate. Sometimes they even resorted to kidnapping.

The Indian Government tried to protect the emigrants by making it necessary for them to sign, or mark, their contracts to labour in the West Indies in the presence of a magistrate, who was to ensure that they understood what they were doing. This procedure reduced the extent to which recruiters could take advantage of possible emigrants, but it did not stop fraud completely. What it did do was to give those Indian officials who were against Indian emigration a chance to obstruct the work of the recruiters. From the beginning, there were always Indians who thought the system harmful to Indian interests or a slur on Indian dignity. They obstructed it in India, and kept themselves informed on what happened to immigrants in Trinidad or British Guiana. When the Indian national movement became better organised, in the latter part of the nineteenth century and in the early years of the twentieth century, their members were very active in obstructing the recruiters and in dissuading would-be emigrants. In particular, they discouraged women emigrants, who were always far fewer in number than men although the proportions changed as the years went by and immigrants became more settled in the West Indies.

The recruiters took the Indians they had collected to the sub-agent and were paid by him. The sub-agent then put the emigrants in a train for the port of embarkation, which was Calcutta in most cases, or Madras or Bombay. At the port they were medically examined and kept at a depot until a ship was ready to sail. Until the beginning of the twentieth century, when steamships were regularly chartered, the voyage was by sail and the ships had to leave India between September and February to escape being becalmed in the Indian Ocean, and so to avoid being too long in the cold weather in the South Atlantic. They came round the Cape of Good Hope and called at the Cape or St. Helena for fresh water and vegetables before embarking on the transatlantic crossing.

The state of recruiting was such that there were always emigrants who were not strong enough to survive the voyage if they became ill. Cholera, dysentery and diarrhoea were prevalent and often fatal diseases. At the beginning of emigration, and even later when it was supervised by the Indian and Imperial Governments, the death-rate was sometimes quite high; it was in time reduced to less harrowing proportions by the close supervision of the traffic. The medical examination ·before embarkation was made very thorough; suitable ships were chartered with good ventilation below decks; the supplies of medicine and the quantity and quality of the food and warm clothing were all increased. There was a surgeon and a dispenser on every ship. Regulations were passed as experience exposed faults; those who had to care for the health of the emigrants, and who were paid a bonus if they landed them in the West Indies alive, learnt from experience too.

When the immigrants arrived in the West Indies, after a voyage which might have lasted anything from seventy-two to a hundred and twenty-six days, they were again examined before being allocated to the estates which had asked for them. Those who were ill were sent to hospital until they were well enough to go to an estate. The immigrant then began to work according to the terms of his contract.

INDENTURED LABOUR

During the years of large scale immigration to the West Indies, the contracts which the immigrants were expected to sign varied in their provisions. The contract stated the period of service, the number of days and hours to be worked, the rate of wages for daily or task work, and the conditions under which a return passage would be granted.

In general, the immigrant had to give five years' service from the day he was allotted to an estate, but any time spent in gaol was not included. He could be called upon to work every day, except Sundays and holidays, at cultivating the soil or at the sugar factory. If he worked in the field for seven hours a day or in the factory for ten hours a day and was a healthy male over sixteen years old, he got 1s. a day. A female or a minor more than ten years old got 8d. a day. For task-work his wages had to be the same as those paid unindentured labour on the same and surrounding estates. During his first three months on the estate, he was provided with rations according to a scale provided by the government, but the planters could deduct 4d. from wages for these rations. The immigrant was housed in barracks free of rent and given medicine and hospital accommodation free of cost.

When he had served five years, the immigrant was usually free to change his employer. The earliest ordinances and laws provided for a free return passage for immigrants at the end of five years' residence, not even necessarily at work on an estate, but after 1854, only when an immigrant had lived ten years in one West Indian colony did he become entitled to a return passage. After 1895, in British Guiana, he had to pay part of the cost, a quarter until 1898 and after that, a half. Only the destitute and the disabled continued to get free passages back to India if they wanted them.

A breach of his contract by an immigrant was a criminal offence to be tried in the criminal court. There he could not give evidence on his own behalf, and usually his friends were afraid to give evidence for him; conviction meant a heavy fine or gaol. But to recover wages due to him the immigrant worker had to go to the Petty Debts Courts, since the Immigration Department did not give him help in this matter. This was a difficult, and often impossible, procedure for an uneducated labourer who spoke little English.

To see that both parties kept to their sides of the contract, a Department of Immigration was established in every colony receiving immigrants from abroad, with an Agent-General as its chief, and sub-agents posted in the countryside to supervise the various estates. In theory, the department was to hold the scales evenly between the employers and their immigrant workers. In practice, however, this happened only when both the Governor and Agent-General were determined to protect the immigrant. In Jamaica Sir John Grant, and in Trinidad Sir Arthur Gordon, took such close interest in the working of immigration that the scales were held fairly even. The work of the Agent-General was also important. Gordon had Dr. Charles Mitchell for this purpose in Trinidad, and he later said of him, 'he never lost an opportunity when he saw it of turning the scale in favour of the immigrant'. The Agent-General in British Guiana, James Crosby, was less fortunate than Mitchell in his chief. Crosby's efforts to help the immigrants were successfully frustrated by the Governor, Sir Francis Hincks, who in effect took over the running of the Immigration Department there himself. Nevertheless, Crosby so managed to endear himself to the immigrants that his successors in office were all known as 'Crosbys' and the sub-agents were called 'little Crosbys'.

205

Sir Arthur Gordon, reflecting in 1909 on his experience as a governor in Trinidad, Mauritius and Fiji, acknowledged that, 'when the employers of labour form, as they do in most of the coolie-employing colonies, the whole of the upper class of society and influence every other class, it requires a very great deal of courage, I will say a great deal of self reliance, to stand up against that influence'. As a committee of investigation observed, the early laws which governed the immigrant in the colonies 'gradually assumed a complexion less and less favourable to freedom and were framed and administered in a spirit of substantial injustice to Indian immigrants'. Particular injustices provoked protest and riots from time to time.

ARGUMENT AND ADJUSTMENT

Riots at Leonora in 1869 provided an occasion for investigating the condition of the immigrant labourers in British Guiana. An ex-Magistrate from British Guiana, William Des Voeux, who had only recently been transferred to St. Lucia as Administrator, was moved by the riots to write a famous letter to the Secretary of State on the condition of the Indians in British Guiana. The Secretary of State for the Colonies appointed a Commission of Enquiry in 1870 to investigate the situation. 'A harsh system of law has been kept up, not so much for use, as that condonation of offences under it might be bartered against reindenture', was the general conclusion of the Commissioners. They confirmed that the Indians mistrusted the magistrates who dealt with their cases and resented a system tilted in favour of the planters. They further suggested that the doctors who served immigrants should be made public servants instead of employees of the estates. They noted that, in some instances, immigrants' wages had been withheld in an arbitrary manner. Finally, they came to the conclusion that the law on immigration as it stood put every indentured immigrant at the mercy of unscrupulous employers.

The Imperial Government after 1870 improved the laws in British Guiana and Trinidad to stop some of the malpractices discovered by the Commissioners. For instance, in British Guiana, the planter himself was now liable to a maximum fine of $24 if convicted after an immigrant worker had made a verbal complaint to a magistrate. But that part of the immigration ordinances which allowed the immigrant to be punished for breach of his contract by being taken before the courts continued to operate against him. He was summoned for failure to be at the daily calling over of names, for refusal to begin work, for absence from work, for being drunk at work, for failure to complete the minimum task.

Because the penalty of a fine or imprisonment was high, the planters would use the system as a threat to keep their workers in order. They would bring charges against them and withdraw them before a conviction, punishing the immigrant by making him pay for the cost of the summons. In 1870, when nearly a quarter of the immigrants in British Guiana were summoned at some time, more than half the cases were withdrawn in this way. The proportion of summonses to indentured population increased steadily, to a peak of 37·8 per cent in 1906 and 1907. It was only following a commission of enquiry appointed by the Indian Government at that time that the number of prosecutions were reduced. In British Guiana, the Agent-General for the Immigrants told the planters he would refuse them any more Indians if the practice continued. The number of summonses then fell to 13 per cent in 1915; but vigilant critics from India felt it was still too high. In the last year of the scheme, imprisonment was abolished as a punishment for offences against the labour laws, and fines, which had been as high as £5 in 1868 but reduced to £1 by the Ordinance of 1873, were now further reduced to 10s.

The attempt to exercise strict control over the movements of the indentured labourer beyond the limits of the estate, made an Indian or Chinese liable to arrest if he was found away from his plantation without a pass. He was required to live on the estate and could be fined for not doing so. Towards the end of the century, these restrictions were removed in Trinidad and relaxed in British Guiana; the immigrant could now go beyond the estate limits outside of working hours, or even sleep away at weekends; but he had to be present on Monday morning. Even so, the law remained and, to avoid arrest or embarrassment, those Indians who were not bound to estates found it wise to carry papers, Certificates of Exemption from Labour, to prove their freedom to move at will.

This close supervision of the life of the immigrant was due in part, especially in the early years, to a desire to protect a helpless, and largely ignorant, worker in a strange country. Lord Harris expressed the official view that 'they are not, neither coolies nor Africans, fit to be placed in a position which the labourers of civilised countries may at once occupy. They must be treated like children and wayward ones too; the former from their habits of religion; the latter, from the utterly savage state in which they arrive.' There is no doubt that many deaths in the early years of immigration, particularly in the case of Europeans, Madeirans and Indians, resulted from a bad diet and insanitary habits. Moreover, the ill and starving Indians, so often seen on the roads of Jamaica and Trinidad in the late eighteen-forties, had demonstrated the absence of adequate supervision of both planter and labourer before immigration was officially organised.

There were thus reasons of common humanity for insisting on adequate supervision. Without it the immigration scheme would have been the near reversion to slavery that the Anti-Slavery Society anticipated. The Indian or Chinese worker, arriving in the West Indies on a defined term of service, had not even the slave's claim of permanency to recommend that he should be well cared for; he was invariably a humble man and did not speak the language of his employers. There was still every chance that his position would be abused even under official supervision and with the services of an interpreter.

For the planter, official supervision of indentured labour gave advantages. He wanted his labour force on the estate, available to him at all times, and he wanted to make sure that he would get the greatest possible amount of work from the immigrant during his years of indenture. At first the Colonial Office would only allow contracts to be signed for one year and the signing was to take place on the immigrant's arrival in the West Indies; some of them, after seeing the conditions, refused to sign. The planters frequently asked the Colonial Office to reconsider this rule, and the contract was extended first to three years in 1848 and then to five years in 1850, and was signed before the immigrant embarked. The planters also frequently asked permission to do away with the free return passages which they had to provide at the end of an immigrant's period of service. The Government of India would not agree to this, but at the end of the nineteenth century, as we have seen, an immigrant had to meet part of the cost of his return passage.

Immigration from India, and to a lesser extent from China, undoubtedly solved the planter's labour problem in Trinidad and British Guiana, but unless he could be assured of a long term of service his expenses were high. Although part of the cost of immigration was met from the public revenues of the colonies, the planters had to pay specifically for the cost of recruiting in India or China, the cost of the voyage from India or China to the West Indies and for the medical treatment of the immigrant indentured on their estates. The planters' part of the expenses was usually met by making them pay a fee for each immigrant allocated to their estate and also by imposing an export duty on all crops commercially grown on estates, whether they used immigrant labourers or not.

Although the planters were continually pleading for adjustments in their favour, they clearly did not regret the arrangement for recruiting their workers from India and China. Had it been left to them, they would have continued the system indefinitely. The end came as the result of the work of supporters of the Indian Nationalist Movement, who attacked the whole policy of emigration because they were particularly incensed by the condition of Indian workers in Fiji and Natal. In 1916 the Indian Legislative Council passed the Abolition of Indenture Act, and in 1918 the Secretary of State for India refused to re-open emigration under indenture. Effectively, Indian immigration stopped in 1917.

In roughly eighty years, 548,000 Indians came to the West Indies under the official immigration scheme. Many returned to India after their period of indentured service, and not all of them were disillusioned by the difficulties they had encountered. Used at first on the sugar estates, they were later employed in cacao production in Trinidad, banana cultivation on the larger banana estates and indeed on any agricultural work which required gangs of hired labourers. It was quite possible for the more enterprising of them to do well during their period in the West Indies. A visitor to Trinidad in 1869 was assured by the Agent-General for Immigration that one worker returning to India at the time was taking away £2,000. This could hardly have been saved from estate earnings, but even one-tenth of the sum would have been wealth to a poor Indian returning to Calcutta.

Most of the Indians, however, stayed and, in Trinidad and British Guiana, were encouraged to do so. The encouragement was not just the negative method of making it hard for them to return to India. Crown Lands were divided into plots which in Trinidad in 1870 could be bought for £5 by any Indian who had completed five years of indentured labour, and who was willing to remain in the West Indies. Furthermore, the Canadian Presbyterian Mission, which, under John Morton, had started work amongst the Indians in the eighteen-sixties, were given government assistance to open schools, churches and homes for Indians. Both in the opportunities for education and the facilities for acquiring land, the Indians in Trinidad were better off than those in British Guiana. In 1909, the Trinidadian Immigration Department could say, 'we have now in practice and at work here clergymen, lawyers, solicitors, merchants, shopkeepers, proprietors, managers, overseers, book-keepers and tradesmen, some of whom came to Trinidad under indenture, the rest of whom had indentured fathers'. In both territories, Asian immigration brought a large new and permanent population into the West Indian community.

NUMBER OF INDIAN IMMIGRANTS TO THE WEST INDIES

To British Guiana . . .	239,000
Trinidad	134,000
Jamaica	33,000
St. Lucia . . .	4,000
Grenada . . .	3,000
St. Vincent . . .	2,700
St. Kitts . . .	300
Guadeloupe ⎱ . . .	78,000
Martinique ⎰	
French Guiana . . .	19,000
Dutch Guiana . . .	35,500

FURTHER READING

Sources of West Indian History, People of the Caribbean, pp. 22–30.
Parry and Sherlock, *Short History of the West Indies*, Chapter XIII, The Best and Worst of Times, pp. 201–204.
Daly, *Story of the Heroes III*, The Luckhoo Dynasty. Chapters XXXI–XXXII.
Ottley, *History of Tobago*, Chapter XIII.

QUESTIONS TO CONSIDER

1. Which reason do you find most convincing for the early failure to find immigrant workers for the estates?

2. Who do you think profited most from the official schemes for Indians' indentured labour?

3. How did the conditions of indentured labour differ from those of slave labour?

4. What role do you consider that the Indian population in the West Indies would be likely to play after the immigration scheme ended?

CHAPTER EIGHTEEN

Competition and its Consequences

THE COMPETITORS

The news of the passing of the Sugar Duties Act in 1846 was received in the British West Indies with gloomy forecasts of utter ruin. By contrast, the Cubans received it with jubilation. In 1847 a British West Indian planter calling at Cuba described the scene in Havana. 'The town was illuminated when I landed,' he wrote, 'in consequence of the news of high prices from England. Three splendid trains of Derosne's machinery, costing 40,000 dollars, had just arrived from France, and were in process of erection. Steam engines and engineers were coming over daily from America; new estates were forming, coffee plantations were being broken up, and the feeble gangs of old people and children were being formed into task-gangs, and being hired out by the month to the new *ingenios.*'

A year later, before a Select Committee of Parliament to enquire into the effects in the West Indies of the Sugar Duties Act, British planters and merchants gave evidence about the differences between sugar production in the British colonies and their main foreign rivals. They were not surprised that the Cubans were jubilant. In 1848, sugar was selling in London at 22s. 6d. per cwt. while they declared the costs of producing one hundredweight of sugar in the various British territories to be as follows:

				s.	d.
Jamaica	.	.	.	22	7
St. Kitts	.	.	.	16	2
Antigua	.	.	.	15	4½
St. Vincent	.	.	.	19	2
Grenada	.	.	.	16	2
Barbados	.	.	.	15	4½
Trinidad	.	.	.	25	0
British Guiana	.	.	.	25	0

To these figures, the merchants claimed, about 7s. should be added to cover the expenses of shipping each hundredweight to Britain. By contrast, they showed that the Cubans and Brazilians had been

211

selling their sugar for the past six years at 20s. per cwt., and had still made encouraging profits.

The British West Indian sugar industry was much affected by what happened to the crops in Cuba and Louisiana. The Louisiana planters sold their sugar in the United States. When they had a poor crop, the Americans supplemented their supplies from Cuba. When the Lousiana crop was good, the Cubans had greater quantities available for export to Europe. The West Indian planters would pray for poor seasons in Louisiana.

In 1844 Louisiana planters owned seven hundred and sixty-two sugar mills, employed about one hundred thousand slave labourers, and produced nearly two million cwt. of sugar per year. Their factories were well equipped with machinery supplied by the foundries of New Orleans, New York, Boston, Philadelphia, Cincinnati and Pittsburgh. Their crop-season was short and early, usually between mid-October and mid-December, before frost could ruin the canes, and the factories had to be efficient to take in the crop so quickly. The cost of producing one hundredweight of sugar and delivering it on board ship at New Orleans for the Atlantic ports was said to be about 15s. In Cuba, as the British planter observed in 1847, the factories were also mechanised and well equipped. The island produced over four million cwt. of sugar that year. The cost, including delivery on board for American and European ports, was said to be about 12s. per cwt.

The superiority of Cuban and Louisiana estates was unquestionable. Partly it can be ascribed to production on a scale which was quite impossible in the smaller Caribbean areas. As one gentleman told the Select Committee in 1848, 'Cuba is on a much larger scale than Jamaica. Jamaica consists generally of narrow valleys, with narrow outlets to the sea, therefore spreading the produce in small quantities round the coast. In Cuba there are vast plains and vast harbours, upon a scale of greater magnitude than is to be found in other colonies.'

With this great area of land went the rapid mechanisation which has been indicated, and the continued use of slaves. In the mid-nineteenth century there were about three hundred and thirty thousand slaves in Cuba, not a large number, considering the area under cultivation and the sugar produced; in 1834 there had been over three hundred thousand slaves in Jamaica alone. But these three hundred and thirty thousand slaves were nearly all bound to estates, and in crop-time they worked in shifts to keep the factories going twenty-four hours a day. Slave labour in Cuba was not cheaper than wage labour in the British islands, but, as the story of Jamaica so well illustrates, the emancipation of three hundred and eleven thousand slaves does not necessarily mean that three hundred and eleven thousand wage labourers have been brought into existence. Crops are worth nothing unless they can be harvested by a steady and dependable supply of labourers.

THE POSITION IN THE BRITISH ISLANDS

In the British colonies generally, the introduction of new factory machinery had taken place much more slowly than in Cuba and Louisiana. There were several reasons for this. First, to obtain equipment the planters needed either money or credit, and they had little of either. Secondly, much of the new factory equipment, such as the steam-mills, the vacuum-pans, and the new centrifugal driers which separated molasses from sugar crystals by rapid spinning, could only be profitably installed on large estates. A vacuum-pan, for example, cost a great deal of money and, unless a planter had a very large cane-crop for processing, he would be unable to use it to its full capacity. Many British West Indian estates were simply too small for the new machinery and equipment available for sugar factories. The main exceptions to this general rule were the larger estates of Trinidad and British Guiana.

The position in the British islands in face of new competition was therefore alarming to planters, and the Select Committee of 1848 recognised their difficulties. After hearing all the evidence, they published 'their conviction that the present distress far exceeds any that ever before occurred in the West Indies'. But the British Government still could not be persuaded to postpone the equalisation of duties on all imported sugar, British or foreign, beyond 1852. Instead, Parliament offered a loan of £500,000 to be shared between Mauritius, Jamaica, British Guiana, Trinidad and Barbados to assist their greatest needs, immigration and a much-needed improvement of communications.

The decision was bitterly disappointing to the West Indians and caused strong protest. In British Guiana, the Court of Policy tried to reduce the salaries of colonial officials by 25 per cent, and then refused to vote supplies when the Governor did not agree. In Jamaica there was talk of refusing to pay taxes and seeking annexation to the

213

United States as there had been just before emancipation. The Jamaican Assembly also at first refused to accept their share of the loan on the grounds that if the sugar industry declined, the island revenue would also decline, so that they would never be able to repay. The sugar industry did decline, and was certainly not helped by the antagonism between the British Government and the West Indian legislatures which now prevailed. The Barbadians, Guianese and Trinidadians accepted the loan. The Barbadians put it into estate improvement; the Guianese and Trinidadians used most of their share for importing more indentured labourers.

The main effect of this decline in sugar was that more estates ceased to function. Sugar production became unprofitable and was more and more confined to areas where special circumstances favoured its production. By the eighteen-sixties, the important British sugar areas in the West Indies were St. Kitts, Antigua, Barbados, Trinidad and British Guiana. The others were either in decline or out of production altogether. St. Kitts, Antigua and Barbados were low-cost producers and they all enjoyed a relatively good supply of workers for the estates. St. Kitts has a magnificently rich soil, and the Barbadians and Antiguans had long established themselves as good farmers and estate-managers. Trinidad and British Guiana forged ahead as their problem of shortage of labour was met by the large importation of workers from the Far East.

But, during the nineteenth century competition increased steadily, especially from Cuba. In 1845, 197,460 cwt. of Cuban sugar were imported into England; in 1864, the figure had increased to 2,887,795 cwt. of unrefined and 61,545 cwt. of refined sugar. So that in twenty years the volume of Cuban sugar imported into England increased twentyfold. In addition, Brazilian, Puerto Rican and Phillipine sugar was finding its way onto the British market. British West Indian sugar, even if confined to the best growing areas and assisted by special loans from the British Government, could not enter into very serious competition with such formidable rivals.

SOCIAL CONSEQUENCES

Everywhere there was a considerable need for social legislation and the spending of public money, if only for those facilities which planters were supposed to have provided in the last years of slavery. If medical services, care for the aged and infirm and education were not publicly provided, people were condemned by poverty to ill health and ignorance. It was not yet a question of raising the standard of living, but simply of giving aid to the helpless.

This need for public services remained one of the main concerns of the Colonial Office reformers, and governors were constantly instructed to see that schools, hospitals, poor relief, almshouses, better prisons, leper hospitals and lunatic asylums were provided or improved in their colonies. In the Crown colonies, the governor could order that these facilities be provided, overriding the obstruction of their councillors if necessary; but in islands where the governors had to cajole the assemblies into providing public services, it was often impossible.

The majority of members of assembly continued to be planters or their agents, merchants and lawyers. They were jealous of their rights as law-makers for their islands, and slow to pass the kind of laws that the Colonial Office thought were most urgent for the benefit of the poorer classes. They were usually more ready to spend money on roads, immigration, the police and fire services and sometimes industrial education, to train young people for work on the estates, than they were to provide or improve medical services, poor relief or prisons, which made less direct contribution to their own prosperity.

The argument of the assemblies was that they did not have the money to provide these services as extensively or as rapidly as the governors urged them to, and so they were justified in providing first such public works as served the interests of the estates and which helped to increase public revenue, before spending money in ways which would not increase the prosperity of their islands. In those years when the price of sugar was low, the assemblies were even more inclined to resist suggestions for expenditure on public services, on the grounds that public money was lacking to pay for them.

Sugar planters all over the Caribbean liked to link the fortunes of their own industry with the size of the public revenue. They argued that if the sugar estates disappeared, the government would be left without money. There was some truth in this argument, particularly in such places as British Guiana and Barbados where the sugar estates provided most of the population with work and money. Although the planters did exaggerate the link between sugar prices and the size of the government's revenue, yet, there was a connection, and it was the result of the way in which the governments collected their money from the people.

The greater part of the public money in the British West Indies was raised from duties on imported goods, and very little from taxing individual persons according to the value of their land or house, or the amount of their income from business. So the governments' revenues were greatly dependent each year on the amount of money people spent buying the goods which were imported from abroad. Some of these were foodstuffs, such as flour, salt fish and salf beef, clothes and shoes, and articles and equipment for use in the home or in the field. With wages from the estates or with money earned as small farmers, the people were able to buy such goods. So the merchants imported them, and the government charged duty on them. But times were hard, wages low, employment difficult to find; when drought or rainstorms ruined the crops of small farmers, people had less money to spend, less was imported, and public revenue decreased. Then the assemblies would say that there was not enough money for public services, or even enough to pay the salaries of civil servants.

The passing of the Sugar Duties Act certainly caused distress to planters, and consequently to their workers and those who lost employment through the closing of estates. The members of the assemblies resented the Imperial Government's action and objected more than ever to direction, even in the form of suggestion, from the Colonial Office through the governors.

There were other hardships to be faced, and they all led to further quarrelling between governors and assemblies about how public money should be spent to meet the difficulties. The eighteen-fifties saw a serious outbreak of cholera which decimated the population of many West Indian islands. The epidemic took hold in Jamaica in 1851 and 40,000 people died before it subsided. In 1854, 20,000 Barbadians and 3,920 people in St. Kitts died of cholera. In British Guiana yellow fever, which had come from Brazil, claimed many victims. The Governor of Trinidad was confronted with a cholera epidemic in Trinidad. These epidemics forced the assemblies to provide some necessary medical and sanitary services, better water supplies, and reform schools for destitute children who had lost their families in the outbreak of cholera.

For the Jamaican Assembly this was a considerable undertaking, and they were in no mood to accept Colonial Office comment that these measures were still wholly inadequate for the social betterment of the Jamaican population. Relations became very strained and, in 1849 and 1853, the assembly refused to vote any money at all, thereby threatening the existence of even those services that they had provided. For instance, in 1853, the governor had no money to feed the prisoners and was forced to give unconditional pardons to about a hundred of them; another two hundred he freed on condition that, for a period of two-thirds of their unserved sentences, they worked as agricultural labourers at 9d a day with lodgings provided.

Not all classes suffered equally from these misfortunes. Estate labour everywhere suffered according to the circumstances of the sugar-planters. Those who had left the estates to become smallholders met with more varied fortunes. Many of them were simply peasants growing their own ground provisions and a surplus to take to the local markets. If they were short of funds they could seek occasional work on nearby estates, but sometimes such employment did not exist and even when it did, the day wages offered were often too low to make it worthwhile.

Other smallholders did better. If they had enough land, they could produce a cheap crop of sugar for sale on the local market, and some of them grew coffee for export to the United States where it was blended with other imported coffee. Such small farmers could make a fair income and were quite independent of the sugar estates. This became a 'superior' lower class, much commended by ministers of all religious denominations for its industry, independence and high moral standards.

The towns were dominated by the coloured groups whose right to vote, if they owned sufficient property, had only been granted just before emancipation. Many notable visitors to the West Indies commented on their prominence as doctors, lawyers, newspaper editors, merchant leaders, in some cases estate owners, often estate managers, and, ever increasingly, members of assembly. The coloured middle class was strong enough for one observer at least to warn his readers of what could happen if these people were slighted or denied opportunities to serve the community as they were obviously fitted to. 'I believe that their ultimate ascendancy is only a question of time,' he wrote.

TACKLING THE PROBLEMS

By the eighteen-sixties all the remaining British West Indian sugar-producing territories, except Jamaica, managed to restore their sugar industry to a profitable undertaking. Nevertheless, the economic changes after the Sugar Duties Act and the stresses of the eighteen-fifties had embittered relations between the governors and their assemblies for a decade. The governors found themselves dealing with particularly aggrieved assembly members when, voicing the views of their masters in England, they spoke for the moral and material welfare of the mass of the people, and claimed that they alone watched their interest.

From the Colonial Office point of view many more of their suggested reforms were achieved in the Crown colonies, where the governors ruled by ordinances, than in the colonies, where the assemblies initiated legislation. Lord Harris in Trinidad administered that developing island from 1846 to 1854 on a pattern which was later to become familiar throughout the West Indies. A list of his measures gives some indication of what could be expected. In the first place, more law-courts were set up. The police were organised. The island was divided into wards to make units of local government for administering new services such as the provision of schools. Roads were improved and such necessary undertakings as drainage and irrigation were much extended.

Under the system of Crown colony government there is no doubt that these necessary reforms were at first more promptly tackled than elsewhere. Trinidad certainly developed steadily, but it had the advantage of starting extensive sugar production in the nineteenth century without the debts and liabilities of the eighteenth century to hold it back. Few landowners there were absentees, and so they remained to give influential and steady advice and criticism in the Legislative Council which was set up in 1831. In particular, they supported from the beginning the policy of immigration which undoubtedly brought increasing prosperity to Trinidadian sugar and, later, cacao producers.

The achievements of the early Crown colony governors were therefore favoured by special circumstances in the developing island of Trinidad. Governors were certainly less harassed there than they were in territories where they had to await the assembly's pleasure before laws could be passed or money voted. It is doubtful, however, whether the Colonial Office view, that dispensing with the assembly was the only way of securing the interests of the unrepresented masses, was in the long run justified. The unrepresented masses certainly had little opportunity or training to voice their own grievances, but they were not without other champions in the West Indies. It was quite beyond the resources of the religious bodies to provide schooling for everybody, but they did maintain schools and training colleges for the families who were not too poor to consider the possible benefits of education. Their teachers, particularly among the non-conformists, were anxious to do their best for the few they could educate. Ambitious lists of subjects appeared at the Mico College in Jamaica, for instance, where, in the eighteen-fifties, the course was 'Sacred and Universal History, Geography, Elements of Astronomy, Etymology, Elements of Science as applied to the Common Purposes of Living, Grammar, Composition, Mental Calculation, and the Higher Branches of Arithmetic, Moral Science, and a thorough acquaintance with the Bible, its precepts, premises, types and figures, and prophecies and its geography, natural history etc.' Obviously students only learnt facts about these subjects by heart, so what was the object? A Moravian pastor, congratulating himself on the results of such a programme in another college, gave the answer. 'It was encouraging,' he reported, 'to every friend and promoter of the sable race to observe this evidence of the capacity of that race for intellectual improvement.' What these teachers were trying to prove was that their West Indian students could do the same as, and were therefore as intelligent as, their English counterparts. From the ranks of those who received such an education were recruited new teachers, minor clerks, policemen and other essential dependable workers.

Another object of the religious bodies was to produce 'a native ministry'. At Codrington College it was hoped that Anglican clergy could be trained in the West Indies for their future work here. The Baptists, who became an independent church and no longer a missionary body as early as 1842, in the following year established their college at Calabar to train Jamaican ministers for work at home and in Africa. This was in effect one branch of secondary education. The Catholics opened secondary schools in Trinidad and Jamaica in the eighteen-fifties, and the Anglicans embarked on secondary schools in British Guiana and, with less success, in Trinidad. In this island, the Queen's Collegiate School was opened in 1859 as a step forward in the government school programme started eight years before. These ventures, while affecting only small numbers, did give some new opportunities to ambitious boys who previously had none.

From the ranks of the newly-educated came additional teachers, journalists, lawyers, doctors and clergy who could add their voices to the expression of public opinion. These were the people who criticised the colonial government, who sent petitions through the governors to England and who maintained a press which seldom failed to discuss current news in a lively and often critical fashion. No governor could fail to know the trend of public opinion, though he might choose to ignore it. Although times were hard in the eighteen-fifties and sixties, new groups were making their way up in society and ridding themselves of the depressed way of life which still remained for the majority.

FURTHER READING

Sources of West Indian History, Economic Life, pp. 68–75, Social Conditions since Emancipation, pp. 222–7, 234–8.

Black, *History of Jamaica*, Chapter XV, The Decline of the Plantation, p. 168.

Hoyos, *Our Common Heritage*, Samuel Jackson Prescod, p. 34.

QUESTIONS TO CONSIDER

1. Why would the West Indian planters pray for a poor season in Louisiana?

2. What arguments can you find for and against the British Government's Sugar Duties Act of 1846?

3. What were the chief acts of government in your territory between 1846 and 1866? How far do you feel that they met the situation at the time?

4. The method of raising revenue for the government was often criticised. What arguments can you find for and against it and who do you think might have held the different opinions in the nineteenth century?

CHAPTER NINETEEN

Who Governs?

TWO WAYS

The officials at the Colonial Office never ceased to worry about the inadequacies of the West Indian assemblies, until the time in the eighteen-sixties when the assemblies began to question their own powers. But the Colonial Office had had a warning in 1839 that it was not easy to rid themselves of the argumentative obstinacy that came from colonial legislatures. In that year the British Government decided to attempt a reform of West Indian prisons by giving themselves powers to close any that were particularly unfit, without the consent of the local legislature. The Jamaican Assembly were up in arms at this threat to their autonomy, and promptly went on strike.

For the Colonial Office reformers this seemed a heaven-sent opportunity to suspend the troublesome members. Henry Taylor, James Stephen's assistant, declared the view of the Colonial Office for many years to come. 'The West Indian legislatures,' he wrote, 'have neither the will nor the skill to make such laws as you want made, and they cannot be converted on the point of willingness, and they will not be instructed.' In the event, the reformers were not supported by the Imperial Parliament. There were not enough members of Parliament who were prepared to abolish a 'representative' assembly, even though it in fact represented only a fraction of the Jamaican population. This resounding failure made the Colonial Office officials very reluctant in future to use the Imperial Parliament against the assemblies. Instead the official policy was now to let the assemblies prove their own incompetence to the point where West Indians themselves would tolerate them no longer and would ask for change.

It was hoped that the more efficient administration of the Crown colonies would arouse the envy of the others so that they would demand the same form of government for themselves. This expectation neglected the fact that some people always prefer to take a part in their own government, almost regardless of the consequences. In the Crown colony of Trinidad, for instance, there were petitions for a representative assembly from the earliest days of British rule there. The Colonial Office even received one in 1846, with seventeen hundred signatures, and this was the first year of Lord Harris's notable governorship. He himself recommended that some members of his Council should be elected instead of all being nominated by him, but this was refused until 'whenever by the diffusion of education and the advancement in civilisation of the inhabitants, they are qualified to take such part'. This was the argument always advanced by the Imperial Government that, as so few people were sufficiently educated to use a vote, they would be at the mercy of the few who were. It was argued that it was in the interest of the many to keep government in the hands of the Governor and a Council nominated by him, answerable to the Colonial Office in London, and that this was an impartial government which would dispense equal justice, and run efficient services for all West Indians alike. But wherever the Crown colony form of government existed, after 1846 there were always some West Indians who resented having no power to govern themselves and, more particularly, no chance to decide what taxes should be levied.

In Trinidad, a Reform Association was formed in 1856 to fight for elected representatives on the Legislative Council and to criticise the Governor's policy at meetings and in the newspapers. Dr. Louis de Verteuil, a member of one of the influential planting families in Trinidad, began a long and distinguished career as a public figure by promoting the Reform Association. Henry Taylor in London told the embarrassed Governor of Trinidad that he saw no reason why his government should not be criticised by 'the educated portions of the colonists' so long as it was done with 'temper and propriety'. The Colonial Office was, however, determined that there should be no elected representatives in a community where only the few had property and education.

THE JAMAICAN ISSUE

After the failure of the Imperial Government to check the Jamaican Assembly in 1839, its life continued until 1865, when in a time of crisis it voted itself out of existence. There was a change in the method of governing the island before that, however. In 1848, the Jamaican Assembly refused to accept the loan offered by the Imperial Government; but in 1854, the island was in such great debt that it was willing to accept a loan of £500,000 on condition that in future the Governor, assisted by a special Executive Committee, composed of two members of Assembly and one from the Council, should always put forward the proposals for government spending instead of permitting the individual members of the Assembly to do so, as had long been the practice. Of course such proposals still had to be passed by the Assembly, so friction between Governor and Assembly was not completely removed. But by the use of the Executive Committee, governors could now put their plans for government more easily before the assemblies; and it was now more difficult for the assemblies to spend more money than the government possessed, as had been done when every member could propose ways of spending public money.

The reform was also introduced into the other islands with assemblies. The Executive Committee was introduced into Tobago in 1855, Grenada in 1856, St. Kitts in 1857 and St. Vincent, Nevis and Antigua in 1859. In practice, the Executive Committee did little to soften quarrels between governors and assemblies when they broke out again. Also, since a member of the Executive Committee gained some power, and in some islands a salary too, jealousy and suspicion increased among members of the assemblies; these feelings in turn affected the way members voted when proposals of the Executive Committee were submitted to them.

This was the system inherited by Governor Eyre when he was sent out to Jamaica as acting-governor in 1862. He was not a tactful man and his strict moral ideas made him criticise what he regarded as the idle and immoral ways of all classes of the Jamaican population. This meant that he was out of sympathy with the people he ruled and unable to accept that their increasing hardships were not altogether their own fault. He was much disliked and those who tried to tell him of the very real difficulties of life in Jamaica had to face his bitter resentment and vengeful spirit.

George William Gordon was one of the first to draw Eyre's attention to various grievances. As a magistrate in St. Thomas, he complained in May 1862, of the inadequacies of the law-courts and the wretched state of the lock-ups where people awaited trial; he also drew the Governor's attention to the absence of medical help, or a hospital, or a poorhouse or an almshouse in his district. He had in fact been driven to writing to Eyre by the death in the lock-up of a sick man who had been placed there by the rector for want of any other public institution to put him in.

Eyre resented this letter and withdrew Gordon's commission as a magistrate. Gordon, who was one of the newly influential coloured landowners, protested vigorously and repeated his case wherever he could, often with the support of the press and occasionally of assembly members; this was not because they approved particularly of Gordon and his campaign for better public institutions, rather it was a way of demonstrating the unpopularity of the Governor. When discontent finally flared into an outbreak of disorder and bloodshed in Morant Bay, St. Thomas, in October 1865, it was not surprising that Gordon was held responsible, although he was far away in Kingston at the time. It was Eyre's final act of revenge to bring him back to St. Thomas in a warship; martial law had been proclaimed there and so Gordon could legally be tried by court-martial for high treason. It was almost a foregone conclusion that he would be condemned and sentenced to death. He was hanged in front of the court house.

THE MORANT BAY REBELLION

The event known as the Morant Bay Rebellion was in fact a local riot. A group of independent smallholders, excited by a Baptist Union preacher named Paul Bogle, marched on Morant Bay Court House on 4 October, 1865, to challenge the Custos of the parish on what they considered an unfair case of arrest the day before. The militia had been called out and, in the heated exchange of argument between Bogle's men and the Custos, they were finally provoked to fire on the crowds. What had been an angry deputation now became a disorderly gang. They burnt down the Court House, and twenty-eight people, including the Custos and some of the rioters, were killed. More property was destroyed and the inmates of the prison released before the band retreated into the country again.

Eyre laid the responsibility at the door of those he called seditious agitators; Gordon, of course, was one. But even more so, in his opinion, was Dr. Edward Underhill, the secretary of the Baptist Missionary Society. Underhill had visited Jamaica for some months in 1859 and had been distressed by conditions in the island. The subsequent reports of Baptist missionaries continued to distress him, and so, in 1865, he addressed a letter to the Secretary of State for the Colonies drawing his attention to the great hardships and poverty prevailing in Jamaica.

The *Underhill Letter*, as it came to be called, pointed out that in recent years there had been a great increase in crime, particularly in praedial larceny, and in applications for poor relief. This was partly because of droughts in 1862 and 1863 which had caused poor crops. Low and irregular wages had reduced many workers to a state of abject poverty. This was accompanied by high prices, largely due to high import duties maintained by the government, and to the great scarcity of those goods, such as food and textiles, which depended on American supplies; this last difficulty was a consequence of the American Civil War which raged between 1861 and 1865.

Underhill maintained that if the government would face its responsibilities for such matters, it could remedy them greatly by organising trade in produce grown by the people, improving communications and then providing vitally needed public services. He declared that the Jamaican legislature had never done its duty, as could be proved by an inspection of the laws they had passed since emancipaton.

The *Letter* was sent to Eyre for his comments and he immediately sent it out to custodes and magistrates so that its contents became generally known. 'Underhill Meetings' were called to discuss the points, and it was obvious that a large body of Jamaican opinion heartily agreed with them. Eyre however only upheld the views of officials, who were not interested in too much criticism of the government. He could then report to the Colonial Office that he had received little confirmation of Underhill's views in Jamaica. The Colonial Office informed Underhill in a short letter that it did not appear that the Jamaican people were 'suffering from any general or continuous distress from which they would not be at once relieved by settled industry'.

This opinion was repeated in June 1865 in the *Queen's Advice* to the people of St. Ann who had petitioned for help to meet their difficulties. This remarkable document ended with the assurance 'that it is from their own industry and prudence, in availing themselves of the means of prospering that are before them, and not from any such schemes as have been suggested to them, that they must look for an improvement in their conditions'. The *Advice* was distributed throughout Jamaica and read by rectors in Anglican churches; the nonconformist ministers refused to pass it on. There is little doubt that such official utterances were much resented in Jamaica and only added to the bitterness over particular grievances, such as the one that led to disorder in Morant Bay.

The disastrous quality of this event was again the work of Eyre.

He regarded this local rising as a Negro insurrection led by discontented coloured dissenters. He declared a state of emergency and so added to the fears of people in the rest of Jamaica that their lives and property were also in danger. Five hundred and eighty men and women were killed or hanged, six hundred were flogged and a thousand houses were destroyed before Eyre declared himself satisfied that the 'rebellion' was over.

CROWN COLONIES

These measures were too extreme, and the criticism of them too great, to pass without investigation. A Royal Commission was sent from England; and in the end Eyre was particularly condemned for his hanging of Gordon, and was deprived of his governorship. This took time, however, and before the enquiry started, the assembly had declared itself unable to govern and had voted itself out of existence. This was partly the result of Eyre's alarmist tactics which deliberately put the members in fear of having to face a rebellion of black Jamaicans against a white planter class. In fact, the assembly was no longer composed only of the white sugar interest, but they were still the majority. In the atmosphere of crisis, there is little doubt that they were persuaded that their interests would be better served by handing over Jamaica to Crown colony government by Englishmen, than by retaining a dwindling influence against an encroachment of rising coloured members whose interests did not coincide with their own.

The Jamaican Assembly had at first intended to keep a majority of elected members on the Council to sit alongside the 'official' civil servants, heads of department, who were also members of the Council in Crown colonies. In this they were seeking to follow the pattern established in Montserrat and Dominica which, in 1861 and 1863 respectively, had merged their two chambers into one, as a means of dealing more efficiently with their parlous finances; there they had retained a majority of elected members. The Jamaican Assembly had second thoughts, however, and decided after all to leave to the discretion of the Colonial Office what type of constitution should follow the two-hundred-year-old representative assembly that they had just abolished. The result was that, instead of a Council with both elected and official members, they were given one in which all the members were nominated by the Governor. This placed Jamaica in the same position as Trinidad where De Verteuil and his associates had for some years been demanding elected members on the Council. Not until 1884 in Jamaica and 1924 in Trinidad was this granted. Some Jamaicans therefore became critics of the new government straight away, but in general it started with good omens and was expected, at least by the Colonial Office, to organise public affairs far better than the assembly had ever done.

The departure of Eyre made room for Sir John Peter Grant, one of the ablest reforming governors ever appointed to the West Indies. His administration from 1866 to 1874 was a promising start for Crown colony government in Jamaica. He and his officials embarked on just those undertakings that had so long been required of the old assembly. The system of justice was overhauled and district courts were set up over the island to hasten the hearing of cases. A unified police force was organised. Indian immigration was renewed after a period of suspension, with a proper department established to administer it. A government savings bank was started, intended as a boon to smallholders. An island medical service was organised. Much was done for road improvement by the newly formed Public Works Department; the Rio Cobre irrigation scheme was also one of Grant's enterprises. Finally, the Anglican Church, which was certainly not the denomination of most of the people, was disestablished. The money saved by not paying for any new clergy was used for a much improved system of education. Grants were no longer given haphazardly but depended on a school satisfying an inspector that the children were actually learning something; this was called payment by results.

This was the form of administration that Taylor and his Colonial Office colleagues had so long thought the answer to problems of government in the West Indies. It was to become the pattern in all territories except Barbados which, like the Bahamas and Bermuda, preserved its elected assembly. Furthermore, the Colonial Office did not feel that they had imposed the new form of government; they were convinced that it was what the majority of West Indians wanted to ensure more efficient spending of public money on essential services for the people.

Difficulties over money were certainly the main cause of other islands first relinquishing their assemblies and, later, their elected members in the Councils. The maintenance of both an assembly and a council had already been abandoned in three small islands before the Jamaican Assembly was abolished in 1865; in Antigua, St.

Kitts and St. Vincent a single chamber was adopted during the three years after Jamaica became a Crown colony. Apart from Barbados, all the islands had reduced their legislature to one chamber by 1875 when Grenada completed the group seven years after the rest.

Governors and Colonial Office civil servants rejoiced in the tidier administration and in the reduced numbers of West Indian members. They had long been of the opinion that the small islands simply had not enough educated, or even literate, candidates for their own government. In 1865, for instance, the Lieutenant-Governor of Montserrat regretted that he was compelled 'to report the total unfitness of the persons chosen to serve in the assembly, the greater number of whom can barely read and write'.

For those who were concerned that West Indians should have a say in their own government, the issue now became, not the abolition of the assembly, but the question of the proportion of elected members to the civil servant official members on the new Legislative Councils. Except in Trinidad and St. Lucia, which had never been granted any representation by the British administration, all the islands which adopted a single chamber legislature, whether for the first time in 1866 or earlier, by that year found themselves with a majority of members nominated by the governor, so that if he or the Colonial Office thought it necessary, he could get his own way in the council.

In 1891 in British Guiana the College of Electors was abolished. The elected members of the Court of Policy, who were all planters, had recently brought the work of government to a standstill by withdrawing from the Court when they were annoyed by the Medical Inspector's criticism of the insanitary conditions for immigrant workers on the estates. The professional and commercial classes in Georgetown now petitioned the Queen for the vote and the incident favoured their plea. Until 1928, British Guiana continued to elect some of its members, and the elected majority in its Combined Court had the power to decide purely financial matters, after they had first voted the necessary money to pay the civil servants. All the other islands, except Barbados, however, lost their elected members and became Crown colonies. A pattern of colonial government was therefore established in the West Indies by which laws were made by a governor and a legislative council consisting of civil servants as official members and planters and merchants as unofficial members chosen by the governor. The former generally sat in council because, like the Colonial Secretary and the Attorney General, they held important offices or were heads of important departments such as the Agent-General for Immigration. The unofficial members were chosen by the governor as the spokesmen for particular groups; for instance, the sugar planters, the cacao planters and the merchants usually had spokesmen in the council.

DECLINE OF THE OLD REPRESENTATIVE SYSTEM

	Old Representative System.	Single Chamber.	
		Some Elected Members.	All Nominated Members.
Barbados	1663	—	—
British Guiana . . .	—	1803	—
Jamaica	1663	—	1866
Leewards			
Antigua	1663	1866	1898
St. Kitts } United 1882	1663	1866	1878
Nevis }	1663	1866	1877
Montserrat . . .	1663	1861	1866
Virgin Islands . . .	1773	1854	1867
Dominica	1775	1863	1898
Windwards			
Grenada	1766	1875	1877
St. Vincent. . . .	1766	1868	1877
St. Lucia	—	—	1803
Trinidad } United 1889	—	—	1797
Tobago }	1803	1874	1877

FURTHER READING

Sources of West Indian History, Government and Politics, pp. 109–20, 121–4, Social Conditions since Emancipation, pp. 227–32.

Black, *History of Jamaica*, Chapter XVII, The Morant Bay Rebellion.

Roberts, *Six Great Jamaicans*, George William Gordon.

Reid, *Sixty-Five*.

Ottley, *History of Tobago*, Chapters X–XI.

QUESTIONS TO CONSIDER

1. Can you account for the information on the chart at the end of the chapter? Why are there gaps in some places? Can you explain the separate dates at which the different territories changed to a government with a Legislative Council and no Assembly?

2. Do you consider that the British Government was justified in wanting Crown colony government in the West Indies?

3. Do you think that the *Underhill Letter* described the position in Jamaica accurately?

4. Do you consider the Morant Bay Riot an important event in West Indian history?

CHAPTER TWENTY

Ways and Means

A NEW RIVAL

The handing of the responsibility for government to the Colonial Office in London could not, and did not, solve the abiding problems in the West Indies. Such measures as were passed in fact still only alleviated distress and inadequacies which might have been removed long before. The provision of public works, hospitals and schools did no more than meet demands that had been made since emancipation by special magistrates, clergy and ministers, and sometimes in the press. It was not a new programme; rather it remained a more efficient attempt to meet old requirements.

Competition for the staple crop of the West Indies was ever-growing. In the second half of the nineteenth century, it was increased again from another source. During the Napoleonic Wars, when it had been difficult for the French to get sugar from their own West Indian islands, their government under Napoleon had encouraged the manufacture of sugar from sugar-beet. During the first half of the nineteenth century, this new industry had grown slowly; it cost more to make sugar from beetroot than from sugar-cane. But there were good reasons for European governments to encourage the beet-sugar industry. In the first place, it helps to make the country independent of imported sugar; this is particularly helpful in time of war when enemy shipping threatens supplies. Secondly, any industry reduces unemployment, and this was an increasing problem in Europe as the population increased steadily from the beginning of the nineteenth century. Thirdly, farmers found sugar-beet profitable and a good crop for the system they used of planting different crops in rotation for the benefit of the soil. Many European governments were therefore persuaded to give subsidies towards the manufacture of beet-sugar, and to raise high tariffs on imported sugar as a protection for their home product. In Europe after 1870 increasing industrial rivalry led governments to protect their national industries and by the eighteen-eighties only Britain and Holland practised free trade.

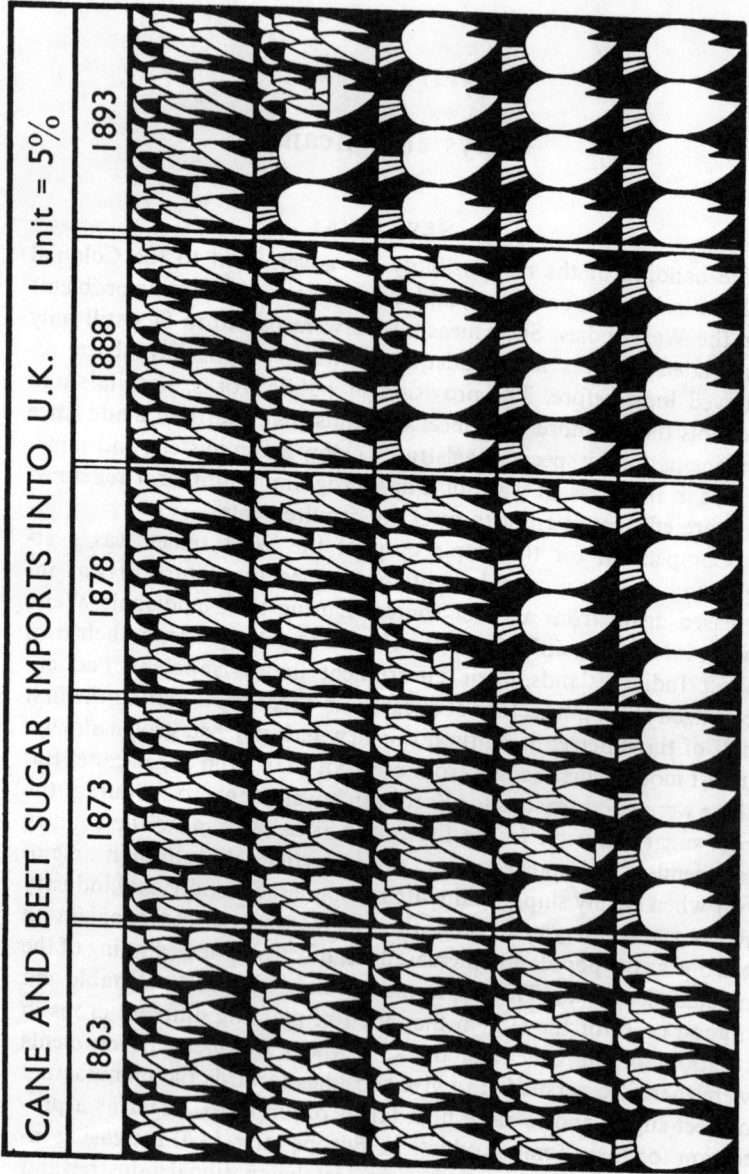

Fig. 11. Proportion of Cane and Beet Sugar Exports to the United Kingdom

In the second half of the nineteenth century, the governments of France, Germany, Austria, Holland, Belgium and Russia increased their assistance to their domestic beet-sugar industries at a time when the manufacturers had greatly improved their refining methods. Encouraged by their governments they were able to sell refined sugar in England at much lower prices than West Indian producers of cane-sugar could possibly compete with. Consequently, as the volume of beet-sugar imported into Britain increased, so the volume of cane-sugar declined. By the end of the nineteenth century, beet-sugar rather than cane-sugar was served on the tables of the United Kingdom.

During the last quarter of the nineteenth century British West Indian sugar, driven by competition from the United Kingdom, found a market in the United States, where demand was expanding and where beet-sugar imports were highly taxed. The American market remained profitable for twenty-odd years.

These were the market difficulties for sugar which had to be met by the planters. There were other misfortunes which affected all cultivators. In the eighteen-seventies there was a disastrous series of droughts, and hurricanes wrought their havoc many times in the last quarter of the century. The combination of natural disasters and new competition caused great suffering in this period.

After the first stage of confident activity under the Crown colony system the governors found themselves with formidable difficulties in the eighteen-seventies. The reforms and services that they had introduced had greatly increased the expenses of government, particularly those with costs that had to be met every year. Hospitals and schools had to be staffed and equipped regularly, for instance; roads and bridges had to be repaired and immigration schemes had to be financed annually. The revenue of these years could barely meet these costs; yet in addition the emergency repairs which storms made necessary and the interest due on loans borrowed long ago had to be provided for.

In these circumstances undertakings such as irrigation schemes, railways, drainage and new roads came in for hard criticism from those people who did not directly benefit from them. Hospitals, prisons, lunatic asylums and other special institutions were short of money, and were castigated for the poor conditions which resulted. Extended education systems in particular proved most costly as they attracted increasing numbers of pupils.

The Governor of Barbados in 1885 summarised the position. 'The increase in the ordinary expenditure,' he reported, 'has been rendered necessary by the natural growth of the population and the introduction of the appliances of civilisation.' The expenditure, he continued, 'has invariably been kept at the lowest possible limit consistent with the efficiency of the service and the proper upkeep of its institutions'. This statement explains the essential points. There was an increase in population in the whole area, and public institutions are expensive to maintain and more expensive to expand.

The last quarter of the nineteenth century became, therefore, not a period of progress under Crown colony government, but a period of problems to be faced with inadequate funds to deal with them, and an ever-increasing population to provide for. Governors and heads of departments frequently knew what was needed, but they were helpless to do anything unless money could be raised. Educational expansion, for instance, was impossible in the Leewards, when in fact money for education was cut by 25 per cent in 1898. For projects, such as markets, waterworks, gaslight for streets, which might be expected to repay the money spent on them, loans were raised. But West Indians without political responsibility became increasingly critical and dissatisfied as they saw the problems, and all too little done to meet them.

ATTEMPTS AT FEDERATION

One way in which the Imperial Government felt that funds could be saved was to unify the administration of the smaller islands. A start was made with the Leewards which had had a General Assembly in the seventeenth century. During not quite forty years of existence, it had never received wholehearted support from the individual islands; after 1711, it did not meet again until 1798, when for a short time unity was found in a common objection to the Imperial Government's interference with the system of slavery.

A new start had to be made, and in 1869 Sir Benjamin Pine was sent as Governor of the Leeward Islands to form Antigua, Dominica, Montserrat, St. Kitts, Nevis and the Virgin Islands into 'one colony with one Governor, one Council, one Superior Court, and one Corps of Police'. The Leeward Islands Act was passed in 1871, but only after considerable objections from the islands, including even a show of force in Nevis.

These objections forced the Colonial Office to accept a Leeward

Islands federation without a common treasury. The Leeward Islands Government was to be concerned with law, criminal and civil, and with the administration of justice, with education, a police force and prison, posts and currency, weights and measures and other items that it would be convenient to administer for the Leewards as a group. But the consent of each island was necessary to each measure as it arose. This had not been the Colonial Office's intention, but the fact that agreement could only be obtained on these terms shows the strength of small island loyalty as well as the reluctance of the Colonial Office to wrangle on details of federal government.

The Leeward Islands federation was intended as the first step towards a larger federation which would include the Windward Islands, with Barbados. The Windwards consisted of Grenada, St. Lucia, St. Vincent and Tobago, all islands more recently acquired by Britain. They had been placed under a Governor-in-Chief in Barbados in 1833, but there was no general assembly and the island legislatures remained quite independent.

Steps towards a more effective Windward Islands federation were taken in 1876. The attempted inclusion of Barbados was a complete failure. It was an old and proud colony which alone had not given up its assembly in favour of Crown colony government. With their plentiful supply of workers and long experience in sugar cultivation, Barbadians had hitherto done better than other West Indians, and were in no mood to be merged with less fortunate neighbours. The resistance was loud and vociferous in the Barbadian Assembly and press, and did not subside before the 'Confederation Riots'.

As we can see from comparing the figures of cane- and beet-sugar imported into Britain in the eighteen-seventies, the new threat to cane was quite obvious by 1876. This was a source of much concern to Barbadian planters. They feared that their inclusion in the Windward Islands federation would mean that they would have to share their workers and their revenue, and they were certainly not prepared to risk either at a time when they were threatened by such serious competition.

Pope-Hennessy, the governor who was sent in 1875 to promote this federation, fared far worse than Pine had done in the Leewards. The white planters formed themselves into a Barbados Defence Association, to protect their independence and their old 'representative' constitution. The mass of the people found themselves in favour of Pope-Hennessy, who had tried to force through the assembly some

235

reforms in prisons and hospitals. The estate labourers thought, no doubt rightly, that the federation would result in higher wages and perhaps make more land available to them. As both these things had been notably lacking in Barbados, feelings ran high and, in March 1876, violence broke out in some country parts. Eight people were killed, and troops had to be brought in from Jamaica and British Guiana before order was restored a month later.

The planters hastened to make capital out of the situation, blaming the Governor for encouraging the Negro workers to rebel and for trying to deprive Barbados of its 'representative' government. This was the issue most quoted, and it was not just a planter excuse. Conrad Reeves was one of the most prominent spokesmen in the assembly. He was typical of the coloured professional men. Of humble birth, he had spent some years as a journalist before he qualified in law. He was elected to the assembly, and in 1874 became Solicitor-General. This post he resigned in the crisis of 1876 so that he could fight the federation issue as an independent member. He was well aware of the justice of Pope-Hennessy's requests for reforms in Barbados, but he was determined that Barbadians should do the task themselves in their own assembly, and that they should not follow the other islands into Crown colony government. He regarded the federation move as a first step in the wrong direction. 'We have declined confederation,' he declared in the House of Assembly, 'because in the form which it takes in the case of the West India colonies it means, and can only mean, the surrender by us, in the long run, of our representative form of government.'

The firmness of this resistance was effective. Pope-Hennessy was removed by the Colonial Office because his presence made the white Barbadians quite intractable. The assembly survived, but the Executive Committee, which had been introduced earlier in the other islands, was now also set up in Barbados to make financial proposals and influence the assembly's spending of public money. In this way, Barbados alone escaped Crown colony government; the Barbados Assembly stepped into the shoes of the old Jamaica Assembly as a robust resister of Colonial Office suggestions, which could not be forced on them in the same way as in the Crown colonies.

The violence of the Barbadian resistance postponed the union of the other Windward Islands for nearly ten years. Although they had given up their assemblies, they had no desire to part with any of their other institutions, so the proposal for sharing their resources was not immediately pressed. The re-organisation of the Windward Islands in 1885 in effect did no more than establish a common governor and auditor general, with their headquarters in Grenada. All suggestions for a joint legislature met with howls of protest from all islands, and any milder proposal for joint officials, such as the eminently reasonable idea in 1891 that two islands could share a chief justice, was met with violent resistance; the British Government even thought it necessary to send a warship to St. Vincent on this occasion. The only combinations that succeeded were the merging of the St. Kitts and Nevis administrations in 1882, and the final fusion of the Governments of Trinidad and Tobago in 1899.

The only results of the attempts at federation by the Colonial Office were that one group of small islands, the Leewards, were loosely federated, and another, the Windwards, now shared one governor. Much more than this had certainly been intended. Because the other important offices were still duplicated in each island, these attempts at federation did not in practice save public money.

FACING THE FACTS

In the eighteen-eighties it became apparent that the West Indian islands were considerably in debt and had little prospect of repaying loans which had been guaranteed by the Imperial Government earlier in the century. A Royal Commission was sent from England in 1882 to enquire into the state of the finances and public spending in Jamaica, the Leewards and the Windwards. The commissioners could only state the obvious facts that the sugar market was in decline, that the competition of beet-sugar was now formidable, and that this threatened the economy of the West Indies. They suggested improvements in the cultivation and marketing of sugar which would help it in competition with other producers. Significantly, they recognised that the army of small farmers that had now grown up in the West Indies might be encouraged to produce more varied crops for export. The small farmers were at last officially recognised as potentially important to West Indian prosperity.

Both of the main suggestions made by the commissioners were worked on. One had already proved its worth when, in the eighteen-seventies, Jamaica found an export market in the United States for the banana which, in consequence, soon became the smallholders' favourite crop. This was not the result of government planning, as Underhill had recommended in his *Letter*, but the sequel when an

237

astute American, Captain Baker, took on a load of bananas at Port Antonio to carry to New York in his schooner. By 1880 he had attracted a newly formed company of fast ships to his business, and so developed the thriving banana trade which rescued Jamaica's economy.

In addition to the banana, there were other cash crops, particularly in those islands where sugar had declined completely. Cacao and nutmegs were grown for export in Grenada, arrowroot in St. Vincent and coconuts in most islands; all became profitable with a developing trade to absorb them. These were crops that would also be grown by smallholders, and the new markets encouraged an increase in their number.

Already in the eighteen-sixties, small farming had been encouraged in Trinidad by the sale by the government of Crown lands in small lots. Elsewhere other methods of land settlement were used; Crown lands and idle estates were sought after to be divided into more smallholdings. We have already seen that a small plot of land was one of the inducements offered to immigrant workers to stay permanently in the West Indies.

In the sugar industry, British Guianese and Trinidadian producers had adopted more efficient methods of production than the other planters, so they competed with greater success in the British market. From emancipation in both these territories there had been much amalgamating of estates and they were by the end of the century owned by companies rather than by individual planters; members of a family, such as the Lamonts and the Tennants in Trinidad, also sometimes found it convenient to turn their estates into limited companies. Most of these estates had been bought cheaply in the difficult years of the eighteen-forties and fifties, and so had made fair returns in the better sugar markets of the seventies, before the competition of beet-sugar had had its effect.

A similar amalgamation of estates took place in Jamaica and Antigua. In the islands which maintained sugar production, Barbadians showed least willingness to turn the estates over to companies as commercial enterprises because the estates there had long been family homes; there were still in existence in 1890, 440 of the 500 estates in the island at the time of emancipation. In British Guiana, by contrast, there were in 1890 only 140 remaining of the 600 sugar estates in 1833. The figures for the whole of the British West Indies reveal the extent to which sugar estates were abandoned or amalgamated during the nineteenth century. At the time of emancipation, there were about 2,200 sugar estates here, by the end of the century there were between 750 and 800.

By the last quarter of the nineteenth century, the sugar industry was constantly threatened by the competition of beet-sugar. The profits maintained by the remaining sugar producers were largely due to improved farming with the advice of agricultural specialists. Government botanists were appointed in Jamaica, Barbados and British Guiana. These appointments brought agricultural specialists here to work on scientific methods for improved farming. In Barbados, for instance, sugar-cane was first grown from seed in 1888 and so a much greater variety of canes could be bred to find the one most profitable for a competitive market. Plant diseases and soil conditions were examined, and information about them was circulated as widely as possible.

The scientific work was on the whole of most benefit to estate owners. The small farmers were less in contact with the new developments, and it was a problem to inform them of the results of the work. Books were published and many lectures given in the chief towns, but they did not reach the general farming public. It was at this time therefore that agricultural education was introduced into the elementary and a few of the secondary schools. Teachers were given short, intensive courses and returned to their schools to show children the best way to grow bananas, vegetables, coffee and such other crops as did well in their particular areas. The attempts were too small to be effective, but they at least informed pupils that some methods of cultivation were more successful than others.

ENTERPRISE AND ADVERSITY

There were other instances of enterprise which also helped to avert disaster. The scarcity of employment increased alarmingly as the population grew, and wages fell as the economic situation deteriorated. The plentiful workers in Barbados, for instance, could still only command 8d. or 9d. a day by the eighteen-nineties. Barbados, however, by the end of the century was not the only territory with too large a population to maintain at a reasonable standard of living. In fifty years the censuses taken showed that the population of the West Indies nearly doubled, from about 863,917 people in 1841 to about 1,607,218 people in 1891. In Trinidad and British Guiana, Indian immigration had established large new groups of people by the end of

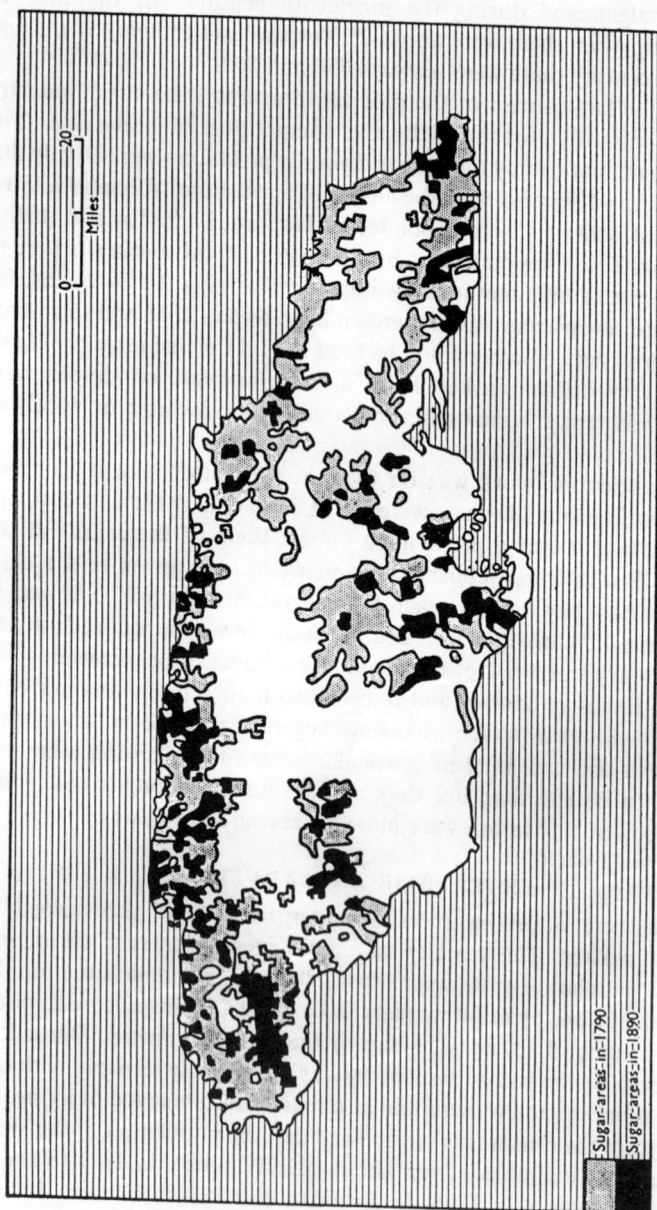

Fig. 12. A Map of the Decline of Sugar Areas in Jamaica, 1790–1890

Sugar areas in 1790
Sugar areas in 1890

the century. Everywhere the number of births greatly exceeded the number of deaths.

Difficulties over employment encouraged individual initiative to meet the situation. The movement from the estates into small independent farming was followed by movement within the Caribbean area as a whole of people seeking work outside their own territories. We have seen the Barbadian tendency to migrate from their overpopulated island. There was a good deal of departure from other small islands too. The Central American mainland provided work on coffee, sugar and banana plantations. When the abolition of slavery was completed in Cuba in 1886, large numbers of West Indians found employment on the far more prosperous sugar estates there. For Jamaicans, in particular, the various enterprises in Panama acted as a magnet. They helped to build the railway in the eighteen-sixties, were casualties of the abortive attempt to start the canal in the eighteen-eighties, and were a large part of the labour force in the successful effort at the beginning of the twentieth century. In all these places, West Indians settled as agricultural workers, construction labourers, shopkeepers and provision merchants.

This was the emphatic beginning of the continuous West Indian emigration in search of work. Some of the emigrants never returned, but others returned to buy smallholdings with the proceeds. They all sent money back to their families, and so indirectly supported the section of the community that needed it most. Those who returned also brought back an experience of working conditions that had not reached the West Indies; they knew how workers could be organised, what wages were considered suitable elsewhere and some of them, who went further afield to America and Great Britain, came into contact with trade unions. In addition to their earnings, some of the returning emigrants brought useful experience of better working conditions back with them.

Education was another way of spreading better standards of living and this continued to expand, at least for the few, in the last quarter of the nineteenth century. The increased tasks of government created much new work in the civil service, such as the paying out of funds, the administration of buildings and services and a vast increase in government correspondence and accounts. These were mainly clerical tasks and were, of course, not done in the top posts of the civil service, but they required more education than could be obtained in the very deficient elementary schools. Parents knew that if their sons got these 'white collar' jobs, they had a respectable place in the community, so they sought secondary education to achieve it. Many English teachers were imported and, with the coming of the Cambridge Local Examinations to the West Indies in the eighteen-eighties, the kind of curriculum was decided. Most pupils could expect to achieve at least a third-class certificate in the Junior Examination, and this alone would put them head and shoulders above the mass of their fellows.

The governments and the religious bodies, sometimes in conjunction, provided secondary schools. In Jamaica and Barbados, the officials found neglected charities, left in the past by wealthy estate owners for the education of poor white boys. By supervising the use of the funds, they were able to establish several new secondary schools. Munro, Ruseas, Titchfield and Mannings are four examples in Jamaica; in Barbados, Harrison College, Christ Church and Combermere were re-established, as secondary schools, by this means.

The Catholics and Anglicans continued to provide schools, and the nonconformists in Jamaica added to their number. In the first place, the nineteenth-century secondary schools provided an education in the West Indies for white boys, including the sons of British civil servants, as a substitute for sending them to England. The added number of secondary schools, however, provided also for the sons of those coloured families which had been increasing in numbers. The Jamaican nonconformists particularly had this group in mind in providing their schools.

It was a considerable enterprise in a period when the prospects for the West Indies were increasingly doubtful. The spread of Crown colony government (except in Barbados, where in any case secondary education was well supported by the assembly) in fact postponed for many decades the time when well-educated West Indians could assume high public responsibility in politics, administration and justice. The prospects for most secondary school graduates were strictly limited to the lower paid white collar jobs. This was a serious and increasingly criticised limitation; but the professions of law, medicine and teaching were open to the few who could obtain higher education.

There were serious attempts to develop university colleges both in Trinidad and Jamaica, but it proved impossible at that time for the schools to educate enough students to university standard. Codrington College, which prepared a few students for classical degrees as well as for the Anglican ministry, alone maintained a precarious existence. Other Protestant denominations had their seminaries, and their churches were increasingly staffed with West Indian ministers.

For the rest, only a few could afford to go to England or North America for further education. The island scholarships, usually for one boy a year, were established in the larger territories in this period and were the much coveted only opportunity that bright pupils had to go to a university. In the circumstances most of them chose to study either medicine or law, since they could practise these professions here; some preferred not to return, since their prospects were so limited.

For events and circumstances were still defeating all the attempts to restore the West Indian sugar economy. A widespread outbreak of cane disease in the eighteen-nineties, for instance, ruined the crops for several years in succession. The Secretary of State for the Colonies at the turn of the century was Joseph Chamberlain, who regarded the British colonial empire as a vast area to be developed profitably, if necessary with imperial assistance accompanied by imperial direction. In 1896 he sent a Royal Commission to the West Indies to discover ways of restoring the sugar industry and to find if the competition of European beet-sugar, still subsidised by government bounties in the countries where it was grown, was in fact the principal cause of distress in the West Indian sugar industry.

The commissioners were not agreed on the effects of competition from beet-sugar, but they were agreed that there was an economic depression in the West Indies and they strongly urged on the Colonial Office 'the encouragement of all measures having a tendency to maintain the well-being of the population'. They suggested that only in Barbados, Antigua and St. Kitts should sugar remain the staple crop. In the other islands, where a variety of crops already existed, farmers should be encouraged and assisted to produce more than at present. To that end the commissioners advised that land settlement schemes should be introduced to increase the number of small farmers; that agricultural banks should be established to assist such farmers; that improved systems of cultivation should be devised in agricultural departments, and made known through popular schemes of agricultural education. Communications between the islands should be improved and a better steamer service should be run to New York, and later to London, to encourage the fruit trade.

The commissioners recognised that the West Indian governments would only be able to act on many of their recommendations if the Imperial Government made grants and loans for these purposes. They therefore recommended that the Imperial Government should spend £60,000 to clear the public debts of the small islands, and also make a grant of £20,000 for five years to relieve existing distress, to aid emigration from small islands where possible and to build roads and prepare land for settlement by small farmers, particularly in St. Vincent and Dominica. The cost of the experimental and educational work in agriculture, and that of improving communications both within and without the Caribbean, would be met by money granted over ten years.

But before the recommendations of the commissioners were acted on, a short, sharp war between the United States and Spain in 1898 brought the crisis to a head. The war lasted ten weeks and, when it was over, the Philippines and Puerto Rico were ceded to the United States. Cuba became an independent republic, with doors wide open to American capitalists who wanted to enter into sugar production. With this new encouragement to Cuba the benefit to the British West Indies of the American market for the past twenty-odd years was lost. At the end of the nineteenth century there seemed little hope for the British Caribbean.

FURTHER READING

Sources of West Indian History, Economic Life, pp. 75–9, Social Conditions since Emancipation, pp. 239–45, Attempts at Unification, pp. 269–80.

Black, *History of Jamaica*, Chapter XVIII, The New Jamaica Takes Shape.

Hoyos, *Our Common Heritage*, John Pope-Hennessy, Conrad Reeves.

Roberts, *Six Great Jamaicans*, Robert Love.

Daly, *The Story of the Heroes*, Alfred Thorne.

Ottley, *History of Tobago*, Chapter XIV.

QUESTIONS TO CONSIDER

1. What attempts to meet the economic difficulties of the West Indies in the last quarter of the nineteenth-century would you think offered the most hope?

2. What differences can you discover between the history of Jamaica and Barbados at this time? How would you expect them to continue?

3. What arguments for and against federation have emerged in this chapter?

4. At the turn of the century the West Indies faced the prospect of financial ruin. Can you account for this and can you predict the measures taken to avert disaster?

CHAPTER TWENTY-ONE

The United States in the Caribbean

FROM ISOLATION TO INTERVENTION

The Spanish American War, as the short spell of fighting in Cuba in 1898 was called, was a turning point for the United States as well as for the Caribbean territories which were affected by the result. It was also the end of the Spanish American Empire when Cuba was granted independence and Puerto Rico was ceded to the United States; in the Pacific, the Philippine Islands also passed into American hands in 1899. This meant that the United States became an imperial country after over a century of criticising and checking the imperial activities of European countries, especially in Central and South America.

The attitude of the United States towards European intervention in the Americas had been clearly stated by President Monroe in his famous message to the American Congress in 1823. In 1820, the last of the Latin American countries in South America had successfully won independence, after years of heroic fighting against Spanish forces. But congresses of European statesmen were still discussing whether they should not help to win back some of these new Latin American republics for Spain. President Monroe intended to discourage any such scheme when he declared that the American continents 'are henceforth not to be considered as subjects for future colonisation by any European powers'. Furthermore, any European attempt to oppress or control the South American countries would be regarded as an unfriendly act towards the United States.

For the half century after their famous declaration against European interference the Americans were fully occupied at home extending their frontier to the west coast and absorbing many millions of immigrants, mainly from Europe. In the eighteen-sixties, they were engaged in the civil war between the southern states, with their plantations and slaves, and the commercial northern states which were concerned with developing the iron foundries of Philadelphia, Cincinnati and Pittsburgh and in making machinery for transport, agriculture and further industry. The victory of the north ensured

246

the industrial progress of the nation with the employment of ever increasing numbers of immigrant wage-earners.

The industrial revolution in the United States really gained momentum only after 1865; the flow of immigrants, mainly from Germany, Scandinavia, Ireland and other Western European countries, increased accordingly, as impoverished workers in a new country sought employment, wages and opportunities which did not exist in their countries of origin. It was the age of business enterprise, and the national heroes were those whose success made them millionaires. They had often themselves started as penniless immigrants, like Andrew Carnegie, who as a boy of twelve came from a Scottish weaver's home to join relatives in the booming industrial town of Pittsburgh. He worked for the telegraph company, the railroads and in the oil and iron industries before he was in a position to launch out for himself in iron and steel, the great resources for American expansion in industry and transport. He made his fortune. So did Rockefeller who slowly bought up a large number of oil refineries and the means of transporting oil, until his Standard Oil Company became the biggest monopoly in the United States. Both these millionaires are now internationally known because, both during their lifetime and after, they gave much of their money to promote education and social welfare wherever it was needed in the world. The Carnegie Libraries in Barbados, British Guiana and St. Lucia bear witness to the fact that the West Indies has benefited, and the foundations which now allot the remaining funds still make many grants for research in West Indian medical, social and educational matters.

In addition to those who made fortunes, there was an army of small investors of all kinds in the United States. Some of them bought schooners and looked for trade in the Caribbean area, where European shipping had become increasingly scarce as the slave trade died. They visited the sugar islands and the still struggling Latin American republics of Central America, and some of them picked up cargoes of coffee in Brazil and cacao in Trinidad. These small shipowners were the first to carry bananas. They would collect them in the Bay Islands, off the coast of Honduras, and from Panama in Colombia, for sale at auction in New Orleans. We have seen that Captain Baker was the first to run a cargo of bananas from Jamaica as far as New York in 1870. Many of these individual enterprises succeeded and attracted American shareholders to finance their development.

By the end of the nineteenth century, $50,000,000 were invested in Cuba, mostly in sugar, and a further $55,000,000 in property in Mexico and other Caribbean areas. This investment was worth defending, and so were the American employees who came out as foremen, accountants and managers on the various estates in the Caribbean and Central America. When there were disturbances in any of these places, American lives, property and capital were all threatened. This became an increasing concern of the American Government.

Relations with the Latin American countries were still friendly when the United States Government called the first Pan-American Conference in 1889, to discuss mutual interests and plans for development. In 1895 a dispute about the boundary between Venezuela and British Guiana caused the American President, Cleveland, to become very aggressive towards the British Government in defence of the independent republic of Venezuela. He sent to London that summer what he called a 'twenty-inch gun note' accusing Britain of violating the Monroe Doctrine and demanding that the British Government should arbitrate with the United States Government on the position of the boundary. 'Today the United States is practically sovereign on this continent,' declared Cleveland. In December, he threatened war if the British Government did not comply. Both the British and the American publics were shocked at the turn of events, and relieved when the arbitration was finally accepted. The importance of the episode lay in the claim of the United States to 'be practically sovereign on this continent' and consequently to be concerned in defending the rights of any independent state in the hemisphere. Cleveland's statements over the Venezuelan border issue showed that they were now ready to intervene, if necessary with armed forces, in disputes and disturbances anywhere in the Americas.

In 1895, the Cubans revolted against Spanish rule, which had drained the island of much of its revenue and had maintained a tyrannical form of government with cruel and arbitrary punishment of any Cuban resisters. An American tariff against Cuban sugar was causing great depression on the Cuban estates. José Marti, the leader of the revolt, found a ready following of underpaid and underemployed estate workers in the country.

There were $50,000,000 of American capital invested in Cuba and trade with America amounted to $100,000,000 a year, mostly in tobacco and sugar. American lives and property were in danger in the savage fighting and Spanish attempts to put down the revolt.

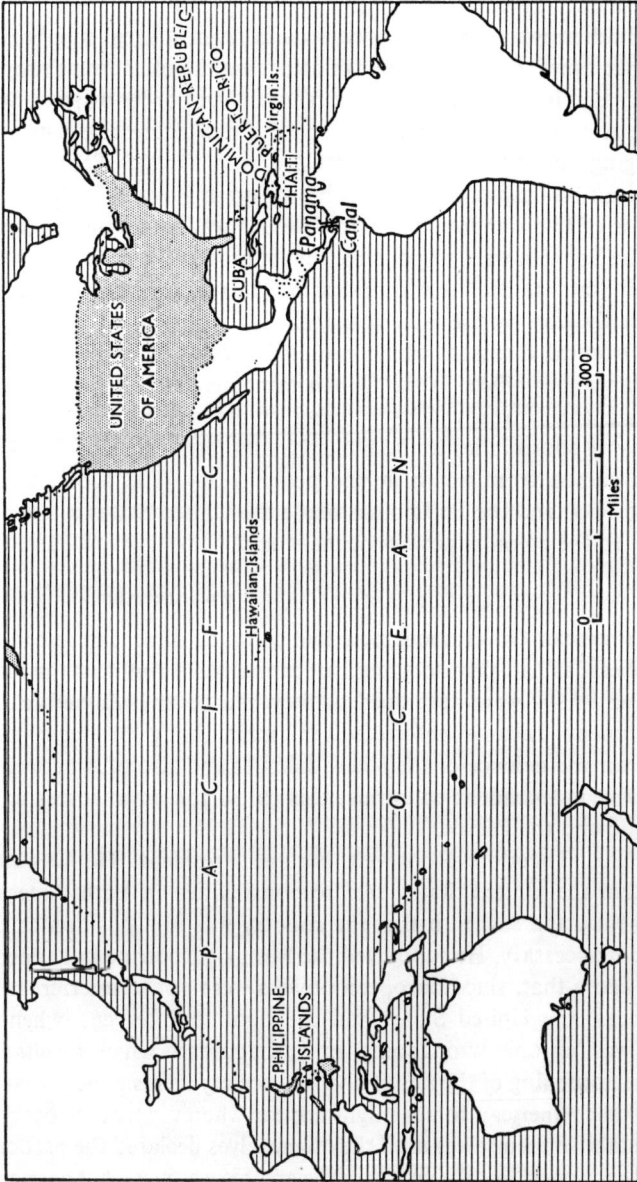

Fig. 13. A Sketch Map of the Pacific Ocean, marking the chief areas of American interest.

Furthermore, Americans were greatly shocked at the stories of Spanish outrages and of concentration camps filled with men, women and children who died of starvation and fever in great numbers.

Public opinion was in favour of attacking the offending European power, as it had not been over the Venezuelan border dispute. Some of the American newspapers played on a new aggressive patriotism in urging the government to declare war. On 15 February, an American battleship, *Maine*, was blown up in Havana harbour with the loss of two hundred and sixty lives. It was by no means certain that the Spanish were responsible, but it proved the occasion for the United States to declare war on Spain. The war lasted ten weeks and was easily won by the Americans, though not without great losses from tropical diseases, which caused Theodore Roosevelt, then a popular young officer in the Cuban campaign, to call it the War of America the Unready. The winning of the war brought new and serious responsibilities to the United States Government in the territories gained from Spain at the peace treaty. The acquisition of Puerto Rico and the Philippines made the United States a late newcomer to the colonial powers of the world.

PERIOD OF AMERICAN EXPANSION

The American Government now had as much direct interest in the Caribbean as had private American capitalists. From this time their army and navy were developed as they had never been before. The government became interested in maintaining strategic naval bases for the defence of their new colonies and also of American interests in independent countries; this called for naval forces in the Atlantic and the Pacific.

In 1901 Theodore Roosevelt became President. He was quite sure that the United States held responsibilities in both American continents, and saw to it that the country was in a position to take action if necessary. He supported the Monroe Doctrine but added to it the claim that, since European powers were not to interfere in the Americas, the United States had the right to intervene whenever there was 'chronic wrongdoing, or an impotence which results in a general loosening of the ties of civilised society'. This policy meant in effect that American forces might appear wherever trouble occurred and establish themselves until they themselves declared the particular emergency over. For the next thirty years this was just what happened.

In this period of expansion the Americans were very interested in reviving the Panama Canal project. Disease amongst the workers had been the main cause of the French failure to complete the canal in the eighteen-eighties. As yellow fever was also prevalent in Cuba amongst the American forces during the Spanish American War, scientists investigated the causes of the epidemic and found it to be a mosquito-borne disease. It could now be eradicated, and the only obstacle remaining for the Americans was the matter of winning the right to undertake the project. To get this Roosevelt set out on a diplomatic adventure which shocked many people. The French were prepared to sell their rights and the British, who were alarmed at growing German competition in industry and trade, were willing to accommodate a new friend by renouncing any rights in the Panama Canal. The country which was not willing to co-operate so easily was Colombia, through whose northern state, called Panama, the canal was to be built.

Years later Roosevelt boasted 'I took Panama', and this was very nearly the truth. He accused the Colombian Government of greed and corruption for asking a higher price than the Americans offered for the strip of land for the canal. The French were anxious for an early sale so that they could get profitable terms for their rights, and their agents in Panama incited some of the local people to restlessness, by saying that the canal might be built elsewhere if the Colombian Government refused the price offered. American newspapers talked of possible revolt in Panama and American warships arrived on the scene. In the excitement that followed American marines landed to restore order before the Colombian troops could intervene, and a tiny new republic with an independent government was proclaimed in Panama. This new government, not surprisingly, gave the United States the strip of land through which the canal was to be built on very favourable terms. With American engineers, American medical officers and a great deal of West Indian, as well as local, labour the canal was in use ten years later.

Roosevelt was criticised at home and abroad for his high-handed action. The Latin American republics became particularly uneasy after an affair in which the hesitation of Colombia had been so roughly dealt with. Many Americans were hardly more happy and ten years later, when the canal came into use, President Wilson paid a large sum to Colombia as compensation for the losses sustained.

There were always Americans who disliked their country's imperial activities; they recalled that they had won their own independence from a colonial power and were unhappy to find that they were now a colonial power themselves. On the other hand, there were many missionaries and social reformers who had followed the businessmen to South America and the Caribbean, and they reported disease, poverty and squalor amongst the common people where-ever they went. Some supported their government's activities abroad because they thought that down-trodden people would benefit from American intervention. The politicians claimed as much. President Taft, who followed Theodore Roosevelt, said that American policy in the Caribbean area was 'international philanthropy', another politician called it 'unselfish service'. In fact, however, while argument continued at home, for many years to come the government conducted 'a dollar diplomacy', by which the government intervened abroad only in places where American business was already established.

In Cuba, although the United States agreed that this large Caribbean island should become an independent republic, they did so on such terms that American forces intervened in local disturbances repeatedly. When the American governor of Cuba handed over to the first elected Cuban president in 1902, it was agreed that American naval stations should remain in Cuba and that the United States 'may intervene for the preservation of Cuban independence and for the protection of life, property and individual liberty'. This agreement was called the Platt Amendment and it was appended to the Cuban constitution. The existence of such an agreement and the presence of American capital in Cuba also meant that the Americans seemed to approve of the Cuban Government when they did not interfere; they were much criticised, for instance, for not interfering with the ruthless dictator, President Machado, who ruled from 1924 to 1933. Many Cubans became bitter critics of the United States at that time.

In Puerto Rico, the responsibility of the United States Government was direct. It was an impoverished island in which continuous risings from 1823 to 1898 had been cruelly suppressed by the Spanish Government. The granting of some degree of self-government by the Spanish in 1897, came too late to win Puerto Rican support and they accepted the Americans with hopes of better government and opportunities. In this they were much disappointed. In the first place they were not made American citizens. An Organic Act of 1900 granted a government of one house elected by universal male suffrage, but the island was effectively ruled by an American governor and a team of civil servants in an Executive Council with 'five other persons of good repute', all appointed by the President of the United States and answerable to him. One provision of the Organic Act was wholly ignored for forty years, and this was the main source of discontent. It said that no person or company should own an estate of more than 500 acres. In fact, four large American sugar-producing corporations were allowed to establish themselves as glaring exceptions to the rule, and this was bitterly resented by Puerto Ricans. The granting, by a new Organic Act in 1917, of American citizenship to Puerto Ricans, two elected chambers of government and the reduction of American civil servants to three heads of department, was too late to remove Puerto Rican criticism of American imperial methods; these included open favouritism towards the American business interests as well as colonial control. For the governor in any case retained great powers, including the right to veto budget items, and both the President and Congress of the United States could veto the island laws. No positive programme of government could result from such divided powers. Public works were confined to the roads, bridges and irrigation needed by the sugar industry and although smallpox and yellow fever were eradicated, tuberculosis, the disease of poverty and undernourishment, caused the highest death-rate in the world in Puerto Rico until 1934. This was hard to reconcile with the American claim that their rule was 'international philanthropy'.

In 1917 the United States bought the islands of St. Thomas, St. Croix and St. John's from the Danish Government and established them as the American Virgin Islands. They paid $25,000,000 for their new colony, that is at the rate of approximately $295 an acre, as compared with the approximately $36 an acre they had originally paid in Panama. The value of these arid, over-populated little islands, which had long lost their prosperity as trading stations, was strategic. They could defend the Atlantic approach to the Panama Canal. It was rumoured that the German Government was trying to buy them and, with submarine warfare prevailing in the Atlantic in the First World War, it was worth a great deal to forestall them. The fact that the Virgin Islands were governed by the American Navy until 1931 shows what use was made of them.

During the First World War the United States also intervened in Haiti and the Dominican Republic when local revolutions were threatening millions of dollars of American private investment. The marines were landed in Haiti in 1915 and in the Dominican Republic in 1916. In the former, an American general acted as High Commissioner and appointed his own heads of department until 1934; in the latter American officials and forces remained until 1924. These measures were intended to ensure that the finances of the countries were kept in order and that debts were paid, particularly to the American investors. The people of the country benefited to the extent that their employment was made more secure. Public works in the introduction of sanitation and the building of hundreds of miles of roads were also undertaken; but this was done by a system which the Haitians regarded as forced labour and, on one occasion, resisted to the point of considerable bloodshed. The trade of both countries became practically an American monopoly. Coffee, in particular, and also sisal, sugar and bananas were sent to an assured market in the United States. This was supported in the nineteen-twenties by high tariffs maintained against imports from countries not supporting American interests. The British West Indian coffee and fruit markets, for instance, suffered severely from these high tariffs. The American Government also assisted trade with all the Caribbean territories where American money was invested by generously subsidising private business concerns which were developing more merchant shipping and air connections in the area.

NEW DEAL AND GOOD NEIGHBOUR POLICIES

The policy of the United States Government of aiding and protecting American business interests abroad changed in the nineteen-thirties. The author of the change was President Franklin D. Roosevelt who was first elected in 1933, in the midst of a world-wide depression following a dramatic slump in trade in 1929. There were over 13,000,000 Americans unemployed when he took office. In this crisis, Roosevelt, who was already well-known as the Governor of New York, was swept to office on a wave of public confidence that he could deal with the crisis. He was sure that the wealth of America should be better distributed and should serve more than private ends. 'Plenty is at our doorstep,' he asserted in his inaugural address, 'but a generous use of it languishes in the very sight of plenty.' He committed himself 'to recommend the measures that a stricken nation in the midst of a stricken world may require'.

The programme that followed both assisted recovery and distributed relief on a pattern that was later copied in the Caribbean.

Under the New Deal, as it was called, banks were closed, to be re-opened under government supervision and government loans were made to hard-pressed businesses. A nation-wide programme of public works was embarked on, with government loans advanced to create employment in the building of houses, roads, bridges and other im-provements. A vast sum was spent on direct relief, such as allow-ances to the unemployed and food distribution in the worst areas of unemployment.

Abroad the new administration had a positive policy too. The Latin American countries, which had watched American interven-tion in the Caribbean area with great suspicion since the Panama incident, were relieved when American forces withdrew from Haiti in 1934 and when the American 'rights' of the Platt Amendment were relinquished in Cuba at the same time. A deliberate Good Neighbour policy with the Latin American countries bore fruit. In 1940, the first year of the Second World War, Roosevelt was able to make an agreement with the Latin American countries for collective protection should hostilities affect any of them.

In the American colonies, the New Deal was also applied to meet distress. In 1934 a division was set up in the American Department of the Interior, for the Territories and Island Possessions. Despite the 'big stick' activities for which they were much criticised in their first decades as an imperial power, Americans have never considered them-selves permanent rulers of empire and so have not set up a separate government department, like the British Colonial Office, to control their oversea possessions. They prefer to see their colonies either moving towards independence, like the Philippines in 1946, or destined to be further states in the Union.

There has always been an independence movement in Puerto Rico, but the present constitution is a special relationship with the United States suggested and voted for by the Puerto Ricans them-selves, at the invitation of the American Government in 1950. They have chosen the same form of government as an American state, with two elected houses. Since 1947 the governor has been made an elected official. He has in fact been a Puerto Rican since 1946 and Muñoz Marin has been governor since 1948. The Puerto Ricans still have no effective representation in the American Congress but they now control their own internal government.

From the American occupation in 1898 till the end of the Second World War in 1945, $580,000,000 were granted to Puerto Rico by the

United States Government but, most strikingly, nearly all of this was given after 1933 when the New Deal began. Progress in Puerto Rico was often called the Little New Deal. In the Virgin Islands, since 1917, about half a million dollars were spent on relief and then $10,000,000 on their development, largely as tourist centres as well as American bases.

The American Government in the last quarter of a century has conducted an expensive fight against poverty and unemployment in their dependencies. Even so, some Puerto Ricans have declared that they would prefer independence from the United States. Others have taken advantage of their American citizenship to emigrate to the mainland; fifty per cent of the population of the Virgin Islands have emigrated, and Puerto Ricans have increasingly migrated in search of better wages and employment. Their emigration was slow in starting and migrants returned home as soon as they had made a little money because, as Spanish speakers, they could not easily make themselves understood in the United States; also, since most Puerto Ricans regard themselves as white, they have been particularly disturbed by the colour bar. Nevertheless, since the end of the last war when there has been employment available in the United States again, migration has become an important possibility for the Puerto Rican worker. Between 1945 and 1952, 283,214 Puerto Ricans went to the United States.

The United States would now be a force in the Caribbean even without their formal possession of Puerto Rico and the American Virgin Islands. The development of Cuban iron ore and nickel and of oil and bauxite confirmed their interest in investment in the region and there are now American concerns of all sorts throughout the Caribbean area. This is one of the most important facts of West Indian affairs in the twentieth century.

FURTHER READING

Parry and Sherlock, *A Short History of the West Indies*, Chapter XVII, The United States and the Independent Islands.

QUESTIONS TO CONSIDER

1. Which event described in this chapter seems to you to have most effectively brought the United States into the Caribbean area?

2. Which Caribbean territory has been most affected by United States direction in your opinion?

3. How far would you agree that 'international philanthropy' has resulted from American activities in the Caribbean area?

4. From the description of difficulties in Puerto Rico in the nineteen-thirties can you work out what needed attention under the 'Little New Deal' there?

CHAPTER TWENTY-TWO

Twentieth-century Endeavour

KEEPING SUGAR IN PRODUCTION

'Had circumstances been more propitious, I should have liked to mark this eightieth year of our proprietorship by the commencement of some work of a nature urgently needed. One is the provision of better houses for the people, and the other is the provision of a better and purer water supply, both of which have long been near my heart; but I regret to say that under present conditions, and with the prospect of another severe loss this year, owing to the bad prices, it is impossible even to begin to carry out these works.' So spoke Sir Norman Lamont to his estate workers in April 1901. Lamont, a Scotsman who regularly visited the family estate in Palmiste, Trinidad, was a Member of Parliament and a spokesman on West Indian affairs in London. His experience, and its results for his employees, were common at the turn of the century. In the previous twelve years, seven of his crops had sold at a loss and five had made only a moderate profit. As he said, he anticipated another loss in 1901; in fact the loss was £8,000 that year, £11,000 in 1902 and £3,000 in 1903. Not surprisingly, he did not plant sugar in 1904.

In 1903 the beet-sugar producing countries of Europe agreed in the Brussels Convention 'to suppress the direct and indirect bounties by which the production or exportation of sugar may profit'. As a result the British West Indian sugar producers expected to be relieved of the formidable competition of European beet-sugar in the British market. 'I make a free gift to my opponents,' said Lamont in a speech to his Scottish voters in 1905, 'of the admission that to the West Indies the Brussels Convention has been the greatest boon for a generation. Three hundred thousand people who are employed directly in the West Indian sugar industry have been saved from being thrown out of employment. Hundreds of thousands of pounds of capital invested in the factories have been saved from total loss.'

In fact Lamont was exaggerating. Although the European beet-sugar producers were no longer heavily subsidised by their governments, beet-sugar could still sell more cheaply in the United Kingdom than British West Indian cane-sugar. Lamont himself, with many other planters, finally abandoned sugar a few years later. Those who remained in production found their new market in Canada rather than in Britain after they lost their trade with the United States to Puerto Rico and Cuba after the Spanish American War. This was because increasingly favourable terms were offered for the import of West Indian sugar into Canada in 1898, 1900 and 1907. In 1897, before these terms were arranged, 11,000 tons of sugar were exported to Canada, but, in 1909, 133,000 tons were sent; so the quantity sold in Canada multiplied eleven times with the help of preferential terms.

Canadian–British West Indian trade was the subject of a Royal Commission which reported in 1910; since then this trade has been encouraged by a series of mutual agreements giving preferences to each other's products. With the trade in fruit, cacao and sugar going to the United States and Canada, there was a great reduction in West Indian trade with the markets in Britain. This is shown by the proportions of imports and exports in Jamaica in 1891 and 1912:

PLACE	1891		1912	
	Imports from	Exports to	Imports from	Exports to
	%	%	%	%
U.K.	48·9	32·7	43·7	13·2
U.S.A.	41·7	50·9	41·7	59·8
Canada	6·7	3·5	9·6	5·5
Other	2·7	12·9	5·0	21·5

While the markets of Canada and the United States sheltered British West Indian, Puerto Rican and Cuban sugar from competition with European beet-sugar, French West Indian sugar producers found no such havens. They exported to France, where they were at a disadvantage against French-grown beet-sugar. Prices for French West Indian cane-sugar fell from 84 francs a kilo in 1900 to 16 francs a kilo in 1902, and recovery was slow until the industry was boosted by the First World War.

But profits still depended on cheaper production by West Indians. There were three main ways of doing this. In the second half of the nineteenth century and in the early twentieth, they reduced wages whenever possible, they improved cultivation, and they improved the manufacturing process. In the process of doing these things the producers separated the planting and grinding of canes as enterprises. The planters improved their cultivation by increased use of fertilisers and selective cane-breeding. The development of agricultural societies and associations helped to spread knowledge of scientific farming to an interested public. In 1898, immediately after the Norman Report, the Imperial Department of Agriculture was opened in Barbados and became the headquarters for the development of scientific cane-farming in the British West Islands.

But in this century, by far the most important saving has been made in the manufacturing process. The planters had long realised that they could economise, and at the same time make much better quality sugar, by abandoning their individual estate factories and introducing a central factory system. The chief advantage of a well-equipped central factory is that it can grind a relatively large quantity of cane each year, produce better quality sugar, and the cost of this quicker and more efficient manufacturing can be shared by all those planters who use it. Individual estate-owners simply could not afford to set up large and efficient modern factories of their own, and in their smaller 'works' there was much wastage of cane and consequently a loss of sugar and of profits.

The British West Indian sugar producers were slow to embark on central factories because they lacked the essential cash and credit in the nineteenth century. Also, a central factory requires a comparatively large supply of cane. This means that there must be sufficient land planted in canes, and transport to the factory must be easy and not too expensive. The French islands had the advantage of cash and credit in the nineteenth century. La Société de Crédit Colonial was formed in France in 1860 to advance money for central factories and also to enable existing factories to be improved. In 1862 two were built in Martinique with the credit provided. The smaller islands found it harder to produce large quantities of cane to feed a central factory than the larger islands and British Guiana. In Cuba cane was planted by the *colonos* who were settled on land surrounding the *central*. In Martinique and Guadeloupe, grinding ceased on many an old estate, which now only supplied canes on contract to the Usine. In those British islands where the sugar producers found it cheaper to do so, an increasing proportion of cane cultivation was left to cane-farmers who rented land from the estates.

The first central factories in the British islands were the Colonial Company's Usine Ste. Madeleine in Trinidad (1871) and the

Grand Cul de Sac Usine in St. Lucia (1873). In Barbados, the introduction of central factories was delayed by the reluctance of estate owners to give up their proud position as masters of their own fields and factories, however inefficient the latter might be. In Antigua and St. Kitts, although the planters were impressed by the great advantages of centralised manufacture, it was not until 1904 and 1912 respectively that central factories were established in these islands, with the help of imperial funds as recommended by the Norman Royal Commission.

In these several ways, by selling in favourable markets in Canada and the United States, improving cultivation and manufacturing, paying low wages, Caribbean sugar producers survived the formidable competition of European beet-sugar until the First World War, when all West Indian producers benefited from the rise in prices which generally comes in wartime. These high prices brought high profits everywhere, but nowhere more than in Cuba where in 1919 sugar cost 5ȼ. a pound to make and was being sold for at least four times that amount in New York.

The boom came to a sudden end in November 1920, and hard times once again overtook the West Indian sugar producers. From 22½ȼ. in March 1920, the price of raw Cuban sugar in New York fell to 3⅝ȼ. in December 1920, to below 1ȼ. in September 1930. One reason for the fall in prices was that sugar production stimulated, particularly in Cuba and Java, by the demands of the First World War was now greater than its consumption in the world. The American refiners had provided the money for Cuban expansion, expecting to supply Europe with her sugar after the war. But the European sugar-beet industry quickly recovered, and so only small quantities of cane-sugar were imported.

The British West Indian sugar producers continued during the First World War, and afterwards, to sell most of their sugar to Canada, attracted to that market by the preferences fixed by the successive trade agreements. At the end of the war, however, the United Kingdom market had been made more attractive for the British West Indies than it had ever been since the eighteen-eighties. This was because Britain had then abandoned the principle of free trade and had given sugar from the British colonies and dominions a preference of 4s. 3d. for white and 3s. 8d. per cwt. for raw sugar. Not until 1932 did the British West Indian islands again export more sugar to the United Kingdom than to Canada.

Nevertheless, British West Indian producers were also affected by the fact that altogether more sugar was being produced in the world than people consumed. As a consequence, prices were falling. They were saved from ruin in 1934 by the increase of the preference on their raw sugar to 6s. 9d. per cwt. on the British market. A quota system was also introduced by which the United Kingdom undertook to buy a certain quota annually from each colony, so that a market was now guaranteed.

DEVELOPING ALTERNATIVES

Wherever sugar planters found it impossible to continue profitably, both land and workers were used for other crops. In some of the small islands sugar practically disappeared. Grenada, for instance, adopted cacao and nutmegs and grew no sugar at all, so that Grenadians themselves had to import it; other small islands only grew enough sugar for local consumption. Most sugar planters did not sell their land. They gave up sugar production and rented their estates, as a whole or in parcels, to farmers who paid rent in cash, or sometimes in produce. Paying rent in produce was a system of share-cropping which had been widely used in the Windward Islands even as early as the eighteen-forties. Since that time, small farmers have become the biggest single occupational group in the West Indies. Even in Barbados a few returning emigrants had enough money to buy land from large planters at very high prices.

As the Norman Report had suggested, in the first quarter of this century much effort was put into the cultivation of still more varied export crops, which could be grown by the increasing number of small farmers. Even in Barbados, St. Kitts and Antigua, where sugar remained the staple crop, experiments in other cultivation were encouraged. The new Imperial Department of Agriculture worked at demonstrating alternative crops to cane; it was established particularly to advise on farming experiments in the Windwards and Leewards, as well as to improve cane cultivation. By a succession of grants from the Imperial Government, it was maintained for this purpose until 1922, when it was succeeded by the Imperial College of Tropical Agriculture in Trinidad. Each island had its Botanic Department, also subsidised by the Imperial Government, to demonstrate to their own farmers new methods of cultivation, to distribute seeds for new cultivation at nominal prices and in general to see that the work of the Imperial Department reached the small farmers. With this encouragement, the more varied crops that had been tried in the last quarter of the nineteenth century were much extended and new ones introduced. In addition to the cacao grown extensively in Trinidad and Grenada, for instance, smaller quantities were produced in Jamaica, St. Lucia and Dominica. Lime cultivation was extended in Dominica and encouraged in St. Lucia. Sea Island cotton was introduced into Montserrat and St. Vincent in 1906, and in the latter island the cultivation of arrowroot was extended.

In 1908 Departments of Agriculture were founded in Jamaica, Trinidad and British Guiana, and the advice of the staff of the Imperial Department was also available to them. They too sought for a greater variety of crops. British Guianese farmers grew increasing quantities of rice for export, in addition to producing sugar, rum and molasses still as their chief exports. In 1899, British Guiana had imported 24,000,000 lb. of rice and exported none; but, in 1913, a mere 13,000 lb. were imported while 17,000,000 lb. were exported. In Trinidad, the high prices obtained for coconuts between 1918 and 1921 encouraged cultivators to increase acreage under that crop. For a time both Trinidad and British Guiana also experimented with the growing of rubber trees. Jamaica of all the territories probably produced the largest number of different export crops, as can be seen from a table of the island's exports in 1912 (p. 264).

Encouragement for this considerable activity was given by finding new markets and by improving communications, both between the islands and abroad. Bananas are probably the best example of production stimulated by new markets and communications. In an earlier chapter you read of the beginning of the trade with Jamaica when in 1870 Captain Lorenzo Baker first took the fruit to New York. Fifteen years later Baker and his colleagues formed the Boston Fruit Company to export bananas to the United States from Jamaica, Cuba and Santo Domingo. At the same time, along the newly constructed railway in Costa Rica, Minor Keith, the railroad contractor, was planting bananas, and had formed his own company. In 1899, Baker and Keith joined together and formed the United Fruit Company. Keith wanted to use Baker's marketing organisation and Baker wanted to have crops in different areas of America so that they would not all suffer at the same time from hazards such as hurricane damage.

The United Fruit Company, by its control of markets and ships,

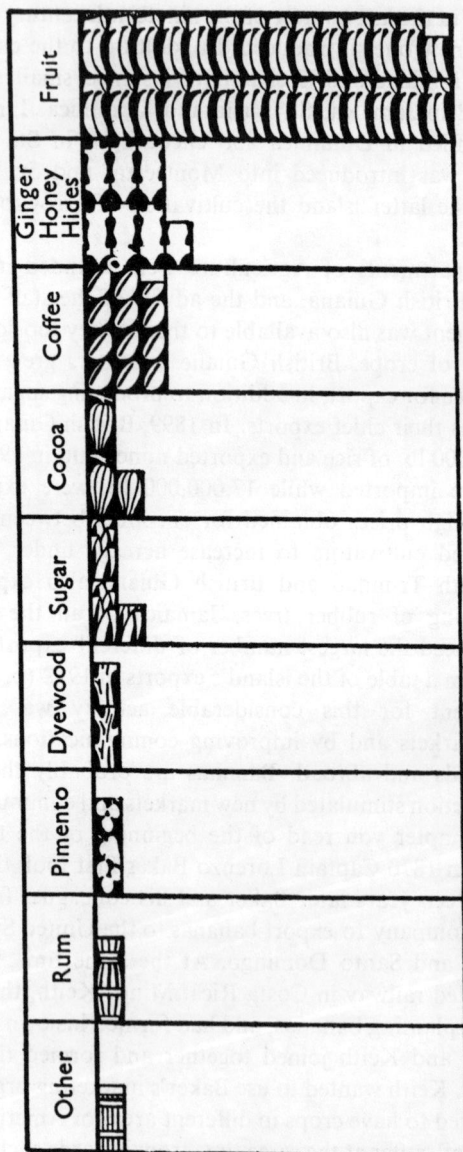

Fig. 14. Percentage Table of Jamaican Exports in 1912. 1 unit = 2% of the earnings for the year

264

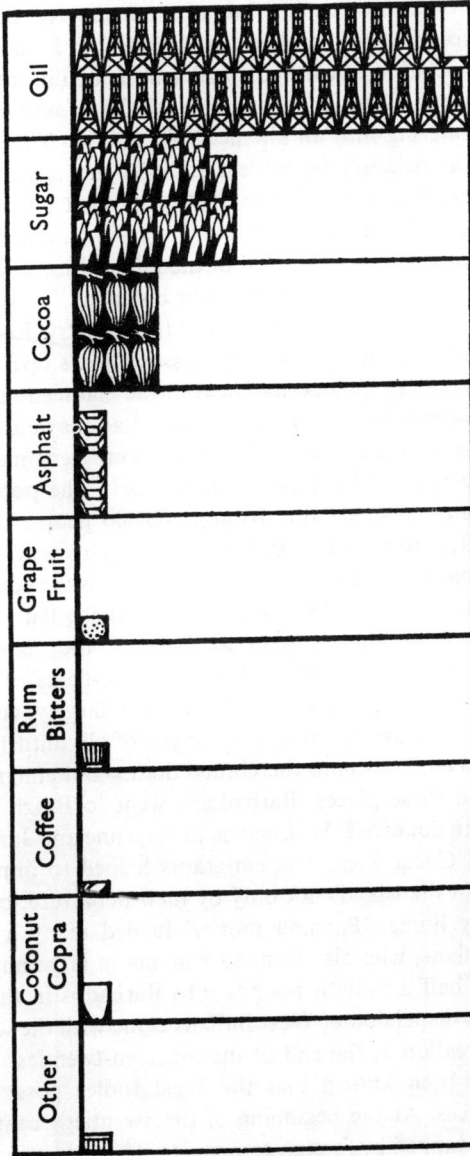

· Fig. 15. Percentage Table of Trinidad's Export Earnings in 1936. 1 unit = 2% of the earnings for the year

now dominated the trade in the islands and in Central America. The company controlled the Jamaica banana industry for thirty years, until in 1929, six thousand smallholders formed the Jamaica Banana Producers' Association to transport and sell their fruit in the United States and Europe. With the assistance of the Jamaican Government and by entering into an alliance with another American fruit company, the association succeeded. In 1932 the chairman could say to members, 'Since its start in 1929 your fruit has realised an average of 2s. 6½d. per payable bunch . . . in addition you are owners of a half share in four ships of the Direct Line . . . you have two new ships . . . you have a marketing company . . . is there any previous four year period in the history of the industry that can stand comparison with the four years of the Association's operations?'

There was moderate prosperity between the eighteen-nineties and the nineteen-twenties for the small man who had his land planted in bananas, cacao, limes, coconuts, but there were very many others who were both without land and without work. The population of the British islands rose steadily from 1,600,000 people in 1891, to 1,950,000 in 1911, to nearly 2,000,000 in 1921. This was a period of great emigration in search of work. First, there was the cutting of the canal in Panama between 1904 and 1914; in these ten years, over 20,000 British West Indians went to Panama, the majority from Jamaica. Secondly, there was work in the cane-fields of Cuba between 1911 and 1921. This emigration was largely confined to Jamaicans and Haitians. Thirdly, and largest of all, until 1924, there was the general emigration to the United States. But emigration was not confined to these places. Barbadians went to Brazil and other South American countries, St. Lucians to Cayenne and Jamaicans to Honduras and Costa Rica. The emigrants helped to improve conditions of life in the islands not only by their departure, but also by sending money home. 'Panama money' helped many a Jamaican family. Barbadians, who also went to Panama in large numbers, introduced over half a million pounds into Barbados in those years. The end of this dispersion of West Indians came with the world-wide economic depression at the end of the nineteen-twenties.

It had long been known that the West Indies possessed some mineral resources. At the beginning of the twentieth century these resources were tapped by foreign companies. The industries which resulted were not of such size that they could relieve unemployment; nowhere have they employed more people than are engaged in agriculture. But they have supplied the governments of the Caribbean with increasing amounts of revenue. Cuba possesses the largest mineral deposits, of which high-grade iron ore and nickel are particularly important. But it was in Trinidad that mineral resources first contributed large sums to a Caribbean government's revenue.

Sir Walter Raleigh is credited with the European discovery, in 1595, of the large pitch lake at La Brea, but not until a geological survey was carried out in the eighteen-fifties was an asphalt industry in any way established. In 1886 A. L. Barber, an American businessman, secured a concession of the whole lake for twenty-one years from the Government of Trinidad, in return for export duty and royalty payments which would yield to the government not less than £10,000 a year. In 1925 the concession was given to the Trinidad Lake Asphalt Company and the government was to receive at least £24,000 a year. This industry was severely hit by the depression, but by then the oil industry had developed.

Oil had been found at Aripero in 1866, but the serious prospecting for oil did not begin until 1905 and production was not sufficient for export until the formation of the Trinidad Oilfields Co. Ltd. in 1910; the first large shipment of Trinidad oil was made to the United States two years later. By 1936 Trinidad oil and asphalt exports were worth £3,800,000 and £240,000 respectively; the oil alone was worth more than half of the island's total exports in that year.

Oil refining also brought prosperity to the agriculturally barren Dutch islands of Aruba and Curaçao. They have developed with the oil industry in Venezuela which has flourished since 1914. The Venezuelan drilling companies claimed that the sandbanks at the mouth of Lake Maracaibo made it inaccessible to ocean tankers, so first in Curaçao and later in Aruba they built refineries which they often increased in capacity.

The bauxite deposits of British and Dutch Guiana attracted foreign attention at about the same time. In British Guiana, the deposits along the Demerara River had first been noticed by government geologists in 1868 and 1873, but it was not until 1910 that Sir John Harrison, the colony's Director of Science and Agriculture, analysed them and determined their composition. Five years later, an American, George MacKenzie, arrived in the same area to buy land. He said he wanted to grow oranges, but all the extensive areas he purchased were found to be rich in bauxite. It was MacKenzie who in 1916 founded the Demerara Bauxite Company, now a subsidiary of the

Aluminum Company of Canada; the exports of crude ore began from Three Friends in 1917 and in 1922 from Moengo, the Dutch field which was worked by the Surinam Bauxite Company, a subsidiary of the Aluminum Company of America. The bauxite industry in British Guiana was badly affected by the depression, and production fell sharply between 1930 and 1935.

HAZARDS AND DEPRESSIONS

The considerable endeavour to foster the cultivation of several export crops in the British West Indies was maintained until a combination of economic depression in North America and Europe and the enterprise of new foreign competitors made it difficult for the British West Indies to sell their products overseas. Furthermore, crop diseases which had first been noticed in the early years of the twentieth century increased in virulence and added to the hazards of the West Indian farmer. Cacao producers not only had to face the competition of the extensive plantations of West Africa, but to fight witchbroom disease. The pink boll worm attacked cotton, which was also affected by the fall in demand following changes in women's fashions in the nineteen-twenties; from 1922 to 1932 Sea Island cotton was unsaleable. Banana producers, who had contended with Panama Disease since 1912, had in 1934 also to meet leaf-spot disease. Palestine and South Africa rapidly extended their production of oranges and grapefruit, and from Burma and Thailand rice poured out for export. The limes in Dominica and St. Lucia suffered from root wither-tip diseases, and the industries which had bought their concentrated lime juice to make citric acid now found a cheaper way to make that acid without lime juice.

The consequence of the general economic depression was hardship for the majority of West Indians. They could no longer emigrate to the United States after 1924. Those who had worked on Cuban sugar estates had to return home because there was now no work for them. The amounts of money sent home by emigrants still abroad decreased. The population of the islands increased, but jobs did not. Because it was the largest employer of labour, the sugar industry received special assistance from the Imperial Government, and in Jamaica and Trinidad the island governments also made special grants to the sugar industry. A report to the Secretary of State said that 'labour contributed its share by continuing to accept a standard of wage and living conditions far below what is desirable'.

On the lands of the smallholders, farming practices were still inefficient, and there were now too many people attempting to live off an acre for its produce to support them all. The movement of the people from the country to the towns was accelerated, but in the towns the people found only irregular employment, whether they worked for the government or for private firms. The Public Works Department in Jamaica, for instance, gave work to a man two or three days a week, and in Trinidad, work was doled out for three or four days in a fortnight. The island governments were, like the sugar industry, large employers of labour; but in neither Jamaica nor Trinidad did the government increase wages until workers had rioted. Throughout the West Indies very few workers, and those mostly in the towns, had organisations of their own to bargain with employers.

FURTHER READING

Sources of West Indian History, Economic Life, pp. 79–83, Social Conditions since Emancipation, pp. 245–53.

QUESTIONS TO CONSIDER

1. Why was Sir Norman Lamont exaggerating in claiming that the Brussels Convention was 'the greatest boon for a generation'?

2. How far do you think that the development of the British West Indies was affected by events outside the area during the period discussed in this chapter?

3. What would you consider to be the most promising economic development in the West Indies in the first quarter of the twentieth century? Discuss the reasons for your choice.

4. A Royal Commission came to the West Indies in 1938. In their report, the commissioners included discussion on *The Problem of Population*, *The Problem of Employment* and *Agricultural Policy*. What points would they have raised?

CHAPTER TWENTY-THREE

Trade Unions and Representation

EARLY TRADE UNIONS

West Indian workers first began to organise themselves into groups to protect their own interests at the turn of the century. In Cuba the tobacco and port workers set up the first organisations in 1889 and 1890. In 1898 in Jamaica, a Carpenters, Bricklayers and Painters Union was formed and in 1907, there was the Jamaica Trades and Labour Union as well as organisations of printers and cigar makers. The Working Men's Association started in Trinidad at the end of the eighteen-nineties. In 1906 in British Guiana, Hubert Critchlow, a stevedore, led a strike of dockers in Georgetown.

These were early efforts at a difficult time for trade unions to take root. It was a time of wholesale emigration from the British West Indies and of immigration into Cuba. Moreover, the law did not protect trade unionists from charges of conspiracy or against action for damages by employers. But these early, weak attempts at trade unions were known outside the West Indies. Their leaders made contact with the labour unions in the United States; the Jamaica Trades and Labour Union, for instance, was affiliated to the American Federation of Labour.

These were mainly organisations of town workers, who were steadily increasing in number. Estate-workers had not even this means of demanding higher wages as a body. They were exploited by native and foreign companies, particularly in Cuba, where immigrants from the West Indies and from the Spanish Canary islands and Madeira were swelling the number of estate workers. In 1911 Cuban Negroes attempted to redress their wrongs by revolt. Three thousand died, but their working conditions were not improved.

Immediately after the First World War, there was another attempt to organise workers in the larger British colonies. In 1919 Hubert Critchlow formed the British Guiana Labour Union. In 1918 the Jamaica Trades and Labour Union was re-formed and Bain Alves formed the Jamaica Longshoremen's Union No. 1 of the Jamaica

Federation of Labour. In Trinidad, the Working Men's Association was revived after a period of relapse. There was an immediate response in larger membership, but there were too many workers still outside for the unions to be strong, and they went into decline with the depression of the nineteen-twenties.

In Cuba and the Dominican Republic the unions did not merely decline; they were attacked. Their attempts to raise the very low wages of workers on the sugar, sisal and tobacco plantations were unsuccessful. When Presidents Machado and Trujillo established their dictatorships, they assassinated the prominent labour leaders and both destroyed the unions in their countries. But Cuban workers also had some political supporters and under Dr. Ramon Grau San Martin, who undertook the government after Machado's expulsion in 1933, an eight-hour working day and minimum wages for estate-workers were established.

It was just such effective political support that the infant unions in the British islands lacked in the early years of the depression. Trade union laws were passed in Jamaica in 1918, British Guiana in 1921, Trinidad in 1932 and St. Vincent in 1933. The Labour Party when it governed England in 1929 urged governors to give legal recognition to trade unions. The Secretary of State said that trade unions were 'a natural and legitimate consequence of progress', but a source of disturbance if they were not officially recognised.

But despite this formal encouragement from the Colonial Office, the laws passed in the islands did not fully protect trade unionists. For instance, they could not legally post pickets when on strike. The compulsory registration fees for official recognition were difficult for small, new unions to raise. Moreover, the views of the Secretary of State in London did not effectively alter the hostility of the employers and the island governments. Police detectives shadowed trade unionists as they would conspirators against the government.

The trade unionists received some measure of assistance from members of the middle class in their efforts to draw attention to the condition of the workers after the First World War, notably from Captain Arthur Cipriani in Trinidad. Cipriani was an ex-officer of the West Indian contingent, which served abroad in the First World War, and an unofficial member of the Legislative Council. Alfred Thorne was a Barbadian who had made his home in British Guiana and became a public figure as headmaster of the Middle School, a newspaper editor and an elected member of the Combined Court.

O'Neale was an older man who had become sympathetic towards working people while training to be a doctor in Edinburgh and later practising in the industrial north of England. When he returned to his native Barbados, he joined the newspaper editor Clennel Wickham to form the Democratic League in 1924 and later a Working Men's Association. Jacques Palache and his associates in the Jamaica League supported the working-class movement there. In 1919 a speaker for the League advocated 'four reasons why wages should be increased immediately'. He also spoke of the duty of the better-paid to provide leadership for the trade unions, and finally he warned Jamaicans that they were sleeping beside the centre of a volcano. The volcano did not in fact erupt until late in the nineteen-thirties.

CHANGES IN GOVERNMENT

In the meantime the middle classes, discontented with Crown colony government, asked the Colonial Office for a greater share in the governments of the islands. Representative Government Associations were formed in most of the islands with a membership which the Colonial Office called 'a coloured and black intelligentsia', many of whom had recently returned from service in the First World War. Their common purpose, the Grenada Association said in 1921, was to get 'such a measure of representative government as will enable them to have an effective voice in their own government'. They wanted elected members in the legislative councils, and in greater numbers than the civil servant members. They did not intend to give everybody a vote, but they wanted the qualifications for voting low enough for the electorate to be large. These associations were not demanding self-government.

The petition of the Grenadians was the first to be answered. Early in 1921, the Secretary of State agreed that they should have some elected members in their legislative council; his reason was that, since 1886, the six District Boards which administered local government in the island had had some elected members, and these Boards had worked well.

Later in 1921, Major Wood, the Under Secretary of State for the Colonies, toured the British West Indies to see how far the demands of the Representative Associations should be met. Jamaica already had the elected members granted in 1884; so the argument there was how to give them a still more effective voice in their own government. The elected members in the Jamaican Legislative Council did not agree with Wood's proposals and the constitution was not changed.

St. Lucia, St. Vincent and Dominica were allowed three elected members in 1924. In Antigua, St. Kitts and Montserrat the demand of the Representative Associations for elected members was opposed by the more prominent planters and merchants, and their opposition was effective. In the Leeward Islands too, Wood found a strong dislike, particularly in Dominica, of the Federation which had been established in 1871. He only recommended that Dominica should be detached from the Leewards but this was not done until 1940.

Since it had become a British colony, Trinidad had never had elected members, although it had frequently asked for them. Now the Legislative Reform Committee and the Working Men's Association prepared to answer the arguments which the Colonial Office had always used before to deny representation to Trinidadians, namely, that the mass of the people were ignorant, and that the petitioners represented only themselves. They claimed to represent the peasants, middle classes and workers, and asserted that education in Trinidad had now gone forward by leaps and bounds. But new factors made the Colonial Office hesitate to grant Trinidadians an 'effective voice in their own government'. Now that money had come from outside to develop the oil and asphalt industries, Wood reported that some people regarded it as 'important that no action should be taken which would disturb the confidence felt by such capital in the stability of the local government'. The other new factor was the appearance of Indians in the political life of the island. The East Indian Association asked for their own special representatives. This Wood did not recommend. In 1924, seven elected members took their place for the first time in the history of the Legislative Council in Trinidad.

The sequel to Major Wood's visit was the introduction of elected members to the Legislative Councils of Trinidad, the Windwards and Dominica, but in all the islands, the powers of the governor remained intact. Only in British Guiana did the elected members have some control over the government's revenue and expenditure, and this control the Colonial Office was able to abolish in 1928 when the depression in trade had caused the British Guiana Government, in every year from 1920, to spend more money than it had received in taxes. The Secretary of State had already told the governor in 1914 that before he could ever request any loan from the Imperial Government for British Guiana he 'must be in a position to exercise in the last resort complete control over the raising and the spending of the colonial revenues, as well as over all legislation'.

In 1926 a commission was appointed to report on the economic conditions in British Guiana and on measures to promote its development. Major Wood in 1922 had found nothing wrong with the colony's constitution, but in 1926 the commissioners said the government in British Guiana had 'never been able to govern'; and, in the debate on the subject in the House of Lords, it was called 'the worst in the world'. So in 1928 British Guiana was given a new constitution, which kept the fourteen elected members of the old constitution, but left them without the control of expenditure which had been theirs ever since British Guiana became a British colony. The new constitution also abolished the old Court of Policy and the Combined Court and replaced them by a Legislative Council.

CROWN COLONY GOVERNMENT UNDER ATTACK

As the feelings of frustration and, for some, of desperation mounted during the depression years, the weakness of Crown colony government was emphasised. British West Indians were allowed to criticise the government, but were not allowed to govern themselves. While in Cuba men were in revolt against dictatorship, violence in the British colonies was limited to occasional riots in town and country by hard-pressed labourers. There were not yet any effective alliances of the labourers and the middle classes against Crown colony government. The mass of the people, particularly those in towns, were most impressed by organisations, such as the United Negro Improvement Association, the Negro Progress Convention in British Guiana and the Negro Welfare and Cultural Association in Trinidad, which sought to instil in their members pride of race and also sought, in some cases, to help them to better their conditions of living.

The most widely known leader of such a group was Marcus Garvey who already had an international reputation as President of the United Negro Improvement Association when he returned to Jamaica after having been deported from the United States in 1927. He continued his U.N.I.A. activities in the West Indies with a very loyal following. He was a colourful figure who could move large crowds by impassioned speeches. His U.N.I.A. with its 'back to Africa' slogan caught the imagination of Negroes in the United States and the West Indies, and in many ways put them further in touch with each other. In 1929 he decided to stand for election to the

Jamaican Legislative Council. He attempted to introduce the idea of party politics; candidates should be 'men with a programme' he declared. In his criticisms of authority during the campaign he accused the judges of corruption. For this he was convicted and imprisoned. He lost the election mainly because he quarrelled with some of his supporters.

Garvey had been against American Negroes joining trade unions because he thought that they would lose their jobs; the fact that they were paid less than white workers was the only thing that made them attractive to employers. In Jamaica, however, he held meetings to promote the idea of trade unionism; his slogan was that workers should fight for a wage of 'a dollar a day'. He ended his career in Jamaica as a vocal member of the Kingston Corporation Council, where he constantly but ineffectively urged the Corporation to improve the city's services 'as a means of relieving the present and continuing state of unemployment and hardships among the people'. In 1940 he died in England where he spent his last years.

'Men with a programme', even men with a single measure to propose, continued to be ineffective in the legislative councils of the British islands. For instance, in Trinidad Captain Cipriani tried for many years to have a law passed establishing a minimum wage, but he could get no support for it from the government. Not until the same day in 1937 that the leader of striking oil workers declared that he was unable to get the men back to work did the governor telegraph the Secretary of State to say that 'I have long felt that unskilled labour's rates do not give a living wage and I have been trying to rectify this. . . . I have taken the opportunity of this unrest to fix a minimum government wage . . . and to establish an 8-hour day . . . other employers are following suit.'

Even the best of governors seemed able to do no more than watch expenditure and see how large a loan the Secretary of State would make to their colony. In 1929 the Imperial Parliament had set up a Colonial Development Fund to make grants or loans to colonies 'for the purpose of aiding and developing agriculture and industry and thereby promoting commerce with, or industry in, the United Kingdom'. Some of the governors in the West Indies, notably Sir Edward Denham in British Guiana, proposed to use it. But, before much could be made of the Colonial Development Fund, governors throughout the Empire were reminded by the Secretary of State in 1931 'that the interests of the United Kingdom and of the Colonies are inseparably bound up with one another' and that therefore it was reasonable to look for a common sacrifice from all who now faced the common peril of bankruptcy. Colonies receiving grants-in-aid from Imperial funds were told to make 'drastic economies'. The other colonies were not to attempt to raise loans in London. The Secretary of State said that 'the common interest of the United Kingdom and its Dependencies' would weigh more 'with any colony than its own individual advantage'.

As a consequence, schemes to provide Trinidad with a central water supply and to provide Port-of-Spain with a deep-water wharf were postponed. In October 1931, by fourteen votes to four, the Trinidad Legislative Council made the remarkable move of voting £5,000 per year for five years 'with a view to rendering assistance in the present financial crisis to His Majesty's Government'. In Jamaica, the Development Committee of the Legislative Council in 1931 recommended a loan of £400,000 to spend on public works, public buildings and land settlement. But the Secretary of State reported that 'in the present circumstances it is impossible to raise a loan on reasonable terms and therefore it is not practicable to proceed with the programme'.

It was soon clear to the elected members of legislative councils that they had not gained 'an effective voice in their own government' after 1924. The seeming inability of Crown colony government to ease the hardships brought by the economic depression now made some members of the middle class willing to go further in their demands than in 1924. At the beginning of the nineteen-thirties these men called for self-government. But, feeling that the Imperial Government would refuse to grant to each island the right to rule itself, they asked for self-government for the islands within a federation of the West Indies.

In 1932, a group of West Indians, who referred to themselves as the West Indian Unofficial Conference, met in Dominica to discuss the matter. One of their main criticisms was the neglect by the government of the poorer sections of the population. The criticism was levelled forcibly by Cecil Rawle, a public figure in Dominica and chairman of the conference. 'Indifference to the welfare of the people,' he said in his opening speech, 'is frequently shown in all the islands, but is particularly prevalent in the smaller ones. Witness the hovels and squalid conditions in which the labouring classes live. The want of any serious effort to ameliorate such conditions is the measure of the interest shown in the welfare of the West Indian peoples by Crown colony government.'

Present at the conference were Cipriani, Ebenezer Duncan, editor of *The Investigator* in St. Vincent, other newspaper editors from Antigua and St. Lucia, elected members of the Councils of Grenada, St. Lucia and Dominica, the President of the St. Kitts Workers' League and two lawyers from Barbados. T. Marryshow, already well-known for his championship of political independence and West Indian federation, was absent because he was in London discussing with Colonial Office staff the very matter that had called the conference together in the first place. The Imperial Government was once again urging federation on the West Indies, and these politically alert West Indians had decided to make the promise of representative government the only condition on which they would even discuss the proposals.

The persistent depression of the nineteen-thirties provoked the growth of such groups. They did not, to begin with, meet regularly but they knew each other and, increasingly, criticism of the colonial government spread throughout the West Indies.

FURTHER READING

Sources of West Indian History, Government and Politics, pp. 124–36, Social Conditions since Emancipation, pp. 253–9.

Sherlock, *Caribbean Citizen*, Chapter III, On Being a West Indian, p. 43, Cipriani and Garvey, Pioneers.

Hoyos, *Our Common Heritage*, C. D. O'Neale and Clennel Wickham.

Daly, *Story of the Heroes*, Chapter XXV, A. R. F. Webber, and Chapter XXXIII, A. A. Thorne.

QUESTIONS TO CONSIDER

1. How did trade unions develop in your territory and how have they affected its history?

2. In what ways was the work of the representative associations limited? How does it compare with the demands of the members of the Dominica Conference?

3. Which reasons for criticisms of the Imperial Government given in this chapter do you find justified?

4. Which of the West Indians mentioned in this chapter do you think played the most important part in West Indian history?

CHAPTER TWENTY-FOUR

End and Beginning

THE DISTURBANCES

The nineteen-thirties were uneasy years throughout the world. The decade began with a financial crisis in New York and London, with confidence in banks and governments undermined. It was marked by ill feeling between different classes of society, the workers against the employers, the 'haves' against the 'have nots'. Relations between nations in Europe, Africa and Asia were so tense that war seemed about to engulf the world. By the end of the decade the major European countries were engaged in the Second World War. Colonial agricultural countries, such as the West Indies, shared in the economic depression of the imperial and industrial countries. The large scale unemployment in the United Kingdom and the United States following the trade slump lasted throughout the nineteen-thirties until the outbreak of war created enough work for all idle hands to do. For the first time the British and American Governments had to provide relief for large numbers of their unemployed citizens, either through the distribution of food, clothing and money or through public works.

By contrast, governments in the British islands neither had the money for large scale relief, nor the men to capture the confidence of the people. Government policy was not made in the West Indies. Robert Kirkwood, as a nominated member of the Jamaican Legislative Council, in 1942 described the situation for the West Indian unofficial member. 'No wonder that the critics nag,' he said, 'it is all we can do today. We do not like nagging, but our function is the function that is purely negative. We are not allowed to take responsibility ... the present system is turning us all into a pack of irresponsible critics and nagging nursemaids. It is not we that are to blame; it is the system that is to blame. It is wrong.'

The elected unofficial member was usually an active man in other aspects of public life. A steady stream of candidates came from the press, the professions of law, teaching and medicine. The nominated unofficial member was there to represent some economic interest, such as sugar, cacao, commerce or oil. There were practically no spokesmen from the labouring classes and their case was only presented by unofficial members such as Cipriani and Thorne, who were active in their interest. As a group, the men who sat in the legislative councils, whether elected or nominated, were able men. But within the system of Crown colony government, responsibility for governing the islands did not belong to them, but to the British Government; their job was to see that the governor and Secretary of State did not forget their industry or parish or ward when they made decisions.

There was an increasing number of people in all the islands who did not feel themselves a part of this system of government and who felt that the governments neglected their difficulties. It is easy to show that the legislative councils were concerned about the depression and unemployment. They appointed committees to make recommendations, some of which, such as subsidies to sugar and cacao products, were acted on and were beneficial not only to the landowners, but also to the labourers in those industries. What the legislative councils did not do was ensure that the workers benefited as much as was possible; for instance, they did not insist that some of the profits from sugar and oil be used to pay the labourers higher wages. It is not surprising that in the circumstances what impressed the mass of the people was not the limited action which the councils took, but what Cipriani referred to in 1937 as 'the humbug and platitudes of the past many years'.

In the last chapter some of the earliest critics of 'the humbug and platitudes' in the councils were mentioned. In the later years of the depression they were joined by others both in the islands and abroad, notably by the group of West Indians then living in New York. In 1938 the Jamaican Progressive League had the assistance of Adolphe Roberts, the writer, and the Barbados Progressive League had the support of Hope Stevens, the lawyer. The West Indians from New York found that there were men in the islands already at work. In Jamaica, for example, there were O. T. Fairclough and W. G. McFarlane, and, in Barbados, J. A. Martineau and W. A. Crawford, and they were not alone. In fact, the task at this time was less to find men dissatisfied with Crown colony government than to find agreement on what should replace it, because not all the West Indian critics of Crown colony rule agreed with the demand of the progressive leagues for self-government based on universal suffrage.

This political activity of some members of the middle classes in the British islands was given strength by the eruption of the workers which had long been predicted.

A series of strikes and riots touched off by local grievances in individual islands started in the bad year of 1934. They were a protest both against low wages and against the Crown colony government which made it impossible for West Indians to do much about their own hardships. Sometimes these riots were inspired by the working men's movements and the struggling trade unions; more often they were outbursts by unorganised groups of workers. There was a strike on some sugar estates in Trinidad in 1934. In the following year came the first of a series of riots in which people were killed and wounded. This was in the sugar island of St. Kitts, where conditions were probably the hardest in the British West Indies and where the highest death rate obtained. In 1935 the sugar workers struck for more wages and wandered through the estates in disorderly gangs; several of the strikers were killed when the police disbanded these groups. In British Guiana at the same time, sugar workers raided the estates and set fire to canes. Exasperation over conditions in St. Vincent led to the formation of a Working Men's Association there, with an active programme to secure land settlement and a new constitution. In St. Lucia the coal carriers in Castries went on strike.

The unrest spread to Trinidad, Jamaica and Barbados in 1937 and 1938. City riots were added to strikes and disorders in the country. Disturbances broke out on the Trinidad oilfields where the leader was Uriah Butler. A Grenadian who had migrated to Trinidad in 1921 after serving in the First World War, he was typical of the large number of migrant workers from other West Indian islands to be found in the Trinidad labour movement. Until 1936 Butler was a member of Cipriani's Trinidad Labour Party and first came into public notice when in 1935 he led a hunger march of 120 men into Port-of-Spain. This kind of action led to his expulsion from Cipriani's group. He then formed his own British Empire Citizens' and Workers' Home Rule Party. Like Garvey before him he was a champion of Negro rights against white employers and a fiery orator; he soon secured a following of a thousand Negro workers in the oilfields. A strike was called in 1937, two oil wells were set on fire and two policemen were killed in a clumsy attempt to arrest Butler. The strikes spread to the sugar estates and rioting was only quelled in

Port-of-Spain and San Fernando when British battleships were summoned by the governor and armed sailors landed.

It was Clement Payne, a follower of Butler's, who caused disturbances in Bridgetown, Barbados, when he arrived there with the claim that he was 'Minister of Propaganda' from Trinidad. Payne's fiery speeches stirred the populace of Bridgetown. At his nightly meetings he urged them to 'organise' by forming trade unions. As the number of his supporters increased, the government of Barbados decided to deport him on the grounds that he had made a false declaration of his place of birth. The truth was that, although Payne had Barbadian parents and had lived as a boy in Barbados, he was born in Trinidad. Not knowing this, he had said he was born in Barbados. Payne was found guilty, but won an appeal against the verdict. His young lawyer on appeal was a journalist and a member of the House of Assembly, who had himself already been criticising the privileges of the planters and merchants in Barbados; this was Grantley Adams, twenty years later to be the first Prime Minister of the West Indies. Despite the fact that Payne won on appeal, the Barbadian Government deported him. Incensed by this act, and prey to all sorts of rumours of brutality by the police, the Bridgetown populace rioted; in the mêlée fourteen people were killed and fifty-nine wounded.

In Jamaica the Jamaica Workers and Tradesmen Union was started in 1935. The leaders Coombs and Bustamante did much to agitate public opinion in mass meetings and, in 1937, sent a petition to the King complaining of the poverty of the Jamaican people. The union agitated workers rather than organised them, and excited gatherings of unemployed men were broken up in Kingston in 1937. From January to May 1938 there were outbreaks of rioting both in Kingston and on some of the sugar estates. In May there was a disorderly strike at the Tate & Lyle Company estates in Frome in which some of the overseers were attacked; the police killed four workers in trying to arrest one. Disorders began again in Kingston when a general strike of waterfront workers was called at the end of May. Strikers paraded the streets forcing shops to close and sometimes looting. Again, eight people were killed, 171 wounded and more than 700 arrested before order was restored.

After the riots the value of trade unions was widely appreciated; membership of existing unions became much larger and new ones were formed in all the islands. In the five years after the riots, 58 unions were registered with about 65,000 members. Another important consequence was that the middle-class politicians now demanded not only self-government for their islands, but also higher wages and better social services for the workers. In Jamaica, Barbados, Antigua and St. Kitts, political parties were founded in association with the new trade unions and the support for the parties came from the members of the unions. This conjunction of political party and trade union was not easily accomplished. In some cases, the political leaders were too timid to press the demands of the workers on employers and governments. Where this was the case, as in Antigua, they were replaced by more determined men. In other instances, conflicts arose from differences of method, differences of aims and from the clash of personalities.

The Barbados Progressive League managed to survive such conflicts even though it lost some of its original supporters. After the Payne affair, the League became a popular group, with a following of 23,000 paying members in 1938. It registered as a trade union, later dividing its activities into the political Labour Party and the Barbados Workers' Union. Those who broke away successfully fought the League at elections as the Congress Party, offering the workers almost the same programme as the League. Lack of comparable trade union support has prevented them from winning a majority over the Barbados Labour Party.

In Jamaica a mass meeting was called in September 1938 to form the People's National Party, and Norman Manley was elected its leader. Some of the founders of the People's National Party were active trade unionists, but Bustamante was the man who dominated the working class in the developing Bustamante Industrial Trade Union. The alliance between the P.N.P. and Bustamante was uneasy from the beginning, although when Bustamante was interned for encouraging strikes early in the war, his trade union was kept alive by the P.N.P. The alliance did not survive the stresses of mutual suspicion after Bustamante was released from prison in 1942. In 1943 he founded a political party of his own and the P.N.P. had to seek popular support by organising their own trade union.

In Trinidad the differences of method between Cipriani and Butler had not been healed and, even when Butler was jailed for his part in the oilfield strikes, Cipriani did not find it any easier to win the confidence of the new trade-union leaders such as Rienzi. So in Trinidad there was not a close and stable alliance between political parties and trade unions.

THE MOYNE COMMISSION AND ITS SEQUEL

The riots moved the Colonial Office, in August 1938, to appoint a royal commission under the chairmanship of Lord Moyne 'to investigate social and economic conditions in all the West Indian territories, and to make recommendations'. For fifteen months the commissioners were at work in the area. They heard formal evidence from 370 individuals and groups in twenty-six centres; they had 789 memoranda of evidence to consider and 300 communications of individual grievances. It is interesting to note that the commissioners interviewed representatives from many bodies which had only recently come into existence, such as the trade unions in all territories, the Barbados and Jamaica Progressive Leagues, and the Guianese and West Indies Labour Congress, the Bustamante Industrial Unions and, everywhere, the unofficial members of the legislative councils.

Out of all this evidence the commissioners produced a long and comprehensive report concerning all aspects of West Indian life. In many ways it was the biggest indictment of Crown colony government in the West Indies made by anybody in the nineteen-thirties, just because there was so much detail to reveal the inadequacies of the system. They described the plight of the workers on the estates, on smallholdings, in towns and special industries. They revealed the distressing hovels that many people lived in, the great extent of malnutrition and chronic ill-health, the inadequacies of education, the amount of infant mortality and juvenile delinquency. They were clear that the ever-rising population would aggravate these hardships more and more.

The proposals to remedy the situation were definite and extensive. The main suggestion was the creation of a West Indian Welfare Fund of £1,000,000 per annum for twenty years from the Imperial Government, with a comptroller and staff of specialists in the area so that a realistic programme for spending the money could be worked out on the spot, instead of by remote control from the Colonial Office. The Report did not mince words. 'The efforts of Your Majesty's Government and of the Colonial Governments concerned,' it ran, 'have failed to make for radical reform. We therefore conclude that the means do not exist for effecting improvements on an adequate scale.' Education, health services, housing and slum clearance, the creation of labour departments, social welfare facilities and encouragement for land settlement were all to be served by the

Fund, and in each field there would be an administrator of long experience to advise the island governments on the best way to spend the money.

The commissioners were anxious to encourage the trade unions and wanted them to cater more for the depressed agricultural workers. They recommended that the compulsory registration of trade unions and the audit of their funds should be done by the governments free of charge. They also called for laws permitting peaceful picketing and for protecting the unions from actions for damages after strikes. While the trade unions were gaining strength the commissioners recommended that wage boards should be established as a means of fixing wages.

The United Kingdom, however, could not be expected to subsidise the West Indies for ever, so the real solution was to provide more opportunity for work in the islands. For this the commissioners recommended more efficiently organised farming, with the products sold to well controlled markets; but they did not encourage West Indian governments to 'conduct or finance speculative industrial enterprises'. Part of their argument was that if the standard of living, especially food, was raised for the ever-expanding population, there was plenty of room for an internal West Indian market in agricultural products, in addition to the export markets. Apart from a cement works in Jamaica and the development of coconut products in the West Indies, they had no new industries to suggest.

The commissioners did not support immediate and complete self-government, nor immediate universal adult suffrage. They thought that such a suffrage should be granted in the near future, but the West Indies should move towards self-government gradually. To help the individual islands move towards self-government the commissioners looked for ways of inviting West Indians to share in the daily routine of government. They urged that 'all important sections and interests of the community' should be represented in the executive council which advised the governor. In the legislative councils they argued, only the three important officials, the Colonial Secretary, the Attorney General and the Financial Secretary, should attend; the elected members should be put on committees which would advise the governor on the running of the administration. In this way the commissioners sought to modify Crown colony government without passing to self-government.

The Moyne Report was actually written in the first months of the

Second World War and only the recommendations were published at the time; the long discussion of conditions was not made public until 1945. The recommendations had a mixed reception here. The suggestions for social improvement in such matters as health, housing and education were well received; but the limited recommendations for political and economic development were criticised. The Mayor of Port-of-Spain called the report 'the biggest hoax ever perpetrated by the British Government on a colonial people in the twentieth century'. For those who had long wanted to organise their own government the report offered only very delayed prospects of political responsibility.

In 1940, by a Colonial Development and Welfare Act, the British Government voted a sum of money for the relief of all the British colonies which had suffered during the thirties. A special Comptroller for Development and Welfare, with a staff of advisers stationed in Barbados, was appointed to assist the West Indian governments, and up to 1950, nearly a quarter of the Development and Welfare funds voted by the British Government had been spent in the West Indies. In the smaller islands this has been the largest source of income for public spending in the last twelve years and advice was given extensively until the functions of the Development and Welfare Organisation passed to the new Federal Government in 1958.

NEW PROSPECTS

In the early years of the war the protest against the Crown colony system continued strongly, but since 1944 the movement towards greater participation of West Indians in their governments has gone forward fairly steadily. The gradual transfer of responsibility from the Colonial Office to elected members has been the key to the new constitutions in recent years.

In 1944 the form of government in Jamaica was changed to create a House of Representatives in addition to the Legislative Council, which was now to consist only of senior government officials and the members nominated by the governor. The House of Representatives was to be composed of forty-eight members, all elected by universal adult suffrage. This made it similar to the Barbadian House of Assembly, which alone had survived as a wholly elected body throughout the period of Crown colony government, although the Barbadian assembly members were not elected on a universal suffrage until 1950.

In all the other British Caribbean colonies the steps towards self-government have been marked first by the grant of universal adult suffrage; this was achieved in British Guiana and British Honduras, the last colonies to get it, in 1952 and 1954 respectively. Then the number and powers of the elected members in the governor's executive council have been increased by stages until that council, which decides on the policy of each island's government, is composed entirely of elected members and is called the Cabinet. The governors, who under Crown colony government could reject the advice of the executive council, can now only act according to the advice of the Cabinet. Full internal self-government is achieved when the Premier of the island government presides over his Cabinet of ministers. There remain, however, two limitations on the power of West Indian cabinets; the British Government is still responsible for defence and foreign policy.

The notable exception to this order of progress towards self-government has been British Guiana, where the Imperial Government in December 1953 suspended the constitution under which a government, led by Dr. Cheddi Jagan of the People's Progressive Party and elected by universal adult suffrage, had taken office. The party had been in power for only six months. The Imperial Government charged the party with attempting to establish a Communist government in British Guiana and sent British troops to suppress the riots which were expected to follow the overthrow of the government. In fact no disturbances happened. For a time British Guiana was governed by men who were the nominees of the governor. The People's Progressive Party split into factions; but when elections were again allowed, the party led by Cheddi Jagan was again elected to office, but this time under a constitution which gave the British Guiana Government less power than in 1952.

The political changes in the British islands which have taken them towards internal self-government and federation, have occurred at the same time as political changes in the French, Dutch and American colonies, which also gave their inhabitants a greater degree of responsibility for their own affairs without giving them independence. Some of these islands possessed political advantages before the British colonies. For instance, Martinique and Guadeloupe have had male adult suffrage since 1875. In these French islands the voters in each case elected a General Council of thirty-six members; In Puerto Rico since 1917 the voters have elected the members to the

Senate and to the House of Representatives. In Surinam and Curaçao from 1922 there was a legislative council of fifteen members, ten of whom were elected by the few people qualified to vote. The French islands also elect one Senator and two deputies to the French Parliament, and the Puerto Ricans elect a Commissioner who can speak in the United States Congress but has no vote.

As colonies, all these territories had one thing in common, namely, that their governors and their senior officials were appointed from overseas, and the local legislatures, however constituted, could not wholly determine the policy of the government. It is not surprising that their social and economic conditions were very similar to those in the British islands and that they were aggravated by the depression of the nineteen-thirties.

The nationalist movement emerged in Puerto Rico in 1935. This was organised by a group of intellectuals led by Campos, a Puerto Rican graduate of an American university. They started a small private army, assassinated the American Chief of Police in the island, proclaimed Puerto Rico a republic and in 1937 finally paraded in Ponce against the orders of the police. Nineteen people, mostly Puerto Rican students, were killed in 'the Ponce Massacre'; this shocked that section of the American public which was always anxious not to be regarded as empire-builders and oppressors.

This was the high point of the movement to make Puerto Rico into a country independent of the United States. The cry for independence lost much of its force when the Little New Deal was started to attend to the lamentable social and economic conditions, and when a Puerto Rican party was formed able to change them. The Popular Democratic Party was organised by Luis Muñoz Marin in 1938 with a programme for economic progress. The new party won the 1940 elections; after the 1944 election, Muñoz Marin became President of the Senate. He found an ally in R. G. Tugwell, the American governor of the island, and was thus able to embark on the programme of the Democratic Party even before the United States had granted Puerto Rico internal self-government.

A newly created Land Authority confiscated part of the estates of the unpopular American sugar companies, leaving them only the 500 acres each permitted by the Organic Act of 1900, but paying them generous compensation. These companies, owning vast tracts of the best land, exclusively producing sugar, dominating Puerto Rico, had for the critics become symbols of what the American flag over Puerto

287

Rico meant. Minimum wages were declared in consultation with other trade unions and the Labour Relations Board. Finally the first of the industrial undertakings, cement and glass factories, were started with government funds by the new Puerto Rico Development Corporation. There was also a Development Bank to encourage further investment in the island. After the war investment was further encouraged by granting American industries exemption from local taxes while they established themselves, and also by providing them with factory buildings. By 1958 the industrialisation programme had encouraged 498 factories, and over 40,000 direct new jobs had been created.

Puerto Rico was not the first island in the Caribbean to attack the precarious social and economic conditions which have come from dependence on one crop. The Cubans have tried since 1929; and particularly during the second administration of Grau San Martin from 1944 to 1948, the government's programme was to diversify agriculture, encourage industries by tax exemptions, attack illiteracy and fight malaria and typhoid. But it is Puerto Rico which has become the model for the other islands of the Caribbean. Puerto Rico is more like the others in size and resources. 'Operation Bootstrap', as the Puerto Rican programme was called, could be an example to equally poor colonies. Puerto Ricans too, unlike Cubans, were not independent. Jamaica and Trinidad now have their Industrial Development Corporations, Barbados its Development Board and Martinique its Economic Expansion Committee. Puerto Rico's Industrial Incentives Act has spawned Pioneer Industries Acts all over the British Caribbean.

Because of their membership in the Caribbean Commission the work of the Puerto Ricans has become known to the other islands. The Caribbean Commission was an organisation established in 1946 by the governments of France, Holland, Britain and the United States to help foster social and economic development in the Caribbean, by providing the local governments with technical assistance or advice, and circulating information among them. In July 1959, at a conference in the Virgin Islands, control of the Commission was transferred from the imperial to the Caribbean countries and it was renamed the Caribbean Organisation.

The governments that have taken over the Caribbean Organisation are at different stages of independence from their former rulers; but they all now have practical responsibility for the standard of living of their own people. Assistance in eradicating poverty is sometimes thought a more pressing need than independence. Governor Muñoz Marin expressed this view when, in 1952, he accepted that his country should remain an American territory 'for a period of time in order to use all our energy once more in a great effort to solve our grave economic problems, and abolish extreme poverty in Puerto Rico'. Some benefits of the United States Social Security Act apply directly to Puerto Rico and the American Virgin Islands.

In the British Caribbean independent Jamaica and Trinidad are now responsible for seeking their own resources for development. By contrast, some of the smaller islands are still grant-aided and controlled to a corresponding degree by the British Colonial Office. British colonial territories can apply for assistance from the British Development and Welfare Fund for special development projects.

The French islands became Overseas Departments of France after the Second World War; they are governed by Prefects and other officials as if they were departments in France itself, and they benefit from social services, old age pensions and allowances similar to those which all Frenchmen receive from their government. In addition France has provided an Investment Fund for Overseas Departments to assist their development.

The new position of the Dutch islands was defined in 1954 when the 'Netherlands Kingdom' was described as now consisting of three co-equal partners, Holland and her former colonies of the Netherlands Antilles and Surinam. The Dutch Government has provided a Surinam Fund for Economic Development.

POST-WAR DEVELOPMENTS

The advance in social and political affairs in the British territories has been enormously helped by better economic conditions since the dark days of 1938. The outbreak of war immediately brought boom conditions for West Indian sugar. From 1939 the British Government bought all available British Caribbean sugar at a price which would cover the average cost of production. After the war the British Government promised to buy all the sugar produced in the five years after 1944, and renewed the offer in 1948. Consequently, since 1939 the sugar industry has returned to relative prosperity. When the wartime system of bulk purchase ended, it was replaced by the Commonwealth Sugar Agreement of 1951, by which the United

Kingdom promised to buy 1,550,000 tons of sugar a year 'at prices to be negotiated annually and reasonably remunerative to producers'. The total tonnage was to be divided between the commonwealth countries which produced sugar; only the West Indies criticised the offer. After meeting first in Grenada in February 1950, a delegation composed of political and labour leaders and the sugar producers went to London to argue that the quantity allotted to Australia was unduly large and that the West Indian allocation should be raised. It eventually was raised by 30,000 tons.

The world sugar producers having learnt the lessons of uncontrolled production after the First World War, a new International Sugar Agreement was also signed in 1953 dividing world markets.

Protected by these agreements, West Indian sugar sells for the most part in markets which pay it a profitable price. But the annually negotiated price is paid only on the stated quantity of sugar. Surpluses must be sold in the world market in competition with foreign producers whose greater output allows them to fix the price. Cuba can produce five million tons a year. By contrast, the entire British Caribbean production is about 1,200,000 tons, of which 900,000 tons have a guaranteed sale in the United Kingdom and Canada.

The boom of the war years was also helped by the placing of American air bases in the islands. Because permission was given by the British Government without any consultation of West Indian governments, the move was widely resented. On the other hand, the appearance of American dollars in the area was welcome, the bases provided employment for all sorts of workers, including the clerks who had been over-produced by the secondary schools in the nineteen-thirties.

The war also made it necessary to expand considerably the oil refineries in Curaçao and Aruba. Here again was a new source of employment and during the war and for some time after there was a small but steady emigration from the Leewards and Windwards to the American bases in Trinidad and the oil refineries in Curaçao and Aruba. The results can be seen in St. Vincent, St. Lucia and Grenada in the houses built by the money sent back. The need for farm workers in the United States has provided another outlet, but the men cannot stay in the United States. Recently Canada has admitted an annual quota of 250 women for domestic work.

Most British West Indian emigrants since the war have gone to the United Kingdom where British subjects could enter unrestricted until the Immigration Act of 1961, which was passed to control entry for three years in the first instance. There has been a large emigration from Puerto Rico to the United States; this has been facilitated by cheap air fares and the fact that Puerto Ricans are United States citizens. Full employment abroad immediately after the war attracted a great variety of workers, who went for the higher wages and, in some cases, for the training which is not available here. Emigration is a mixed blessing. It certainly reduces the numbers to be provided for in the West Indies, but it also tends to attract the more enterprising and the more skilled workers, who are not the people who can readily be spared. Moreover, emigration is not a substitute for economic development. A slight drop in business in the United States made Puerto Rican emigration to the United States decline by 68 per cent in 1953-4. Occasional depressions and the working of the Immigration Act have also caused fluctuations and decline in the number of emigrants from the British islands in recent years. Furthermore, in the depressed city districts where poorer migrants have settled in England there are hooligans who will bait and, on occasion, fight strangers, particularly coloured people, whom they regard as foreigners. In the summer of 1958 incidents in parts of London and Nottingham caused considerable concern both in England and here. Most West Indian governments have tried to regulate but not to depend upon emigration as part of their policy; Barbados has helped emigrants to take up jobs as transport workers in England and the Canadian and American quotas of workers are selected by the West Indian governments. The Jamaica and Trinidad Governments both maintain High Commissioners in London who help their migrants to Britain; but these services are not on a large scale and do not apply to other West Indians.

It has now become quite clear that manufacturing industries are necessary in the West Indies to offer alternative employment to depressed agricultural workers. The natural resources of Trinidad and British Guiana have proved very beneficial to these territories. Jamaica has found similar assets in the bauxite which was discovered in the centre of the island in the last years of the Second World War. Mining began in 1952 and there are now three companies, one Canadian and two American.

We have now moved in a very short space of time into a much greater variety of economic activity, in which the sugar industry, though still of vast importance and now highly efficient, exists alongside a variety of other profitable agricultural pursuits particularly in fruit and cacao. Enterprises in oil, bauxite and tourism, with the growth of many other smaller but no less important industries, are welcomed as employment for people so that gradually standards of living can be raised after many years of great poverty in the British Caribbean.

FURTHER READING

Sources of West Indian History, Economic Life, pp. 83–8, Government and Politics, pp. 136–40, Social Conditions since Emancipation pp. 259–68.

Parry and Sherlock, *A Short History of the West Indies*, Chapter XVIII, The Caribbean Colonies 1918–1954.

Nembhard, *Jamaica the Awakening*, Chapters II–V.

Hoyos, *The Story of the Progressive Movement*.

QUESTIONS TO CONSIDER

1. What would you consider to be the most important consequence of the riots in the West Indies in the nineteen-thirties?

2. To whom would you give credit for the granting of more responsible government in the West Indies?

3. What have been the developments in trade unions, political affairs, social services and employment in your territory since 1938?

4. What plans would you recommend for the development of your territory and how might they be organised?

CHAPTER TWENTY-FIVE

Attempts at Unification

ADVOCATED BY ADMINISTRATORS

British administrators have always thought that the West Indian islands are too small for each to have its separate machinery of government, and attempts to group the islands for purposes of government and administration have been made almost since the beginning of English settlement. We have already noticed two partly successful attempts at a federation of the Leeward Islands, one at the end of the seventeenth century, and the other which began in 1871 and lasted to our own day. On both occasions the Leewards had a legislature in common, making laws for all the islands in the group. By contrast, the first attempt to confederate Barbados and the Windwards in 1876 was a complete failure; the second attempt, in 1885, resulted only in giving them a governor and auditor general in common.

In these instances, and also when the governments of St. Kitts–Nevis and Trinidad–Tobago were fused, the initiative came from the British administrators either in the West Indies or in England. The outstanding governors dealing with a group of islands, have noticed the similarity of their problems, the weaknesses of several poorly-staffed government departments, and such governors have thought how much more effective government in the islands could be if their talented citizens were assembled in one government. Notable examples of such governors are Sir William Stapleton and Sir William Colebrooke of the Leewards and Sir William Robinson of the Windwards. Capable administrators of individual small islands such as Sir Benjamin Pine in St. Kitts, Gideon Murray in St. Vincent and Sir R. B. Llewelyn in Tobago were, from their point of view, struck by the hopelessness of administering such islands individually, and have also been advocates of federation.

But governors such as Stapleton and Colebrooke were not only concerned with making the most of limited West Indian talent and with tidying up the routine of administration. They were the agents of the Imperial Government responsible for carrying out instructions from the Colonial Office; and this they also saw could be done with greater efficiency if there was only one assembly to deal with. But Stapleton at the end of the seventeenth century, Colebrooke in 1837 and, later, Pope-Hennessy, in the Windwards in 1876, were attempting to carry out instructions unpopular with influential West Indians, that is, the planters and merchants who still controlled the houses of assembly.

Stapleton in the sixteen-nineties wanted to get a permanent revenue act from the Leeward Islands and to make sure that their laws did not contradict imperial policy. Colebrooke in the eighteen-thirties wished to make sure that the newly emancipated slaves would have the kind of assistance from the legislature which would help them to make the most of freedom. In the Windwards in the eighteen-seventies, the Imperial Government policy was to abolish the houses of assembly and make the islands into Crown colonies. The Barbadians in the House of Assembly felt that to accept the federation with Grenada, St. Vincent, St. Lucia and Tobago, which Pope-Hennessy offered them, would be to accept the fate that had already befallen the assemblies in three of these islands.

These were all such unpopular issues to associate with federation that there is little wonder that it was resisted in each case. In addition, the Leeward Islands planters were afraid that the coloured group, which could be controlled in a small community, might in a federation become stronger than the island plantocracies. On such points the resistance was too great to be ignored.

LIMITED CO-OPERATION

Although suggestions for a federation to suit the British administration have been resisted, groups of West Indians have seen the need for co-operation between the islands for certain special purposes. Not surprisingly, for a long time it was co-operation against imperial policy, or co-operation in order to survive against outside competition when no protection was forthcoming from the Imperial Government. This was true even before Stapleton had proposed a Leeward Federation at the end of the seventeenth century; the assembly men of the islands were already holding small meetings with each other to decide on a common reply to the new imperial policy of tighter control over colonies and, in particular, a reply to the request for a permanent revenue.

In the eighteen-forties, when Britain was embarking on the policy of free trade, the Jamaican Assembly sent a delegation to London to argue Jamaica's case. They soon realised that their case could only be made effectively in conjunction with all the islands; so on their own initiative they addressed the assemblies of the other islands asking them also to send delegates to London, to make the case for all the West Indies together. A hundred-odd years later, after the Second World War, when the terms on which West Indian sugar was in future to be admitted to the United Kingdom had to be negotiated, it was done by a West Indian delegation including, not only the representatives of the sugar producers, as in the nineteenth century, but West Indian politicians as well.

But limits have been set to the degree of co-operation by poor communications, by the insularity which the resulting isolation brings, and by the tendency of these islands to be competitors for the same oversea markets or foreign capital. All these things fostered a certain degree of distrust of each other among West Indians, a distrust which was aggravated by mutual ignorance of conditions of life in more than one or two islands. In such circumstances it has been easy for West Indians to exaggerate the differences which certainly do exist between the islands. In 1885 the editor of the *Voice of St. Lucia* could claim that among the Windward Islands there were 'the most radical differences between them of race, language and religion, and the rivalry incident to their insular position precludes the possibility of identity of requirements'. In these circumstances, too, proposals for a federal government were interpreted as a challenge to an island's self-importance. One St. Lucian's objection to the proposed federation of the Windwards expresses this outlook. 'What is worse,' he protested, 'our beautiful St. Lucia is to be classed as and sunk into a Majesterial District under Grenada.'

The distrust that has its seeds in rivalry is the most difficult to overcome. The British islands have long competed with each other on the British sugar market. Calamities in one were advantages to others because less sugar produced meant higher prices for those who had it. In the nineteenth century Barbadian planters saw in proposals for a Federation of the Windwards, the dispersal of their labourers to other islands to build them up into competitors. The fusion of St. Kitts–Nevis, and Trinidad–Tobago after a time brought well-founded complaints from Nevis and Tobago that their interests were being neglected. With these complaints to reinforce its pride, St. Vincent in 1905 resisted, almost to the point of rioting, a similar fate in the attempts by the Colonial Office to fuse its government with that of Grenada.

There has been, then, some reason for mutual distrust, and it has worked not only to limit co-operation, but also to weaken such closer political unions as have taken place. In particular the islands in such unions have been very reluctant to share a federal system of law. They also successfully prevented the federal government from levying its own taxes. The Leewards Government both in the seventeenth and in the nineteenth century had to depend for its revenue on contributions from the islands. In the nineteenth century in the Windwards, this was the major obstacle. The editor of the *Grenada Chronicle* wrote that 'the principal objection . . . to federation is raised on the ground of finance. The leaders of the people object— and, we think, naturally—to a common or federal treasury'. That feeling was strong enough for the islands concerned to resist an offer of elected members to sit in the legislative council, an offer which the Secretary of State made clear was only to apply to a federal council.

PRACTICAL CO-OPERATION

After the refusal of the Windwards to be federated in 1885, the Colonial Office declared that its policy now would be to wait until West Indians themselves were willing to federate. Not until 1945 did the Colonial Office decide the time had arrived once more to test West Indian opinion, and then they asked the West Indians themselves to propose what form federation should take, Between those dates, the West Indies did not revert to isolation. Very slowly West Indians came to know one another better. How slowly can be seen from the comment of the Royal Commissioners in 1939 that even well-informed witnesses claimed that no good could come to their territories from institutions set up in other parts of the West Indies.

Such insularity was diminished by the increase of regular communications between the islands. Yet that too was of very slow growth. Steamships were an improvement on sail, but they were intended to link the West Indies with England, Europe, Canada and America, and only incidentally to link the islands together. In 1922 when Major Wood came to investigate West Indian demands for representative government, he pointed out that his own group could never have done a tour of the West Indies if they had not had a British naval ship at their disposal. Mail between Jamaica and Trinidad and

Barbados usually passed through either London, New York or Halifax; it was certainly quicker to communicate with the latter cities than between the West Indian islands. Many complaints were made to the Colonial Office about the performance of the Cable and Steamship companies, which were subsidised by the island governments to some degree but mainly by the Imperial Government. The 'Lady Boats', subsidised by the Canadian Government, substantially increased the inter-island travel. But, at the beginning of 1929, when the West Indian Conference, the conference of the Associated Chambers of Commerce and a meeting of the West Indian Press Association were all being held in Barbados together, it still took the Jamaicans attending thirteen days to get there. They went by steamer via Cristobal, La Guaira, Wilhelmstad and Port-of-Spain. In recent years air travel has made a great difference, despite the high cost of fares.

Insularity was also reduced by some action largely taken outside the West Indies. It had become clear to the leading producers of agricultural products that the islands were no longer competitors. During the first two decades of the twentieth century it was the commercial interest, represented in England by the West India Committee, and in the islands by Chambers of Commerce, which advocated the use of standing associations, councils or committees to present a united voice on matters affecting the West Indies. Norman Lamont wanted federation in the interests of free trade between the islands. In the nineteen-twenties Sir Edward Davson, President of the Associated West Indian Chambers of Commerce, put forward a complete scheme for a 'federation by conference', as he called it, with a permanent council of the West Indian governors advised by ten members selected by the Secretary of State; he also wanted panels of the appropriate officials dealing with customs, law, medicine, education and the police from each island to consider uniform legislation for all of them. Co-operation in the interest of commerce and trade was also fostered by having to negotiate as a body with the Canadian Government about the terms for Canadian–West Indian trade.

The Colonial Office built other bridges between the islands. After the 1897 Royal Commission, the Imperial Government was committed to a more active policy in the West Indies. The attempts to improve agriculture and the marketing of crops and to raise the standard of health and education led to a number of conferences and a few common institutions, the two most important of the latter being

297

the Imperial Department of Agriculture and the West Indian Court of Appeal.

The conferences on matters for co-operation between governments had one great disadvantage. In the era of Crown colony government, they were attended overwhelmingly by civil servants who were not West Indians, and the good ideas proposed frequently came to nothing. For instance, in 1920 Sir Richard Popham Lobb, then Administrator of St. Vincent, suggested a combined attack on the problems of education in the area. In particular he wanted a training college in which special enquiries should be made into West Indian educational problems and needs. He hoped that it could be associated with the new Imperial College of Tropical Agriculture, so that teachers could be trained in agriculture, commercial subjects and domestic economy; they could then teach in the schools these subjects so necessary to the improvement of the West Indies.

This plan was thoroughly discussed and much approved of in Trinidad in the following year at a conference of education officers, inspectors of schools, religious leaders, a headmaster from a secondary school and a headmaster from a primary school. It is a good example of the staffing of colonial government that these officers, except the primary-school headmaster, were Englishmen. Outside the meeting the scheme was virtually ignored and did not receive much support from West Indians in the various island councils.

The conferences on commercial and professional matters put some West Indians in touch with each other. During the nineteen-thirties, other West Indians, particularly from the Eastern Caribbean and British Guiana, came together for political purposes. These men wanted federation so that they could have independence. We have seen that the unofficial meeting at Dominica in 1932 was primarily intended to put forward the terms on which federation would be acceptable to its members. At this conference a full working constitution was suggested for a federation of the territories of the Eastern Caribbean. There were twenty-four matters listed on which it was thought that federal laws could be passed; these included agriculture, trade, education, public health, criminal law and immigration. Above all, unification of the civil service and the judiciary was recommended, together with other measures which were 'regarded as essential to the ultimate realisation of Dominion Status'.

Later on in the thirties the Moyne Commission was presented with a draft bill for a federation of the West Indies by trade unionists from the Eastern Caribbean, and they commented on the contact 'maintained by those in each Colony who are most interested in securing rapid political progress'. For this reason they asked most of their witnesses for their views on federation, and found almost everyone in favour. It was through the Caribbean Labour Congress after 1945 that a new group of Jamaicans joined those in trade and commerce in support of the argument for federation.

DRAWING CLOSER

A new attitude to federation came after the Second World War. The Colonial Office was now willing to sponsor a federation whose political aim was self-government, but it was also willing to grant the separate islands responsible governments based on universal adult suffrage. This was asking the island politicians to pay attention to two important developments at the same time. In fact the politicians paid more attention to their individual islands than to federation. The pace at which they moved to establish federation became slower and by the time the Federal Government was established in 1958, island governments, particularly in Jamaica, had already taken the initiative with some success in improving the standards of living in their islands.

By 1945 there were several signs of a new West Indian unity and the Imperial Government gave evidence of their intention to encourage a movement towards independence in the West Indies by setting up the Irvine Commission to propose plans for a university, in order to provide more trained people for service in the area. The University College of the West Indies was referred to as 'the parting gift' of the British Government who provided capital for buildings, leaving the expenses of running the College first to the West Indian governments and then to the Federal Government. About one-third of the federal budget was meant for the University College. Between 1944 and 1945 several organisations declared themselves in favour of federation. The most notable were the Barbados Progressive League, the People's National Party and the Legislative Council of Jamaica, the Associated Chambers of Commerce and the Caribbean Labour Congress. In 1945 the British Government told West Indian governors that they now proposed to promote federation, and in 1947 the Secretary of State invited West Indians to a conference to discuss the matter. This conference was held in Montego Bay.

The delegates at Montego Bay favoured federation and they proceeded to create committees to work out the organisation. The two most important were the Regional Economic Committee, which through its discussion of economic affairs on a Caribbean scale gave valuable experience to West Indian politicians, and the Standing Closer Association Committee, itself to propose a form of federation. Under the chairmanship of Sir Hubert Rance, the Standing Closer Association Committee brought out its proposals in two years. The aims of the federation were no longer given as administrative convenience for the colonial administrator. On the contrary, federation was offered as the shortest cut to independence and Dominion status.

Conferences were held in London in 1953 and 1956 to write the federal constitution and to arrange for its inception. The constitution gave powers to the Governor-General which governors in Jamaica and Barbados no longer exercised, and critical West Indians were able to say that the delegates had accepted a 'Crown Colony Federation'. There were conflicting views among the delegates on how quickly freedom of movement between the islands and a customs union of all the islands should be established. Trinidad, the island to which other West Indians migrated, and Jamaica, the island which received a high proportion of its revenue from import duties, were the ones principally affected by these issues. Although willing to agree that unfettered migration and customs union were practices essential to a federation, neither island was willing to bear immediately the financial burden of adopting them.

In 1957 the peninsula of Chaguaramas in Trinidad was selected for the federal capital. Much of the site was, however, still occupied by an American naval base built there during the Second World War, so Port-of-Spain became the temporary capital. Meanwhile, politicians had grouped themselves in two federal parties in readiness for elections which took place early in 1958 and which were won by the Federal Labour Party by a very slender majority. In April 1958 the first West Indian Federal Government came into existence.

It had been agreed at the London conferences that the constitution would remain unchanged for five years, but it had not been clearly settled what the Federal Government was to do during those years, nor how the unit governments should behave. Within two years of its coming into existence, the Federal Government was subjected to intense criticism by the Governments of Jamaica and Trinidad, both of which also proposed changes in the federal constitution.

The dispute with Jamaica occurred when its government decided to establish an oil refinery by granting concessions to the company which built and operated it. The Prime Minister alarmed many in Jamaica by speaking of the possibility of federal 'retroactive legislation' after 1963 to counteract such concessions, and so focused attention on the fact that the Federal Government could use the financial powers promised it by the 1956 constitution in such ways as to regulate the economies of the units.

Jamaica, fearing that the exercise of such powers might jeopardise its economic development, proposed to rewrite the federal constitution to deny to the federal government powers of direct taxation and power to control the economy of any unit unless invited to do so. As a further safeguard Jamaica asked for an increase in the number of its representatives.

The dispute with Trinidad flared over the exercise of federal powers in external affairs. The Trinidadian Government, eager for West Indian independence before 1963, but doubtful that the Federal Government were moved by the same spirit, and doubtful that it could be relied upon to safeguard Trinidad's interests in Chaguaramas, asked for independent representation at the talks with the United Kingdom and the United States on the future of the naval base. Trinidad, however, proposed changes in the federal constitution which would extend the functions of the Federal Government and increase the revenues at its disposal.

In September 1959, the unit governments met in Trinidad to begin the revision of the constitution. They enlarged the House to sixty-four members by increasing Jamaica's seats to thirty and Trinidad's to sixteen. The conference then created two committees to study the political, economic and financial implications of independence and adjourned to await their reports.

The committees met at intervals during 1960. While they were at work decisions were taken by the British, United States and Jamaican Governments which affected the Federation. The British amended the constitution to give the Federation full internal self-government. The Americans signed a new agreement with Trinidad for the Chaguaramas Naval Base. The Jamaican Government decided to hold a Referendum to settle whether or not Jamaica would continue in the Federation.

The referendum was held in Jamaica in September 1961, and the electorate voted for withdrawal from the Federation. Four months later the head of the Trinidad Government declared that, in the case of the West Indian Federation, one from ten was not nine, but nought, and 80. The 1958 Federation had ended. Shortly after the Federal Government and Civil Service were disbanded. In August 1962 Jamaica and Trinidad each became independent states. The other islands immediately began discussions on the formation of a new federation, and at a meeting in Barbados in May 1963 proposed that such a federation should be independent from the outset.

In July 1963 the heads of the Governments of Barbados, British Guinea, Jamaica and Trinidad held a first meeting in Port of Spain to confer on matters of common concern. These were trade and communication within and beyond the area, migration to the United Kingdom and the United States, economic and technical aid and the University of the West Indies. They agreed to press for increased aid from the United States and Great Britain, to set up a working party to study the services now run by the West Indian Shipping Corporation, to press for amendments to the British Commonwealth Immigration Act and to seek ways of offering legal aid to migrants in the United Kingdom. The Governments agreed to consult one another on their future policy on these and other matters, such as tourism, air services and the university, which they had discussed during the meeting.

FURTHER READING

Sources of West Indian History, Attempts at Unification, pp. 280–96.

QUESTIONS TO CONSIDER

1. What have been the main arguments against a federation of the West Indies?

2. Which seems to you the strongest argument presented at any time for federation?

3. Why do you consider that the Federal Government of 1958 to 1961 failed?

4. Over what matters do you think that the British West Indian territories might act in co-operation?

A NOTE ON SUGGESTED BOOKS

AT the end of each chapter there is a short list on further reading. The first reference in every case is to *Sources of West Indian History* compiled by Augier and Gordon, Longmans, 1962. This is a series of extracts from contemporary writings on West Indian history and is intended as a book to be explored in class with the guidance of teachers' questions to help pupils in finding facts from often unfamiliar language. Eric Williams, *Documents of West Indian History*, 1492–1655, P.N.M. Publishing Co., Trinidad, 1963, provides further source material for the early period which can be similarly used in class.

TEXTBOOKS

J. H. Parry and P. M. Sherlock, *A Short History of the West Indies*, Macmillan, 1956.
This is written for undergraduates and senior students, but descriptive chapters make good general reading for the School Certificate candidates.

E. H. Carter, G. W. Digby and R. N. Murray, *History of the West Indian Peoples*, Books III and IV, Nelson, 1953 and 1959.
These more simply written textbooks give a general account of West Indian history with some good descriptive chapters, particularly in Book III.

C. V. Black, *History of Jamaica*, Collins, 1958.
An excellent history by the Government Archivist in Jamaica. We have referred to those chapters on Jamaican history which are important to the history of the West Indies as a whole.

E. Williams, *History of the People of Trinidad and Tobago*, P.N.M. Publishing Co.

D. C. Somervell, *A History of the United States*, Heinemann, 1942.
This history has been selected because it draws most clearly the parallels between American and West Indian history in the colonial period.

D. Richards and A. Quick, *Britain 1714–1851*, Longmans, 1961.
Particularly for the chapters on British social history in the period when the West Indies were profitable colonies.

P. M. Sherlock, *Caribbean Citizen*, Longmans, 1957.

BIOGRAPHIES

F. A. Hoyos, *Our Common Heritage*, Advocate Press, Barbados, 1952.
> *Short biographies of famous Barbadians.*

A. Roberts, *Six Great Jamaicans*, Pioneer Press, Jamaica, 1952.

P. H. Daly, *Story of the Heroes*, III, "The Daily Chronicle", British Guiana, 1943
> *Short biographies of famous British Guianese.*

A. Roberts, *Sir Henry Morgan*, Pioneer Press, Jamaica, 1952.

BOOKS ON TOPICS

Non-Fiction

P. M. Sherlock, *West Indian Story*, Longmans, 1960.
> *This is largely a description of the settlement of different peoples in the West Indies and incorporates a fair amount of source material.*

A. Roberts, *The French in the West Indies*, Bobbs-Merrill, 1942.

C. R. Ottley, *Spanish Trinidad*, College Press, Trinidad, 1955.

F. A. Hoyos, *The Story of the Progressive Movement*, Beacon Printery, Barbados, 1947.

L. S. Nembhard, *Jamaica the Awakening*, The Jamaica Times Ltd., 1943.

Rev. C. Jesse, *Outlines of St. Lucia's History*, Voice of St. Lucia, Castries, 1956.

C. R. Ottley, *The Complete History of Tobago*, Guardian Printery, Trinidad.

C. R. Ottley, *The Story of Port of Spain*, Trinidad, 1962.

F. A. Hoyos, *The Rise of West Indian Democracy*, Advocate Press, Barbados, 1963.

Douglas Hall, *Letters from Monville*, Ministry of Education Publications Branch, Jamaica, 1963.

Fiction

Evan Jones, *Protector of the Indians*, Nelson, 1958.

S. A. G. Taylor, *The Capture of Jamaica*, Pioneer Press, Jamaica, 1951.

S. A. G. Taylor, *Buccaneer Bay*, Pioneer Press, Jamaica, 1952.

V. Reid, *New Day*, Heinemann, 1950.

C. V. Black, *Tales of Old Jamaica*, Pioneer Press, Jamaica, 1952

INDEX

305